Reading Texts in Music and Literature
of the Long Nineteenth Century

Reading Texts in Music and Literature of the Long Nineteenth Century

Edited by
Phyllis Weliver and Katharine Ellis

THE BOYDELL PRESS

© Contributors 2025

All Rights Reserved. Except as permitted under current legislation
no part of this work may be photocopied, stored in a retrieval system,
published, performed in public, adapted, broadcast,
transmitted, recorded or reproduced in any form or by any means,
without the prior permission of the copyright owner

First published 2025
The Boydell Press, Woodbridge

ISBN 978 1 83765 183 2 hardback
ISBN 978 1 83765 184 9 paperback

The Boydell Press is an imprint of Boydell & Brewer Ltd
PO Box 9, Woodbridge, Suffolk IP12 3DF, UK
and of Boydell & Brewer Inc.
668 Mt Hope Avenue, Rochester, NY 14620–2731, USA
website: www.boydellandbrewer.com

Our Authorised Representative for product safety in the EU is Easy Access System Europe,
Mustamäe tee 50, 10621 Tallinn, Estonia, gpsr.requests@easproject.com

A CIP catalogue record for this book is available
from the British Library

The publisher has no responsibility for the continued existence or accuracy of URLs for
external or third-party internet websites referred to in this book, and does not guarantee
that any content on such websites is, or will remain, accurate or appropriate

Contents

List of Figures	vii
Contributors	x
Acknowledgements	xiii

    A Guide to this Book   1
    Phyllis Weliver and Katharine Ellis

1   Vernon Lee's "A Wicked Voice" (1890): Music and Queerness in Decadent Fiction   15
    Fraser Riddell

2   Conjuring Folk Music: George Sand's *The Master Pipers* (1853)   29
    Katharine Ellis

3   Bands of Mercy Music: A Cultural Study of Victorian Animal Welfare Songs for Children   40
    Alisa Clapp-Itnyre

4   The Music of the Women's Suffrage Movement   56
    Christopher Wiley

5   Song and the Political Body: William Morris   75
    Elizabeth Helsinger

6   Understanding Colonial Mission Hymns and Hybridity   91
    Philip Burnett

7   Representing Non-Western Music: Robert Louis Stevenson in Kiribati   105
    Emma Sutton

8   Musical Encounters at the Louisiana Lakeside in Charles Jobey's "Le lac Cathahoula" (1856/1861)   118
    Charlotte Bentley

9   Critical Dislocations: Champfleury's *Richard Wagner* (1860)   133
    Jeremy Coleman

10 Locating Elgar: Nationalism, Landscape and Musical Biography   146
    Daniel M. Grimley

11　Musical *Ekphrasis* and Intermedial Form in Walter Pater's
　　"Duke Carl of Rosenmold" (1887)　　　　　　　　　　　159
　　Elicia Clements

12　Women, Music and Tennyson's *The Princess* (1850 edn)　　170
　　Phyllis Weliver

13　Reading Whitman, Hearing Vaughan Williams: Sexuality,
　　National Politics and the Role of the Artist in Society　　186
　　Sarah Collins

　　Coda　　　　　　　　　　　　　　　　　　　　　　　　198
　　Shafquat Towheed

　　Index　　　　　　　　　　　　　　　　　　　　　　　　201

Figures

0.1 Wilkie Collins, *The Moonstone*, instalment 1, *Harper's Weekly* 12.1 (January 4, 1868): 5. Illustrations by John McLenan. Public domain. Courtesy, American Antiquarian Society.   5

0.2 Samuel Coleridge-Taylor, *Hiawatha's Wedding Feast*, Op. 30 (London: Novello, 1898) 2. Opening choral entry. Public domain.   8

1.1 Albert Lynch, illustration to Vernon Lee, "Voix maudite," *Les Lettres et les arts, revue illustrée* (August 1, 1887): 138. Public domain.   17

2.1 George Sand, *Les Maîtres sonneurs* [1853] (Clichy: Loignon, Dupont et Cie, 1869). Joseph listens to the master piper Père Bastien. Courtesy, The Picture Art Collection / Alamy Stock Photo.   28

3.1 G.W. Martin, "The Helpless Lamb," words S.W. Partridge, *Band of Mercy Advocate* 1.7 (July 1879) no. 7. Reproduced by kind permission of the Syndics of Cambridge University Library. Photographer: Amélie Deblauwe.   41

3.2 M.W. Seeley, "A Cry for Liberty," words anonymous, *Songs of Happy Life*, ed. Sarah J. Eddy, 1st edn (Providence, Rhode Island: 1897) no. 56. Reproduced by kind permission of the Syndics of Cambridge University Library. Photographer: Amélie Deblauwe.   42

3.3 L.B. Marshall, "Voice of the Helpless," words Carlotta Perry, *Songs of Happy Life*, ed. Sarah J. Eddy, 1st edn (Providence, Rhode Island: 1897) no. 65. Reproduced by kind permission of the Syndics of Cambridge University Library. Photographer: Amélie Deblauwe.   43

3.4 J.C.O. Redington, "Dare to do Right," words anonymous, *Songs of Happy Life*, ed. Sarah J. Eddy, 1st edn (Providence, Rhode Island: 1897) no. 14. Reproduced by kind permission of the Syndics of Cambridge University Library. Photographer: Amélie Deblauwe.   44

3.5 W.M. Bradbury, "Dare to do Right," words anonymous, from program for Church of England Temperance Society Exeter Hall Meeting (April 26, 1898). Public domain.   45

4.1 Ethel Smyth, *The March of the Women*, words Cicely Hamilton. Edition by Christopher Wiley. Free to use or reuse.   56

viii FIGURES

4.2 Herman Paley, "She's Good Enough to be Your Baby's Mother and She's Good Enough to Vote with You," words Alfred Bryan (New York, 1916) opening. Courtesy, Library of Congress, Music Division. Public domain. 59

4.3 Phil Hanna, words and music, *The Anti-Suffrage Rose* (Boston: Women's Anti-Suffrage Association, 1915) opening. Courtesy, Library of Congress, Music Division. Public domain. 61

5.1 "Educate, Agitate, Organize." Walter Crane's design for *The Manifesto of the Socialist League* (London: Socialist League Office, 1885). Reproduced by kind permission of the Syndics of Cambridge University Library. Photographer: Amélie Deblauwe. 78

5.2 Edward Carpenter, *Chants of Labour*, title-page design by Walter Crane for the first edition (London: George Allen & Unwin, 1888). Public domain. 79

5.3 "When Adam delved and Eve span, Who was then the gentleman?" Design by Edward Burne-Jones for the first book edition of William Morris's *A Dream of John Ball* (London: Reeves & Turner, 1888). The Picture Art Collection / Alamy Stock Photo. 83

5.4 William Morris, "The Voice of Toil," no. 27 in Carpenter, *Chants of Labour*, to the traditional tune "Ye Banks and Braes." Public domain. 86

5.5 William Morris, "The March of the Workers," no. 38 in Carpenter, *Chants of Labour*, to the tune of "John Brown's Body." Public domain. 87

6.1 "*Ndiza kuwe wena Mvana*," with the tune ROCKINGHAM, *Amaculo* (Gwatyu: Ishicilelwe e-"S. Peter's Mission," 1875) no. 96. Edited by Philip Burnett. 91

6.2 "All people that on earth do dwell," with the tune OLD HUNDREDTH, *Hymns, Ancient and Modern, For use in the Services of the Church, with Accompanying Tunes* (London: Novello, 1861) no. 136. Edited by Philip Burnett. 92

6.3a "*Ap'ilanga lihambayo*," *Amaculo* (Gwatyu: Ishicilelwe e-"S. Peter's Mission," 1875) no. 51. National Library of South Africa (Cape Town Campus), Grey Collection, G.50.b.56. Used with permission. 93

6.3b "*Ap'ilanga lihambayo*" / [Jesus shall reign], with the tune ST AIDAN, *Amaculo* (Gwatyu, 1875), no. 51. Edited by Philip Burnett. 93

7.1 "A Map to Illustrate R.L. Stevenson's Three Cruises in the South Seas." Prefatory illustration to Robert Louis Stevenson, *In the South Seas: Being an Account of Experiences and Observations in the Marquesas, Paumotus and Gilbert Islands in the Course of Two*

Cruises on the Yacht "Casco" (1888) and the Schooner "Equator" (1889) (New York: Charles Scribner's Sons, 1896). Public domain. 108

8.1 Daniel-Esprit Auber, *La Muette de Portici*, title page from the first edition of the vocal score (Paris: E. Troupenas, [1828]). Bibliothèque nationale de France. 130

9.1 Photographic portrait of Richard Wagner by Pierre Petit, 1861. Courtesy, Maidun Collection / Alamy Stock Photo. 137

10.1 Henry Guy, "Malvern: View from the Worcestershire Beacon Looking South," color lithograph (240 x 725mm, c.1880). Courtesy, Dominic Winter Auctioneers. 152

11.1 Anon., "Johann Sebastian Bach at the Court of Frederick the Great." Woodcut (c.1892) based on a painting by Hermann Kaulbach. Sunny Celeste / Alamy Stock Photo. 167

12.1 Albumen print of Alfred Lord Tennyson and Emily Lady Tennyson with their sons at Farringford, by Oscar Gustav Rejlander, c.1862. Public domain. 183

13.1 Walt Whitman by Samuel Hollyer. Engraving of a daguerreotype by Gabriel Harrison (original lost), 1854, printed as the frontispiece for the 1855 self-published edition of *Leaves of Grass*. Ian Dagnall Computing / Alamy Stock Photo. 189

The editors, contributors and publisher are grateful to all the institutions and persons listed for permission to reproduce the materials in which they hold copyright. Every effort has been made to trace the copyright holders; apologies are offered for any omission, and the publisher will be pleased to add any necessary acknowledgement in subsequent editions.

Contributors

Charlotte Bentley is Lecturer in Music at Newcastle University. Her recent research focuses on musical transnationalism, with a particular interest in the development of transatlantic and intra-American operatic networks in the nineteenth century. Her monograph, *New Orleans and the Creation of Transatlantic Opera, 1819–1859*, was published by the University of Chicago Press in 2022 and won the American Musicological Society's H. Robert Cohen / RIPM Award in 2023.

Philip Burnett is a Leverhulme Early Career Fellow in Music at the University of York, UK. He is an historian of the musical practices found on Anglican missions in South and East Africa in the nineteenth and early twentieth centuries. His work has been published in *Yale Journal of Music and Religion*, *Postcolonial Studies*, and *South African Music Studies*. He recently co-edited with Erin Johnson-Williams *Hymns and Constructions of Race: Mobility, Agency, De/coloniality* (2024).

Alisa Clapp-Itnyre is author of *Angelic Airs, Subversive Songs: Music as Social Discourse in the Victorian Novel* (2002) and *British Hymn Books for Children, 1800–1900: Re-Tuning the History of Childhood* (2016). Her research on Bands of Mercy organizations is found in *British Hymn Books* as well as *Animals and Their Children in Victorian Culture*, edited by Brenda Ayres and Sarah E. Maier (2019). She is Professor of English at Indiana University East.

Elicia Clements is Associate Professor in the Departments of Humanities and English at York University, Canada, and the author of *Virginia Woolf: Music, Sound, Language* (2019). She is co-editor, with Lesley J. Higgins, of *Victorian Aesthetic Conditions: Pater Across the Arts* (2010) and has numerous articles and chapters on the intermedial connections between literature and music. Currently, she is working on a book titled *Modernist Literary Musics* with the aid of a SSHRC Insight Grant.

Jeremy Coleman is a musicologist and collaborative pianist originally from the UK. He is Resident Lecturer in Music in the Department of Music Studies, School of Performing Arts, University of Malta, and Area Director for Research in the School of Performing Arts. His first monograph was *Richard Wagner in Paris: Translation, Identity, Modernity* (2019) and he is currently working on a project about music historiography and performance practice.

Sarah Collins, recipient of the Royal Musical Association's Dent Medal for 2024, has written on the relationship between music, literary aesthetics and politics in the late nineteenth and early twentieth centuries. She is the author of *Lateness and Modernism: Untimely Ideas about Music, Literature and Politics in Interwar Britain* (2019) and *The Aesthetic Life of Cyril Scott* (2013); editor of *Music and Victorian Liberalism: Composing the Liberal Subject* (2019); and co-editor of *The Oxford Handbook of Music and Intellectual Culture in the Nineteenth Century* (2020). Sarah is currently Professor of Music at the University of Western Australia, and co-editor of the journal *Music & Letters*.

Katharine Ellis is the 1684 Professor of Music at the University of Cambridge. A cultural historian of musical France in the nineteenth and twentieth centuries, she is widely published on criticism, women's careers, amateur music-making, listening, and music education. Her books include *Music Criticism in Nineteenth-Century France* (1995), *Interpreting the Musical Past* (2005), *The Politics of Plainchant* (2013), *French Musical Life* (2022, winner of the AMS Otto Kinkeldey Award), and jointly-edited collections on Berlioz (2008) and, with Phyllis Weliver, on music and literature (*Words & Notes*, 2013).

Daniel M. Grimley is Head of Humanities at the University of Oxford and a Professorial Fellow at Merton College. His research centers on late nineteenth- and early twentieth-century music, especially in Scandinavia (Grieg, Sibelius, Carl Nielsen) and England (Elgar, Vaughan Williams, Delius). Recent publications include *Delius and the Sound of Place* (2018), *Jean Sibelius: Life, Music, Silence* (2021), which was named book of the year by the *Times Literary Supplement*, and *Vaughan Williams and his World*, co-edited with Byron Adams (2023).

Elizabeth Helsinger, John Matthews Manly Distinguished Service Professor Emerita in the Departments of English and Art History at the University of Chicago, is the author of *Poetry and the Pre-Raphaelite Arts* (2008), *Poetry and the Thought of Song in Nineteenth-Century Britain* (2015), and *Conversing in Verse* (2022). She is a contributor to *Song Beyond the Nation* (eds Bullock and Tunbridge, 2021) and has written numerous articles on William Morris and on the relations between literature, art, and music in the nineteenth century.

Fraser Riddell is Associate Professor of English and Medical Humanities at Durham University. His publications include *Music and the Queer Body in English Literature at the Fin de Siècle* (2022), and articles on music and literature in *Volupté, Journal of Victorian Culture*, and *Victorian Literature and Culture*. A recent chapter on the queer soundscapes of Victorian pastoral literature was published in *The Victorian Idyll in Art and Literature: Subject, Ecology, Form* (2024).

Emma Sutton is Professor of English at the University of St Andrews and an Associate of the UK's Centre for Pacific Studies. Her publications include: *Aubrey Beardsley and British Wagnerism in the 1890s* (2002), *Opera and the Novel* (edited with Michael Downes, 2012), and *Virginia Woolf and Classical Music* (2013). Emma has worked closely with Oceanian artists and scholars for a decade; in 2018, she established a collaboration with National University of Samoa creating public-facing resources on Samoan music.

Shafquat Towheed is Director of Research in the School of Arts and Humanities at The Open University. He has written extensively on nineteenth- and twentieth-century literature, with a particular focus on the history and practice of reading, including its relationship to listening. He is a volume editor for the *Collected Works of Edith Wharton* for Oxford University Press and is currently co-editing a book on Vernon Lee and the future of intelligence.

Phyllis Weliver, Professor of English at Saint Louis University, publishes books and articles that explore literature and music as mutually constitutive with a range of nineteenth-century discourses. She is the author of the monographs *Mary Gladstone and the Victorian Salon: Music, Literature, Liberalism* (2017); *The Musical Crowd in English Fiction, 1840–1910: Class, Culture and Nation* (2006); and *Women Musicians in Victorian Fiction, 1860–1900: Representations of Music, Science and Gender in the Leisured Home* (2000). Her edited projects include *Words & Notes in the Long Nineteenth Century* with Katharine Ellis (2013) and *The Figure of Music in Nineteenth-Century British Poetry* (2005).

Christopher Wiley is Head of Music and Media at the University of Surrey, UK. He has published six books, including the co-edited *Women's Suffrage in Word, Image, Music, Stage and Screen* (2021); articles in *The Musical Quarterly, Music & Letters, Women's History Review*, and other journals; and book chapters on a wide range of subjects. He is an internationally recognized expert on Ethel Smyth, about whom he is currently editing volumes for both Cambridge University Press and The Boydell Press.

Acknowledgements

In a book such as this, the research of individual authors transforms into seminar and classroom material as if via alchemy. Yet, backstage, the process requires patience and understanding on all sides, because cross-disciplinary study of literature and music demands authors to accommodate their work to the pedagogical needs of a second discipline. Things that are self-evident in the home discipline suddenly require explanation. Our contributing authors have consistently risen to these challenges and have been an inspiration and a pleasure to work with. We are immensely grateful to them. On the editorial side, our work on the book has been helped by two people in particular: research assistant Nate Meshau, who did fact-checking and bibliographical work on advanced drafts of the essays; and Michael Middeke at Boydell, whose enthusiasm for this project was matched only by his patience in waiting for its delivery.

Several authors would like to express gratitude for scholarly help and for permissions relating to their chapters. Without the support of Rosemary Lloyd, translator of George Sand's *Les Maîtres sonneurs*, Katharine Ellis's contribution (Chapter 2) would not have got beyond the drawing board. Emma Sutton (Chapter 7) would like to signal Mary (Lisa) Lawson Burke, Elfriede Hermann and Wolfgang Kempf for their generosity in sharing expertise on Kiribati music. Elicia Clements (Chapter 11) extends warm thanks to Lesley J. Higgins, co-General Editor of the *Collected Works of Walter Pater*, for reading of a chapter draft and for responsiveness to queries.

Permission was generously granted by Oxford University Press for Katharine Ellis's use of the extracts from George Sand, *The Master Pipers*, trans. Rosemary Lloyd (Oxford: Oxford University Press, 1994). With the publisher's generous waiving of specific permissions, Chapter 8, by Charlotte Bentley, contains ideas that previously appeared in her *New Orleans and the Creation of Transatlantic Opera, 1819–1859* (Chicago: University of Chicago Press, 2022). The translation of Champfleury by Palomba Paves-Yashinsky in Jeremy Coleman's contribution (Chapter 9) is drawn from Paves-Yashinsky's article "*Richard Wagner* and *After the Battle*: Champfleury," *19th-Century Music* 13.1 (Summer 1989): 20–5 and is reused with permission from the University of California Press. Chapter 13 is a modified version of Sarah Collins, "Nationalisms, Modernisms and Masculinities: Strategies of Displacement in Vaughan Williams's Reading of Walt Whitman" in *Nineteenth-Century Music Review* 14.1 (2017): 65–91. © Cambridge University Press, 2016. Relevant passages are reprinted here with permission.

A Guide to this Book

Phyllis Weliver and Katharine Ellis

As readers and listeners, we frequently have responses to music and literature that are difficult to put into words. In fact, they are so closely linked that in some cultures they are impossible to separate: music is poetry and poetry is music. In the West, when nineteenth-century authors searched for ways to express the inexpressible, they turned to music more than to any other art form. They did likewise to indicate subtle aspects of identity or political allegiance, and hierarchies of social class. When critics of the same period wanted to convey the emotional power of music, they turned to prose poetry or to other explicitly literary forms of expression. And in a period of high colonialism, nationalism and social injustice, when agents of political, religious and social change – on all sides – sought to intensify the power of their message, they turned their poetry into song.

This historical richness of literary sensitivity to music sits in inverse relationship to current tendencies in universities and even the culture at large to foreground the visual (and the historical) rather than the aural, and to leave the soundscapes and musical facets of nineteenth-century literature to a close-knit group of specialists. While recent essay collections and handbooks indicate an upsurge of interest in music and literature at the highest levels of research practice, there has until now been no stepping-stone to allow students interested in these sister subjects to develop their skills in studying them together. How, then, do we talk about artistic forms that express meaning that is difficult to paraphrase? In one sense, the answer is to learn the "codes" that are expressed in literary texts and musical scores.

This book is a cross between a reader, a workbook and a DIY manual for students and instructors. Its aim is to act as a foundational text to help demystify, and even normalize, the study of music as a literary topic of the nineteenth century. Likewise, it helps students of music to engage with poetry and prose texts of various kinds where layers of meaning need to be painstakingly uncovered. It focuses on a period when the crossovers of music and literature take many different forms and speak to some of the most important, and enduring, issues of the time. Using a combination of the thematic and the analytical, each of the book's thirteen chapters takes a case-study genre or work, contextualizes it, and shows ways towards detailed readings of the music/text relationship. The result is a series of model approaches illustrating the kinds of music-related questions one can ask of a particular literary text or genre, with a view to inspiring robust discussion in the seminar room and catalyzing new directions in independent research. Chapters focus, via case studies, on issues of:

- Gender and sexuality (Chapter 1 on Vernon Lee, Chapter 4 on suffrage songs, Chapter 12 on Alfred Lord Tennyson and Chapter 13 on Walt Whitman);
- Race, ethnicity and empire (the editors' "Guide to this Book" on Wilkie Collins, Samuel Coleridge-Taylor and Zitkála-Šá; Chapter 6 on mission hymns; Chapter 7 on Robert Louis Stevenson's Pacific travelogue, and Chapter 8 on a Charles Jobey short story about Louisiana);
- Cultural politics and aesthetics (Chapter 2 on George Sand, folk song, and Otherness; Chapter 9 on Wagner as an aesthetic misfit in Paris; Chapter 10 on Elgar, place and belonging; and Chapter 11 on Pater, aestheticization and national musics);
- Activism (Chapter 3 on Bands of Mercy, Chapter 4 on suffrage and Chapter 5 on William Morris).

These categories necessarily overlap, their inter-relationships signaled by the keywords at the beginning of the chapters. Via their case studies, the chapters also broach technical questions that students of word and music studies will find useful. For instance, Chapters 2 and 7 deal with unwritten types of music, Chapters 3 to 6 are concerned with the setting of poetry to music in songs and hymns, and Chapters 9 and 10 deal with intermediality (interactive relationships between different art forms).

The importance of the listener's perspective – both the listening character within a novel or a poem and the modern reader (an imaginary listener) – is constantly brought to the fore. While the long nineteenth century was the era that made "self-improvement" a life's work, and easy forms of musical notation were invented in that spirit, the original audiences for our case studies were likely to be musical amateurs at best. Writers had to use non-technical language to make their point: they did not need musically literate readers so much as readers with a good aural imagination. Our book implies the same, and we hope students will also take advantage of the easy accessibility, via the internet, of much of the music that our authors discuss. Western musical notation has been the most obvious barrier to embedding music/text relationships into pedagogy. In this book our authors do not avoid it; but frequently their case studies show how questions relating to non-notated musics, or issues of performance, are just as important as those requiring the analysis of notation.

Music in nineteenth-century writing acts as a bridge: to carry coded messages; to indicate Otherness, the uncanny, displacement or belonging. But in song, especially when allied to marching or dancing, it also acts haptically, bringing participants and onlookers into solidarity through entrained physical movement, and connoting general "health." With these extremes in mind, our authors explore case studies relating to sexual identity, mental health, exile, landscape and rootedness, colonial interaction, and politics. On the "haptic" side they also discuss songs of political activism aimed at women and children in Britain and the USA, and hymns adapted to Western tunes by missionary converts in South Africa.

Our authors have been encouraged to start at the widest point and move inwards, but students may need to work in the opposite direction, perhaps beginning by noting where music occurs in a novel, and then working outwards. For example, the first English detective novel, *The Moonstone* (1868) by Wilkie Collins (1824–89), begins with a prehistory to the main narrative about the storming of Seringapatam, India in 1799, during which Colonel John Herncastle steals an exotic yellow diamond. The narrator writes that in the midst of the general plundering, "General Baird announced publicly by beat of drum, that any thief detected in the fact, be he whom he might, should be hung."[1] The military drum is a signaling device, usually meant to organize troop movement. Here, Baird states that the plundering must cease, but only after the drumming first permeates the chaos by sonorously demanding that attention be paid. Colonel Herncastle is not hanged, although he has brutally stolen the "Moonstone." He goes on to will the gem to his niece, Rachel Verinder.

Within the first few pages of the novel, then, I have determined that there is a musical moment. I then begin to ask what role music plays in the larger narrative. Because it is a detective novel, I wonder if music will have a role to play in the mystery. It is sometimes helpful to ask who, what, where, why and how questions. In this case, the context for the drumming is military and it is directly linked to cultural plunder. This is what I know so far. But because I have begun to pay attention to drumming, when I see it again, I can link the various occurrences together and ask how meaning develops.

The main plot of the novel explores the repossession of the diamond by three Indian priests who are hereditary guardians of the gem. The gifting of the Moonstone to Rachel occurs early in the novel, as does its disappearance while she is asleep. The mystery in the novel thereafter has to do with discovering not what was done, but how it was done. Notably, the three priests are heard before they are seen in their first two appearances in the novel. They are playing Indian hand-drums. The first time, house steward of the Verinder country seat Gabriel Betteredge tells us:

> Concluding to set myself in the warm summer air next [...] I was stopped by hearing a sound like the soft beating of a drum, on the terrace in front of my lady's residence.

---

[1] Wilkie Collins, *The Moonstone* (1868), ed. J.I.M. Stewart (London: Penguin, 1986) 37. All subsequent citations given parenthetically.

> Going round to the terrace, I found three mahogany-coloured Indians, in white linen frocks and trousers, looking up at the house.
>
> The Indians, as I saw on looking closer, had small hand-drums slung in front of them. Behind them stood a little delicate-looking light-haired English boy carrying a bag. I judged the fellows to be strolling conjurors, and the boy with the bag to be carrying the tools of their trade. (48–9)

Conjurors they are, but not of the wandering minstrel variety. The narrator misinterprets their identity, but the astute reader links the drumming with the initial theft in India. Unlike the martial drum of British troops, however, this is a "soft" drumming that steals quietly into Britain. It is doubly foreign in the sense of environment (one does not usually hear drums of any sort in English country houses of this period) and in being culturally Indian. The latter is highlighted the next time that the drums are heard. Again, these are Betteredge's words:

> I had just ranged the decanters in a row before old Mr Ablewhite (who represented the master of the house), when there came a sound from the terrace which startled me out of my company manners on the instant. Mr Franklin and I looked at each other; it was the sound of the Indian drum. (105)

In this citation, the drumming does not just sound "like" a drum (which the head of the Verinder staff cannot identify as Indian until he sees the players, as in the previous example); here, it is clearly understood aurally as "the sound of the Indian drum." From the larger context, we know that the exchanged look is one of worry, for Betteredge and Franklin already associate the Indians with the threatened loss of the Moonstone. This is reading from the English perspective. If we approach the novel with sensitivity to the Indian position, however, the drumming signals the presence of Indian culture. It is as if the three disguised priests announce audibly (but in code) that they are going to repossess the diamond, and they will do so under the soundscape of their own drumming. Because the original theft occurred despite the signals of the British military drum, the Indian hand-drum becomes an assertion of cultural sovereignty.

My next step with publications that originally appeared in periodicals is to find the original periodical, if possible, because modern versions can hide the contextualized meanings available to original readers (serialized novels are juxtaposed with articles, poems, illustrations, advertisements and more). *The Moonstone* rewards this small bit of research particularly well because it was published simultaneously as weekly parts in *Harper's Weekly: A Journal of Civilization* in America and Charles Dickens's *All the Year Round* in Britain – both of which are easily found on the internet.[2] There is an immediately

---

[2] *Dickens Journals Online*, <https://www.djo.org.uk/> [Accessed October 24, 2024]; and *Harper's Weekly*, The Online Books Page, <https://onlinebooks.library.upenn.edu/webbin/serial?id=harpersweekly> [Accessed October 24, 2024].

FIG. 0.1: Wilkie Collins, *The Moonstone*, instalment 1, *Harper's Weekly* 12.1 (January 4, 1868): 5. Illustrations by John McLenan.

discernible difference between the presentation of *The Moonstone* in these two publications, for *Harper's Weekly* was illustrated (by John McLenan) and *All the Year Round* was not. Thus, American readers encountered a direct tie between the British and Indian drumming on the first page of the first installment, which featured three large images: the diamond in its sacred shrine, Harcourt's violent acquisition of it, and the three Indian priests with the English boy and the hand-drums. This last image is placed a little above the sentence about the British military drum in Seringapatam. The American audience would have seen the Indian aspects of the tale at a glance before beginning to read, including looking at the Indian hand-drum while they read of the military drum of empire.[3] In contrast, British readers of *All the Year Round* encountered the exotic sonority of the Indian drums in a later issue and chapter, like today's readers. This little bit of research helps to establish that the drums are indeed linked, whether we realized this through closely paying attention to how music occurs in the text alone or whether we had a little help from the illustration. Regardless, *The Moonstone* example illustrates how an author's novelistic representation of music and sound can act as a signal of plot development, and how being alive to the resonances of these signals enhances an interpretation of the whole.

What questions are best, though, in cases where a novel or poem has captured the imagination of composers and has been set to music, as song, as opera or as choral music? Poetry immediately raises questions of musicality because of the rhythms set up by a poet's use of rhyme, assonance and meter. We can start with the "interart" question of whether poetic rhythm translates well into musical rhythm. And then, moving beyond internal analysis, we can think about the power relations involved in adaptation, and the ways a new artistic voice and new audiences can change the meaning of the original, creating what are known as its "afterlives."

We can test out this scenario via another mini case study, on an epic poem recounting the life and love of a legendary Onondaga warrior chief: *The Song of Hiawatha* (1855) by the American poet Henry Wadsworth Longfellow (1807–82). This poem, a runaway success, inspired an unusually large number of artistic responses, including musical settings and poetic parodies. By far its most popular musical setting was by the Sierra-Leone English composer Samuel Coleridge-Taylor (1875–1912), who wrote a trio of choral cantatas on selected portions of the poem, starting with *Hiawatha's Wedding Feast* (1898).

Below, I cite a single stanza of the original poem, where the wedding feast is introduced:

---

[3] For more on the American illustrations, see Molly Knox Leverenz, "Illustrating 'The Moonstone' in America: 'Harper's Weekly' and Transatlantic Introspection," *American Periodicals* 24.1 (2014): 21–44.

Canto XI
You shall hear how Pau-Puk-Keewis,
How the handsome Yenadizze,
Danced at Hiawatha's wedding;
How the gentle Chibiabos,
He the sweetest of musicians,
Sang his songs of love and longing;
How Iagoo, the great boaster,
He the marvellous storyteller,
Told his tales of strange adventure,
That the feast might be more joyous,
That the time might pass more gayly,
And the guests be more contented.

Reciting this poetry out loud immediately brings to life Longfellow's choice of meter – trochaic tetrameter – which was possibly chosen precisely for its exotic feel in English. The stresses on most of the odd-numbered syllables run counter to the usual iambic unstress/stress pattern of the English language and make for an incantatory experience when used at such length. (Imagine the effect of reciting in this meter, albeit with some variants and ambiguities, for the whole 250 pages of the poem.) We can also think about Longfellow's use of internal repetition to create the effect of a list. We can notice that the whole stanza has just one period [full stop], and that Longfellow uses various kinds of extension – including the "list-effect" – to keep a single poetic sentence afloat for the entire duration of the stanza. This same process happens with many of the stanzas. All these aspects of the poetry are musical: they play with sound operating in time.

Before turning to Coleridge-Taylor's music, a thought experiment: how likely is it that a nineteenth-century composer of concert music would want to preserve the syllabic rhythm of Longfellow's original? What would that sound like over, say, a thirty-minute cantata? How singable or lyrical would it be? Perhaps unsurprisingly, Coleridge-Taylor has other ideas. Listening to the opening of the first chorus brings home how he substitutes one kind of repetition for another. Yes, he builds repetition in his music; but he does it in ways that conform to nineteenth-century expectations of how music works.

Two phrases, with repetitions across the choir, start the first choral section of the piece. One phrase has wide leaps both up and down ("You shall hear…"); the second has a descending stepwise start and then uses much smaller leaps ("Danced at Hiawatha's wedding"). Neither preserves the rhythm of the poetry: rather, the composer extends some durations to align with stresses and introduces quicker notes than the Longfellow poem implies. Coleridge-Taylor uses variants of these phrases across the entire cantata, changing either the melodies, the rhythms, the harmony or any combination. This procedure comes across as a musical "translation" of Longfellow's poetic repetition.

FIG. 0.2: Samuel Coleridge-Taylor, *Hiawatha's Wedding Feast*, Op. 30 (London: Novello, 1898) 2. Opening choral entry.

Beyond poetic and musical content, what other subjects might be of interest here? One of the key messages in this book relates to context, and to the way that understanding historical background helps to bring the interart relationships of music and literature into relief. Seen through a racial lens, for instance, these two Hiawathas are very different. Longfellow knew and worked with tribal peoples, but his Hiawatha was a composite of several legends, and his epic is written very much from the viewpoint of a United States settler-colonial. It ends with successful missionary intervention (everyone in the tribe converts to Catholicism). Coleridge-Taylor, unique as a London-trained Black composer experiencing everyday racism but successfully integrating himself into Britain's musical life, had a different relationship to the Indigenous subject-matter. Inspired by meetings with the African American poet Paul Lawrence Dunbar, *Hiawatha's Wedding Feast* became a way of celebrating his own racial identity and of navigating an English Otherness. (In 1896 and 1897 Coleridge-Taylor presented poetry and music concerts in London with Dunbar, and they included his *Hiawatha Sketches* for violin and piano.) This conclusion becomes all the more plausible given that when Coleridge-Taylor came to write an orchestral overture to *Hiawatha* in 1899, he evoked the melody of an African American Spiritual, "Nobody knows the trouble I see, Lord," within it. Strikingly, there are no Indigenous melodies in the *Hiawatha* cantatas. There is a parallel here, in that Coleridge-Taylor's favorite composer, Antonín Dvořák (1841–1904), said in an interview of December 15, 1893, that he had evoked the spirit of Indigenous melodies in his Symphony no. 9 "From the New World" (premiered in New York the following day), and that part of it was a sketch for a cantata or an opera on Longfellow's *Hiawatha*.[4] Just a few months earlier, he had encouraged Americans to use specifically African American melodies as the fount for a "national" style;[5] now he said that upon further study, he had found that African American and Indigenous melodies were "practically identical." In other words, two ethnic traditions were conflated (and appropriated) by a white composer, in ways that might make a twenty-first-century reader recoil; but Coleridge-Taylor seems to have accepted the conflation as useful and mirrored it in his own work.

Finally, how might we approach a situation where a poet responds to a familiar tune? This process brings different interart questions to the fore. There is a long practice of writing poems to be sung to existing tunes, often for political reasons. A notable example from early in our period is the enduring *Irish Melodies* of Thomas Moore (1779–1852), published from 1808 to 1834. Norman

---

[4] "Dvořák on His New Work," *New York Herald* (December 15, 1893). Available at https://scalar.oberlincollegelibrary.org/decolonizing-ethnomusicology/media/image-december-1893-article-from-the-new-york-herald-on-dvoks-new-world-symphony [Accessed October 29, 2024].
[5] Interview "The Real Value of Negro Melodies," *New York Herald* (May 21, 1893).

Vance observes that these *Melodies* were "national rather than narrowly partisan or sectarian" because they drew "on a composite and adaptable musical tradition shared by Irish people of different politics."[6] Such practices continued to the end of the long nineteenth century in a variety of cultural contexts, as we see in the poem "The Red Man's America" (1917) by Zitkála-Šá (Gertrude Simmons Bonnin, 1876–1938), a member of the Ihanktonwan Dakota Oyate tribe in North America (Yankton Sioux or Dakota) who had been educated at White's Indiana Manual Labor Institute; Earlham College in Richmond, Indiana; and the New England Conservatory of Music in Boston (she was a violinist). Writing in English, she published legends of her nation, lifewriting and activist writing – often in ways that blur the lines between these categories. She was also the librettist, melodist, costume designer, choreographer and chorus trainer for *The Sun Dance Opera* (1913), with scoring completed by William F. Hanson (1887–1969).

"The Red Man's America" appeared in the journal that was sent to members and friends of the Society of American Indians – a predominantly Native audience. When original readers paged through the spring issue of *American Indian Magazine* in early 1917 and found a poem with the opening line clearly referencing "America" (also known as "My country 'tis of thee"), there was no need to provide the scored music or to instruct what tune to sing it to, for "America" was familiar in US schools, Sunday school hymn books and patriotic events across the country (including on reservations) where singing the song accompanied displays of the US flag.[7] In fact, the tune was popular beyond the US border, too. Decades before Reverend Samuel Francis Smith wrote the words for "America" in 1831, several other Western countries had used the same music as a vehicle for their own national sentiments, including in Britain where it is known as "God Save the King."

Zitkála-Šá's title "The Red Man's America" thus points to two meanings of "America" (the land or country and the song). Then the opening line subverts the first line of "America" by exchanging the word "of" with "to" (the original comma also changes to an exclamation point):

"The Red Man's America"	"America"
My country! 'tis to thee,	My country, 'tis of thee,
Sweet land of Liberty,	Sweet land of liberty,
My pleas I bring.	Of thee I sing.
Land where OUR fathers died,	Land where my fathers died,

---

[6] Norman Vance, "Poetry and its Audiences: Club, Street, Ballad," *Irish Literature in Transition, 1830–1880*, ed. Matthew Campbell (Cambridge: Cambridge University Press, 2020) 225.

[7] Thomas Grillot, *First Americans: U.S. Patriotism in Indian Country After World War I* (New Haven: Yale University Press, 2018) 118.

Whose offspring are denied	Land of the Pilgrims' pride,
The Franchise given wide,	From every mountain side,
Hark, while I sing.	Let freedom ring.
[...]	[...]
Great Mystery, to thee,	Our fathers' God, to Thee,
Life of humanity,	Author of liberty,
To thee we cling,	To Thee we sing;
Grant our home-land be bright,	Long may our land be bright,
Grant us just human right,	With freedom's holy light,
Protect us by Thy might,	Protect us by Thy might,
Great God, our king (lines 1–7, 22–8)[8]	Great God, our King.[9]

Note how closely the new poem follows the original: line 3, for example, only changes one vowel sound: "Of" to "my." It is a masterly achievement. If we think of the musical setting, these small changes do not add difficulty to the execution (composers need to be aware of which vowels are used on high notes, for example). At the same time, the meaning changes. In the hands of the Sioux author, "America" becomes an addressee ("to thee"), not a possession ("of thee") in line 1. These two small words align with cultural beliefs about a person's relationship to land.

Anthologies reproduce Zitkála-Šá's four-stanza poem in isolation, but if we return to the original periodical publication to contextualize its first distribution, then we find that the meaning of this poem deepens. Prefaced by the magazine's motto, *"For the Honor of the Race and the Good of the Country,"* this particular journal issue commences with an article requesting gifts to support the Great War in the months just before the US entered the conflict. The call, "Indians of America awaken!" in the fight "for universal justice," is put thus: "As the Indian fed the hungry Pilgrim on the Atlantic shore in 1620 let him again give of his store of corn. He will not only enrich himself but save the world from misery."[10] Giving services of life and food were central to how Indigenous

---

[8] Zitkála-Šá, "The Red Man's America," *American Indian Magazine: A Journal of Race Progress* 5.1 (January–March 1917): 64, <https://www.aidhp.com/files/original/054f74de756cc2b62a2cba9e031be52a.pdf> [Accessed October 24, 2024].

[9] Samuel F. Smith, "America," 1831, ms copy in Smith's hand (August 4, 1886), *Gilder Lehrman Institute of American History*, <https://www.gilderlehrman.org/history-resources/spotlight-primary-source/my-country-tis-thee> [Accessed October 24, 2024].

[10] [Arthur C. Parker], "America Needs Men," *American Indian Magazine* 5.1 (January–March 1917): 6, <https://www.aidhp.com/files/original/054f74de756cc2b62a2cba9e031be52a.pdf> [Accessed October 24, 2024].

Americans understood participation in World War I, which this article presents as a global war against human rights violations.[11]

"The Red Man's America" can be seen to be part of this war effort because of how it is situated within this journal. As the final item in the issue before the end matter, Zitkála-Šá's poem bookends the appeal of the opening article. The content of the journal thus moves from "America Needs Men" (the title of the opening editorial) to "Grant us just human right, / Protect us by Thy might, / Great God, our king." The message is similar enough to read as a single statement, with the difference that the first is mostly an appeal to logic, whereas the latter – with the well-known tune imagined while reading the fresh words – becomes an emotional argument.

This link with the war effort gains further credibility because of page layout. Rather than the poem being printed on its own, a short article sits just above it on the same sheet. "1,200 Indians from the Canadian reserves have enlisted for active service in the war," reports "Indians at the Front." "Last year Indians contributed over $7,000 to war funds, and Indian women have been noteworthy contributors of knitted socks, mufflers and other comforts for the soldiers."[12] Because the article and poem are both given in full on the page (neither runs over), they seem all the more to exist together.

Situated thus, the cited stanzas renounce settler-invader dominance while they also proudly assert tribal America's continued "Life of humanity" (line 23). "The Red Man's America" thereby communicates survivance, which Gerald Vizenor (Ojibwe) defines as "an active sense of presence, the continuance of native stories, not a mere reaction, or a survivable name. Native survivance stories are renunciations of dominance, tragedy, and victimry."[13] We are analyzing a poem instead of a story, but the idea of survivance is still applicable. "Land where OUR fathers died" in the poem does not just correct the original line 4 ("Land where my fathers died," or the self-enfranchised colonizers) with the insistence of capital letters ("OUR" Indian fathers), but rather makes clear the continuing presence of a vigorous community, who offer valuable service to the world and are demanding the franchise. Nationalist song has potency because it is shared by a nation of people despite their local and political differences (to adopt Vance's observation about Moore's *Irish Melodies*). The music is already known, and it will be known again. Encountering a parody changes original meaning on the spot, and this newfound meaning is future-oriented, too, for singing "America" again in a group will be a collective, "haptic" engagement

---

[11] See Grillot, *First Americans*, 83–122.

[12] "Indians at the Front," *American Indian Magazine: A Journal of Race Progress* 5.1 (January–March 1917): 64, <https://www.aidhp.com/files/original/054f74de756cc2b62a2cba9e031be52a.pdf> [Accessed October 24, 2024].

[13] Gerald Vizenor, *Manifest Manners: Narratives on Postindian Survivance* (Lincoln: University of Nebraska Press, 1994, 1999) vii.

that is layered with individuals' silent memory of reading "The Red Man's America." Greater than the sum of their parts, together the new words with the existing tune insist upon tribal peoples' participation in decisions about their land (before citizenship was legalized with the Indian Citizenship Act of 1924) and, with the replacement of "Great Mystery" for "God," assert Native survivance in the face of attempted invader-erasure.

Note for Instructors

In general, and mindful that students from different disciplines will find different technical aspects of the book challenging, we have tried to order chapters in sequence according to the technical complexity of the questions they pose. In order to maximize understanding of the intellectual aims of the book, we recommend that students read this Guide before embarking on their first chapter.

Our chapters are split into short sections each with a different function. The "Prelude" is always a primary source extract and will form the reference point for the case study. Students might want to study it before reading the rest of the chapter and then return to it afterwards to see how their understanding has changed. Initial keywords help indicate themes that are shared across chapters; and sections on "Further Reading" and/or "Listening" at the end of each chapter allow for independent work. These sections also underpin the dual role of the book: it can be used as a stand-alone set of chapters or, if students are studying the whole of a text that we have excerpted and used as a case study, our book can be used as an entry point to that text.

In the middle of the sandwich, the "Challenge" gives an executive summary of the topic and outlines the kinds of thematic and analytical questions that the chapter raises. The more extensive "Background" and "Case Study" sections then move progressively deeper into the chosen text, its musical content and possible implications. "Backgrounds" can be historical, biographical, aesthetic or genre-based, or a mixture. Part of the function of this section is to enable students to see how prioritizing different contexts can change the questions that might be considered to be important – how they can channel our thinking and, therefore, how important it is to think about multiple possibilities. The "Case Study" sections contain analytical detail, but they will often leave interpretations open-ended, to facilitate discussion and to highlight the value of multiple perspectives. Each chapter of the book accordingly suggests a move from the summary to the general to the particular; but it would be equally valid to reverse the flow and to work outwards from the analysis of "Prelude" material towards identifying relevant cultural contexts for each extract. The design is intended to be flexible.

A Note on Anachronistic Language

This book deals with historical texts, some of which use terms that are offensive in today's world. We have attempted to navigate between historical accuracy and sensitivity to present-day terminology. Language is ever shifting, and we appreciate that the text of this book might not keep up with terminological change concerning colonialism, ethnicity, gender, mental illness, race and sexuality.

Further Reading

Allis, Michael. *British Music and Literary Context: Artistic Connections in the Long Nineteenth Century.* Woodbridge, Suffolk: The Boydell Press, 2012.

da Sousa Correa, Delia. "Music." Eds Dino Franco Felluga, Pamela K. Gilbert and Linda K. Hughes. *The Encyclopedia of Victorian Literature.* Vol. 3. Chichester: Wiley-Blackwell, 2015. 1092–101.

——, ed. *The Edinburgh Companion to Literature and Music.* Edinburgh: Edinburgh University Press, 2020.

Dayan, Peter. *Music Writing Literature, from Sand via Debussy to Derrida.* Aldershot: Ashgate, 2006.

Durkin, Rachael, Peter Dayan, Axel Englund and Katharina Clausius, eds. *The Routledge Companion to Music and Modern Literature.* London: Routledge, 2022.

Fuller, Sophie and Nicky Losseff, eds. *The Idea of Music in Victorian Fiction.* Aldershot: Ashgate, 2004.

Helsinger, Elizabeth K. *Poetry and the Thought of Song in Nineteenth-Century Britain.* Charlottesville: University of Virginia Press, 2015.

Kramer, Lawrence. *Song Acts: Writings on Words and Music.* Leiden: Brill, 2017.

Newark, Cormac. *Opera in the Novel from Balzac to Proust.* Cambridge: Cambridge University Press, 2011.

Prins, Yopie. "Robert Browning, Transported by Meter." *The Traffic in Poems: Nineteenth-Century Poetry and Transatlantic Exchange.* Ed. Meredith McGill. New Brunswick, New Jersey: Rutgers University Press, 2007.

Solie, Ruth A. *Music in Other Words: Victorian Conversations.* Berkeley: University of California Press, 2005.

Weliver, Phyllis. "A Score of Change: Twenty Years of Critical Musicology and Victorian Literature." *Literature Compass* 8.10 (October 2011): 776–94.

——, ed. *The Figure of Music in Nineteenth-Century British Poetry.* Aldershot: Ashgate, 2005.

—— and Katharine Ellis, eds. *Words and Notes in the Long Nineteenth Century.* Woodbridge: The Boydell Press, 2013.

CHAPTER 1

Vernon Lee's "A Wicked Voice" (1890): Music and Queerness in Decadent Fiction

Fraser Riddell

Recommended Text

Vernon Lee, "A Wicked Voice," *Hauntings: Fantastic Stories* (New York: Lovell, 1890) 195–237; <https://archive.org/details/hauntingsfantastooleev/page/n7/mode/2up> [Accessed February 24, 2025]. Numbers in brackets refer to this edition.

Keywords

Body, castrati, eighteenth-century music, fiction, Italy, listening, medicine, opera, sexuality, short story, Venice, Victorian Britain, voice, Richard Wagner

Prelude

Extract

Lee, "A Wicked Voice," 218–21.

The musicians, under their green and yellow and red lamps, held a whispered consultation on the manner of conciliating these contradictory demands. Then, after a minute's hesitation, the violins began the prelude of that once famous air, which has remained popular in Venice – the words written, some hundred years ago, by the patrician Gritti, the music by an unknown composer – *La Biondina in Gondoleta.*

That cursed eighteenth century! It seemed a malignant fatality that made these brutes choose just this piece to interrupt me.

At last the long prelude came to an end; and above the cracked guitars and squeaking fiddles there arose, not the expected nasal chorus, but a single voice singing below its breath.

My arteries throbbed. How well I knew that voice! It was singing, as I have said, below its breath, yet none the less it sufficed to fill all that reach of the canal with its strange quality of tone, exquisite, far-fetched.

They were long-drawn-out notes, of intense but peculiar sweetness, a man's voice which had much of a woman's, but more even of a chorister's, but a chorister's voice without its limpidity and innocence; its youthfulness was veiled, muffled, as it were, in a sort of downy vagueness, as if a passion of tears withheld.

There was a burst of applause, and the old palaces re-echoed with the clapping. "Bravo, bravo! Thank you, thank you! Sing again – please, sing again. Who can it be?"

And then a bumping of hulls, a splashing of oars, and the oaths of gondoliers trying to push each other away, as the red prow-lamps of the gondolas pressed round the gaily lit singing-boat.

But no one stirred on board. It was to none of them that this applause was due. And while every one pressed on, and clapped and vociferated, one little red prow-lamp dropped away from the fleet; for a moment a single gondola stood forth black upon the black water, and then was lost in the night.

For several days the mysterious singer was the universal topic. The people of the music-boat swore that no one besides themselves had been on board, and that they knew as little as ourselves about the owner of that voice. The gondoliers, despite their descent from the spies of the old Republic, were equally unable to furnish any clue. No musical celebrity was known or suspected to be at Venice; and every one agreed that such a singer must be a European celebrity. The strangest thing in this strange business was, that even among those learned in music there was no agreement on the subject of this voice: it was called by all sorts of names and described by all manner of incongruous adjectives; people went so far as to dispute whether the voice belonged to a man or to a woman: every one had some new definition.

In all these musical discussions I, alone, brought forward no opinion. I felt a repugnance, an impossibility almost, of speaking about that voice; and the more or less commonplace conjectures of my friend had the invariable effect of sending me out of the room.

Meanwhile my work was becoming daily more difficult, and I soon passed from utter impotence to a state of inexplicable agitation. Every morning I arose with fine resolutions and grand projects of work; only to go to bed that night without having accomplished anything. I spent hours leaning on my balcony, or wandering through the network of lanes with their ribbon of blue sky, endeavoring vainly to expel the thought of that voice, or endeavoring in reality to reproduce it in my memory; for the more I tried to banish it from my thoughts, the more I grew to thirst for that extraordinary tone, for those mysteriously downy, veiled notes; and no sooner did I make an effort to work at my opera than my head was full of scraps of forgotten eighteenth century airs, of frivolous or languishing little phrases; and I fell to wondering with a bitter-sweet longing how those songs would have sounded if sung by that voice.

At length it became necessary to see a doctor, from whom, however, I carefully hid away all the stranger symptoms of my malady. The air of the lagoons, the great heat, he answered cheerfully, had pulled me down a little; a tonic and a month in the country, with plenty of riding and no work, would make me myself again.

Fig. 1.1: Albert Lynch, illustration to Vernon Lee, "Voix maudite," *Les Lettres et les arts, revue illustrée* (August 1, 1887): 138.

The Challenge

This chapter suggests ways in which students can engage with nineteenth-century literary texts from a queer perspective, while exploring how music can act as a vehicle for expressing queer identities and desires. Vernon Lee's "A Wicked Voice" (1890) is a Decadent short story in which Magnus, a composer of Wagnerian-style operas, is seduced by the ghostly singing voice of an eighteenth-century *castrato*. The short story explores the relationship between music and same-sex desire at the end of the nineteenth century. It raises important questions about how genders and sexualities are categorized, placing a focus on the singing voice as a site of erotic indeterminacy. The story also provides an opportunity to consider the significance of embodied responses to music, whether by placing these in a Sapphic literary tradition of lesbian eroticism or by understanding them in the light of nineteenth-century scientific and medical discourses about homosexuality. Finally, the text also allows for a consideration of the reception of Richard Wagner's music and its association with forms of sexual deviance. Wagner's operas, in particular *Tristan und Isolde* (1857–9), were controversial due to their exploration of intense and often destructive erotic desires. *Tristan und Isolde* portrays the pain and pleasure of its titular characters' intense sexual longing using highly chromatic musical harmonies that challenged the conventions of Western music (such as in the so-called "Tristan chord" in the opera's opening bars). The association drawn in Wagner's works between sexual desire and suffering meant that his operas were understood by some listeners as evoking the challenges of expressing forbidden same-sex love.

Background

Vernon Lee (the pseudonym of Violet Paget, 1856–1935) was born in France to English parents in 1856. She was raised in Italy from childhood and lived in Florence for most of her adult life, though she traveled widely across Europe. Her works cover a remarkably broad range of topics and genres: impressionistic essays on Renaissance art and history, supernatural short stories (such as "A Wicked Voice"), studies on the physiology of aesthetic response, travel literature, anti-war experimental drama – and many others. Her stories and essays are particularly striking for their presentation of gender-non-normative and androgynous figures. Lee's most intense emotional relationships throughout her life were with other women, and her fictional texts often explore the nature of female romantic friendship, same-sex desire and queer forms of identity. While Lee herself seems never to have personally identified as a lesbian, she was widely recognized by her contemporaries as living a life that refused to conform to conventional expectations of gender and sexuality.

Lee wrote a great deal about Western art music throughout her life. Her first book, *Studies of the Eighteenth Century in Italy* (1880), published when she was only twenty-four, is a compendious account of the vocal music of the period.[1] Based on Lee's own research in the archives of Venice and Rome, it is a wonderfully original defense of the artistry of a style of music that was out of fashion in Victorian England. Lee's tastes in music reflected her commitment to what can most simply be called "formalism." Like many writers on musical aesthetics in the latter half of the nineteenth century, such as Eduard Hanslick, she believed that the beauty of music inheres in its abstract formal structures (rather than, say, its ability to elicit strong emotional responses). Her commitment to formalism finds its strongest expression in her essays attacking the music of Richard Wagner. She criticizes Wagner's music as functioning through its emotional manipulation of listeners, who are rendered introspective and solipsistic by the mental strain of Wagner's "confused flux [of] [...] unrhythmical harmonies and elusive modulations."[2] Lee's often strident views about the superiority of one musical style over another are best understood in the context of her deeply held beliefs about the relationships among art, health and the body. Just as the music of George Frideric Handel, Christoph Willibald Gluck and Wolfgang Amadeus Mozart is capable of affirming and enforcing moral and spiritual healthiness, she argued, the music of Wagner renders listeners mentally exhausted and physically enervated. However, Lee's fictional works often complicate and subvert such simplistic oppositions. So it is with "A Wicked Voice," where the music of the eighteenth century takes its revenge on an arrogant Wagnerian in ways that are strikingly *unhealthy* in their emotional effect on the listener's body.

"A Wicked Voice" is a story about music, desire and compulsion. The narrator of the story is a fictional late nineteenth-century Norwegian composer called Magnus. At the opening of the text, he recalls the events that led up to his artistic inspiration being overwhelmed by the uncanny singing voice of a ghostly *castrato*. A *castrato* was a male singer who was castrated before he reached puberty in order to preserve the purity of the voice, a procedure that produced a highly distinctive vocal timbre. Magnus has traveled to Venice to complete the music for his overtly Wagnerian opera, *Ogier the Dane*, which is itself a parable of calamitous seduction that foreshadows the composer's own fate. His views on music are representative of a late-Romantic "follower of Wagner" (196): he derides the virtuoso singing of eighteenth-century Italy as an execrable exercise in vacuous self-indulgence. However, Magnus's ability to compose his own style of music soon founders "in the stagnant lagoon of the past," where the languid atmosphere of Venice throws his ideas into confusion.

---

[1] Vernon Lee, *Studies of the Eighteenth Century in Italy* (London: Fisher Unwin, 1880).
[2] Vernon Lee, "The Religious and Moral Status of Wagner," *Fortnightly Review* 89 (May 1911): 877.

One evening in his boarding-house, he is presented with an engraving of a celebrated eighteenth-century opera singer. This singer is Balthasar Cesari, nicknamed Zaffirino "because of a sapphire engraved with cabalistic signs presented to him one evening by a masked stranger [...] that great cultivator of the human voice, the devil" (199). Although never made explicit in the story, he is clearly Lee's fictional amalgam of other historical *castrati* singers, such as Gaspare Pacchierotti (1740–1821) and Carlo Broschi (known as Farinelli, 1705–82). Another guest at the boarding-house, the elderly Count Alvise, tells the story of how Zaffirino – who boasted that no woman could resist the allure of his singing – killed the Count's own great-aunt merely by the terrible beauty of his voice. Captivated by the Count's story and by the portrait of Zaffirino "with his wicked woman's face," Magnus, too, is soon seduced by the singer's voice, whose "strange, exotic, unique" (210) tones come to haunt his dreaming and waking hours and render him unable to work. The Count urges Magnus to leave Venice for the sake of his health, and to recuperate at his estate on the mainland. But here, too, Magnus is pursued by the uncanny sounds of the "wicked voice, violin of flesh and blood" (237). Leaving his bedroom late at night, he is drawn by a "piteous wail" (234) to the same room where Zaffirino once killed the Count's great-aunt. He stares into the "handsome, effeminate face" (235) of the long-dead singer. As he tries desperately to escape, he relives the scene of the woman's death, only for this hallucinatory vision suddenly to vanish. At the tale's conclusion, Magnus remains possessed by his burning desire to encounter the voice once again. His own creative voice as a composer is completely effaced. "Wasted by a strange and deadly disease," he is now able to write music only in a style that he "despise[s] and abhor[s]" – that of eighteenth-century Italian opera (237).

Case Study

A useful starting point for pursuing a queer reading of a nineteenth-century literary text about music is to consider how the text presents categories of gender and sexuality – in what ways does it complicate clear-cut distinctions between masculine or feminine, "straight" and "gay"? In "A Wicked Voice," part of the reason for Magnus's simultaneous attraction and repulsion to the singing voice he hears is that it resists gender categorization: "a man's voice which had much of a woman's, but more even of a chorister's" (219). The story's interest in this problem of categorization can be situated in the wider context of debates about queer identities at the end of the nineteenth century. One of the reasons that texts of this period can be so interesting to examine for what they say about queer sexual desire is that it was around this time that modern categories of sexual identity, such as "heterosexual" and "homosexual," first emerged. In general terms, before this time, medical and legal language tended to describe sexual *acts* – such as the offense of "sodomy" – rather than describe an innate *identity* that was defined by who you were attracted to. As the influential philosopher Michel Foucault has argued, the emergence of such categories had two important effects: firstly, it gave a category to individuals that allowed them to understand their sexual identities and form shared communities based on those identities; and secondly, it allowed individuals to resist or refuse the terms in which they were categorized by others.[3]

In "A Wicked Voice," the most striking emblem of gender indeterminacy is the singing voice itself. In classical music, we often unthinkingly associate certain voice types with the gender of the singer (e.g. the soprano voice with women or the bass voice with men). Lee's story is interested in the destabilizing effect of being confronted with a voice that resists such easy categorization along gendered lines. Today the prevalence of men singing *falsetto*, particularly in popular music, has done much to undermine any simplistic or inflexible associations between low vocal pitch and hegemonic masculinity. Nevertheless, we might still recognize the ways in which certain vocal timbres have an uncanny or surprising effect, especially when they seem to exist in tension with other aspects of a singer's gender presentation. While Lee's story drops lots of teasing clues that Zaffirino is a *castrato*, his voice type is never actually named by the narrator. The *castrato* tradition had its origins in late sixteenth-century Italy, where it involved singers in chapels and on the operatic stage. By the eighteenth century, *castrati* singers were performing the leading heroic roles in *opera seria* (noble or "serious" opera), and often became international celebrities. By the 1820s, the operatic *castrati* had fallen out of fashion, although there were still *castrati* singers in the Vatican Chapel in Rome as late as the 1920s. Recordings of Alessandro Moreschi, the so-called "last castrato," survive from the early years of the twentieth century – though these can give us little sense of what a star *castrato* in the eighteenth century sounded like. Lee herself was fascinated by the capacity of new sound technologies in the 1880s – such as Thomas Edison's phonograph cylinder – to record and reproduce the sound of the singing voice. Indeed, in its depictions of voices that have become detached from their bodies, "A Wicked Voice" can be understood as a response to the ghostly nature of these new recording technologies. Today, the virtuosity and technical prowess of the *castrati* can best be appreciated by listening to recordings of music composed for these singers by Antonio Vivaldi and George Frideric Handel (particularly as sung by countertenors).

While the *castrati* were obsolete by the time Lee wrote her text, their voices nevertheless remained the subject of historical fascination. Lee's narrator mocks those "learned in music" who determinedly seek a "nomenclature" for Zaffirino's "mysteriously downy, veiled notes": "[T]here was no agreement on the subject of this voice: it was called by all sorts of names and described by all

[3] Michel Foucault, *The History of Sexuality, Volume 1: The Will to Knowledge*, trans. Robert Hurley (New York: Pantheon, 1978) 43.

manners of incongruous adjectives; people went so far as to dispute whether the voice belonged to a man or a woman: every one had some new definition" (220). Her apparent derision at these forced efforts to categorize the voice reflects her broader discomfort with ways in which bodies and desires might be disciplined and controlled. In "The Art of Singing Past and Present" (1880), she singles out for praise the pedagogical techniques of eighteenth-century vocal teachers: in contrast to the "complicated comparative classification of the various sorts of abstract voice" typical of the nineteenth century, the "eighteenth century," she suggests, "never guessed that such nomenclature could exist."[4] Rather than being forced to sing in a manner that best suits a pre-ordained vocal category, Lee's idealized voices of eighteenth-century Venice emerge organically through the careful cultivation of their own unique individuality. In "A Wicked Voice," the urge to categorize prompts the emergence of a profusion of descriptions and terminologies, yet the character of the voice nevertheless succeeds in frustrating definition. Through her exploration of this gender-indeterminate voice, Lee's story also implicitly addresses the categorization of sexual identities more broadly. What if your desires do not fit easily into the identity categories that are imposed upon you?

While Zaffirino's voice disrupts the ways in which bodies and desires are categorized, it also invokes a specifically lesbian literary tradition. As Catherine Maxwell has noted, although the story is ostensibly focused on the male homoerotic dynamics of Magnus's fascination with the *castrato*, it represents this seduction through the language of the Sapphic.[5] Sappho was an Ancient Greek poet, whose work has survived only in fragments. Her surviving works represent sexual desire between women in a strikingly visceral manner. Her poems are also notable for their imagery of music, which often figures metaphorically for sexual consummation. In the nineteenth century, many writers turned to Sappho's works to provide a way of exploring same-sex desire between women. Lee hints at the Sapphic subtext of "A Wicked Voice" with Zaffirino's name – which has its origins in the Italian *zaffiro*, meaning "little sapphire." She also draws upon imagery from Sappho's verse to evoke Magnus's response to the *castrato*'s voice: "I felt my body melt even as wax in the sunshine, and it seemed to me that I too was turning fluid and vaporous, in order to mingle with these sounds as the moonbeams mingle with the dew" (234). In her evocation of Magnus's "melt[ing]" body – which forms part of the text's much wider preoccupation with imagery of the "fluid" and the "vaporous" – Lee draws upon Sappho's Fragment 130, which refers to "Eros the melter of limbs."[6]

---

[4] Vernon Lee, "The Art of Singing Past and Present," *British Quarterly Review* 72 (October 1880): 329.
[5] Catherine Maxwell, "Sappho, Mary Wakefield, and Vernon Lee's 'A Wicked Voice,'" *Modern Languages Review* 102 (2007): 960–74.
[6] See Anne Carson, *If Not, Winter: Fragments of Sappho* (New York: Vintage, 2002) 265.

In doing so, she invites readers familiar with this tradition to recognize that Zaffirino's androgynous voice might also be a site of lesbian identification. Indeed, it seems likely that the short story was at least partially a response to the *female* singing voice – specifically that of Lee's friend, the contralto and composer Mary Wakefield (1853–1910), to whom the text was dedicated.[7] Like Lee, Wakefield's most intimate relationships were with other women, and she also shared her love for eighteenth-century vocal music. Lee was both attracted to and repelled by the emotional power of Wakefield's voice and the physicality of her body in performance. After listening to her perform Edvard Grieg's song "Ich liebe dich" ["I love you," 1864], Lee commented that "[Wakefield] has a marvellous instinct & form & expression […] yet sometimes she shakes one too much." She was particularly troubled by Wakefield's apparent ability to seduce other women, seemingly with the force of her singing voice alone. "She is said to have a great power of fascinating people," Lee observed, "as a bird is fascinated by a snake."[8] Elsewhere, she talks of Wakefield as a "subjugat[or]" and a "magnetiser," with "a vanity of subduing women."[9] After the women spent time together on a holiday in Venice, Lee subsequently complained in a gossipy letter to a friend that the city was "too much for [her] […] because the image of [Wakefield] those afternoons half undressed, unabashed, red, hot, perspiring is vivid before me & seems the image not only of her body but of her soul."[10] Like Magnus's conflicted desire towards Zaffirino in "A Wicked Voice," Lee's response to Wakefield's physicality refracts the complex feelings of rapture, fear and shame bound up with same-sex attraction at the close of the nineteenth century. It reminds us that the story responds not only to the general dynamics of a Victorian queer literary tradition, but also to the fraught nature of specific queer relationships within late-Victorian literary and musical sub-cultures.

An alternative approach for thinking about music and queerness in the nineteenth century is to consider how literary texts represent different ways of listening to or responding to music, and to examine how these are connected to sexual identity. Doctors and scientists who studied human sexuality at the end of the nineteenth century – known as sexologists – insistently drew a

---

[7] See Maxwell, "Sappho, Mary Wakefield, and Vernon Lee's 'A Wicked Voice.'" For an accessible introduction to Wakefield's work as a performer and composer, see Michael Craske, "'The world, what is it to you, dear': Mary Wakefield's *Maytime in Midwinter* (1885)," *Verseandmusic.com*, posted May 16, 2019, <https://verseandmusic.com/2019/05/16/the-world-what-is-it-to-you-dear-mary-wakefields-maytime-in-midwinter-1885/> [Accessed October 24, 2024].

[8] Vernon Lee to A. Mary F. Robinson, February 27, 1886, *The Selected Letters of Vernon Lee, 1856–1935: Volume II, 1885–1889*, eds Sophie Geoffroy and Amanda Gagel (Abingdon: Routledge, 2021) 164.

[9] Vernon Lee to A. Mary F. Robinson, October 29, 1886, *Letters II*, 259; November 8, 1886, *Letters II*, 262.

[10] Vernon Lee to A. Mary F. Robinson, November 8, 1886, *Letters II*, 262.

connection between homosexuality and being "musical." They typically understood homosexuality as a form of illness, with its origins in a diseased nervous system. As such, they were particularly interested in examining emotional or bodily responses to music – which seemed to have their origins in listeners' nerves – as diagnostic indicators of homosexuality.[11]

In *Homosexuality in Men and Women* (1914), the sexologist Magnus Hirschfeld argued that male homosexual listeners "experience music only as an aspect of mood, a purely sensory impression." He suggests that such listeners lack the "intellectual engagement" to follow the complex formal structures of "older, classical music." Although Hirschfeld himself does not offer specific examples, such music might include J.S. Bach's fugues (say, in the opening "Kyrie eleison" of the Mass in B minor, BWV 232 [1749]), or the treatment of sonata form by Joseph Haydn in his symphonies (for example, in the first movement of the Symphony No. 101 in D major, Hob. 1/101 [1794]). They also dislike "classical opera" (such as W.A. Mozart's *Idomeneo* K. 366 [1781]) – "in which the music itself is the ultimate purpose" – because the artificial "closed forms, arias, ensembles, etc." distract from the "dramatics of feeling" that they demand from music. Instead, Hirschfeld suggests, such homosexual listeners prefer the "more colourful or sensual music" of nineteenth-century musical Romanticism, demanding the dramatic immediacy of music "in which the succession of musical structures is determined by clearly defined images, ideas, by a text."[12] Hirschfeld refers here to what we would now call "program music" – instrumental music which follows a story, or responds to some other extramusical idea, such as Hector Berlioz's *Symphonie fantastique* (1830) or Richard Strauss's tone poems *Don Juan* (1888) and *Tod und Verklärung* [*Death and Transfiguration*, 1889]. He also gestures to developments in orchestration – what is sometimes called "orchestral color" – across the course of the nineteenth century. Composers such as Hector Berlioz, Richard Wagner and Richard Strauss experimented with orchestral timbres by inventing new instruments (such as the Wagner tuba, first used in Wagner's *Das Rheingold* [*The Rhinegold*, premiered 1869]) or by combining instruments in unusual ways (such as the piccolo and harps whose sixteenth notes [semiquavers] evoke the shimmering of fire at the end of Wagner's *Die Walküre* [*The Valkyrie*, premiered 1870]). Hirschfeld builds here upon an established scientific tradition in nineteenth-century sexology in which modes of emotional responsiveness and preferences for certain styles of music were both understood to indicate so-called "sexual perversity." His basic argument – eccentric as it now seems – is that homosexual men essentially have a preference for Romantic program

---

[11] See Fraser Riddell, *Music and the Queer Body in English Literature at the Fin de Siècle* (Cambridge: Cambridge University Press, 2022) 20–51.

[12] Magnus Hirschfeld, *Die Homosexualität des Mannes und des Weibes* (Berlin: Marcus, 1914) 510–11. Unpublished translations by Tom Smith, cited with permission.

music because it appeals more directly to their subjective emotions, rather than requiring specialist intellectual understanding of abstract musical forms.

Lee's short story is particularly striking for the way in which it foregrounds the emotional impact of music on the body. In the passage above, for example, the immediate response of the composer Magnus to hearing Zaffirino's voice is that his "arteries throbbed." Later, he is struck by an intense feeling of "repugnance" about the voice, followed by feelings of "inexplicable agitation." This ultimately leads him to consult a doctor, from whom he hides "the stranger symptoms of my malady." At the story's conclusion, as Magnus succumbs to the voice's deadly seduction, sickness itself becomes a paradoxical source of pleasure: "my hair was clammy, my knees sank beneath me, an enervating heat spread through my body; I tried to breathe more largely, to suck in the sounds with the incense-laden air. I was supremely happy, and yet as if I were dying; then suddenly a chill ran through me, and with it a vague panic" (225). The story's continual recourse to imagery of bodily illness to characterize Magnus's response to music gestures towards well-established sexological discourses that view such behavior as symptomatic of homosexuality. Notably, the music that was most insistently associated with homosexuality in the late nineteenth century was that of Wagner – precisely because it was accused of having such a powerful emotional effect on audiences.[13] Many of Wagner's critics argued that his music was so emotionally overwhelming that it could make listeners physically and mentally ill. The philosopher Friedrich Nietzsche, for instance, asserted that Wagner had "made music sick": "the convulsiveness of his affects, his over-charged sensibility, his taste that craves stronger and stronger spices, the instability that he disguises as a principle: [...] taken together, this presents a clinical picture that leaves no room for doubt. *Wagner est une névrose* [Wagner is a neurosis]."[14] One such "neurosis" – at least as understood by nineteenth-century medicine – was same-sex attraction. In a survey designed to allow homosexual men to self-diagnose, for instance, the queer writer Edward Prime-Stevenson included the question: "Are you peculiarly fond of Wagner?"[15]

Lee's "A Wicked Voice" is also keenly aware of Wagner's particular association with Venice. It was in Venice that Wagner composed parts of his opera *Tristan und Isolde* (1858) and it was here that the composer died in 1883. Magnus, it seems, is following in Wagner's footsteps, hoping to find "inspiration in this strange Venice, floating, as it were, in the stagnant lagoon of the

---

[13] See James Kennaway, *Bad Vibrations: The History of the Idea of Music as a Cause of Disease* (Farnham: Ashgate, 2012) 63–98.

[14] Friedrich Nietzsche, "The Case of Wagner: A Musician's Problem," *The Anti-Christ, Ecce Homo, Twilight of the Idols, and Other Writings*, eds Aaron Ridley and Judith Norman, trans. Judith Norman (Cambridge: Cambridge University Press, 2005) 241–2.

[15] Xavier Mayne [Edward Prime-Stevenson], *The Intersexes: A History of Similisexualism as a Problem in Social Life* (Rome: privately printed, 1908) 633.

past" (208). The story's fascination with "acousmatic" sounds – those that are heard without their cause or source being seen – also had a connection with Wagner and his theatrical innovations. In designs for his purpose-built theater at Bayreuth, Wagner lowered the orchestra pit and covered it from view, so that the orchestra would be out of sight of the audience. He also insisted on dimming the lighting in the auditorium, a practice that remained unusual in the mid-nineteenth century. Zaffirino's spectral voice shares something with these Wagnerian visual and aural innovations: it is always divorced from the presence of the singer's body, its source hidden out of sight, and it is always cloaked in darkness as it glides through the nocturnal cityscape of Venice.

Yet Lee's story is more sophisticated than merely presenting a stereotypical portrait of an ardent Wagnerian rendered passive and effeminate by the emotional excess of late-Romantic chromaticism. Lee's story also explores the attractions (and perils) of Decadence itself. Despite the text's notional disavowal of cultural Decadence (not least in its insistent anti-Wagnerism), its literary style nevertheless displays many of the characteristic traits of Decadence. Its long sentences are embedded with richly ornamental descriptions of beautiful objects (etchings, interiors, buildings) or are structured around impressionistic accounts of subjective sensory experiences (sights, sounds, smells). The language is often arcane or archaic, and replete with estranging references to often obscure artworks. Lee's choice of a bitter, ironic narrator who exists on the edge of mental and physical collapse is likewise a familiar feature in Decadent literature. Ultimately, as Carlo Caballero has observed, "A Wicked Voice" stages a sort of queerly Decadent revenge on behalf of eighteenth-century vocal music:

> [Lee] effectively turns the haunting power of the old vocal art she so treasured against the insolent German composer who aimed to obviate it. Where Wagner's music persecutes her with what she would repress (subjective indeterminacy), she persecutes Wagner with what he would repress (a particular culture of the voice).[16]

As a signed-up Wagnerian, Magnus denigrates the eighteenth-century "art of singing" – which he views as a shallow display of vocal virtuosity for its own sake – as "execrable," "degrading" and "corrupting." In depicting his homoerotic seduction by Zaffirino, "A Wicked Voice" reasserts the surprising and unexpected queer pleasures of this vocal style – a mode of singing that escapes categorization in a manner that is both alluring and uncanny. At the same time, the narrative also hints at a specifically Sapphic tradition of lesbian erotic rapture, so that the *castrato* might stand in for a desired woman. Ultimately, Lee's story remains strikingly ambivalent about same-sex desire – not least in the ways it characterizes it with imagery of disease and illness. Yet it nevertheless

---

[16] Carlo Caballero, "'A Wicked Voice': On Vernon Lee, Wagner, and the Effects of Music," *Victorian Studies* 35 (Summer 1992): 401.

creates a space that acknowledges music's power to articulate queer possibility. Indeed, in recent decades, writing about the place of classical music in queer sub-cultures has done much to celebrate and affirm queer identities, whether in Wayne Koestenbaum's explorations of the camp subversiveness of operatic diva-worship or through renewed scholarly attention to the contribution of queer composers, such as Ethel Smyth and Benjamin Britten.

Listening

Handel, George Frideric, and others. *Arias for Guadagni*. Iestyn Davies. Hyperion, 2012.
Alessandro Moreschi – The Last Castrato: Complete Vatican Recordings. Opal, 1993.
Vivaldi: Heroes. Philippe Jaroussky, Jean-Christophe Spinosi, Ensemble Matheus. Erato, 2007.
Wagner, Richard. "O sink hernieder, Nacht der Liebe," from *Tristan und Isolde*. Kirsten Flagstad, Ludwig Suthaus, Wilhelm Furtwängler, Philharmonia Orchestra. Naxos Historical, 2004.

Further Reading

Caballero, Carlo. "'A Wicked Voice': On Vernon Lee, Wagner, and the Effects of Music." *Victorian Studies* 35 (Summer 1992): 385–408.
Feldman, Martha. *The Castrato: Reflections on Natures and Kinds*. Berkeley: University of California Press, 2015.
Franseen, Kristin M. *Imagining Musical Pasts: The Queer Literary Musicology of Vernon Lee, Rosa Newmarch, and Edward Prime-Stevenson*. Clemson: Clemson University Press, 2023.
Kennaway, James. "Modern Music and Nervous Modernity: Wagnerism as a Disease of Civilization, 1850–1914." *Bad Vibrations: The History of the Idea of Music as a Cause of Disease*. Farnham: Ashgate, 2012. 63–98.
Koestenbaum, Wayne. *The Queen's Throat: Opera, Homosexuality and The Mystery of Desire*. Cambridge, Massachusetts: Da Capo, 2001.
Maxwell, Catherine. "Sappho, Mary Wakefield, and Vernon Lee's 'A Wicked Voice.'" *Modern Languages Review* 102 (2007): 960–74.
Pulham, Patricia. "The Castrato and the Cry in Vernon Lee's Wicked Voices." *Victorian Literature and Culture* 30 (2002): 421–37.
Riddell, Fraser. *Music and the Queer Body in English Literature at the Fin de Siècle*. Cambridge: Cambridge University Press, 2022.
Sutton, Emma. *Aubrey Beardsley and British Wagnernism in the 1890s*. Oxford: Oxford University Press, 2002.
———. "Decadence and Music." *Decadence and Literature*. Eds Jane Desmarais and David Weir. Cambridge: Cambridge University Press, 2019. 152–68.
Wilbourne, Emily. "The Queer History of the Castrato." *The Oxford Handbook of Music and Queerness*. Eds Fred Everett Maus and Sheila Whiteley. Oxford: Oxford University Press, 2022. 441–54.

LES
MAITRES SONNEURS

PAR

GEORGE SAND

— Tous droits réservés —

A M. EUGÈNE LAMBERT

Mon cher enfant, puisque tu aimes à m'entendre raconter ce que racontaient les paysans à la veillée, dans ma jeunesse, quand j'avais le temps de les écouter, je vais tâcher de me rappeler l'histoire d'Étienne Depardieu et d'en recoudre les fragments épars dans ma mémoire. Elle me fut dite par lui-même, en plusieurs soirées de *breyage*; c'est ainsi, tu le sais, qu'on appelle les heures assez avancées de la nuit où l'on broie le chanvre, et où chacun alors apportait sa chronique. Il y a déjà longtemps que le père Depardieu dort du sommeil des justes, et il était assez vieux quand il me fit le récit des naïves aventures de sa jeunesse. C'est pourquoi je le ferai parler lui-même, en imitant sa manière autant qu'il me sera possible. Tu ne me reprocheras pas d'y mettre d' l'obstina-

tion, toi qui sais, par expérience de tes oreilles, que les pensées et les émotions d'un paysan ne peuvent être traduites dans notre style, sans s'y dénaturer entièrement et sans y prendre un air d'affectation choquante. Tu sais aussi, par expérience de ton esprit, que les paysans devinent ou comprennent beaucoup plus qu'on ne les en croit capables, et tu as été souvent frappé de leurs aperçus soudains qui, même dans les choses d'art, ressemblaient à des révélations. Si je fusse venue te dire, dans ma langue et dans la tienne, certaines choses que tu as entendues et comprises dans la leur, tu les aurais trouvées si invraisemblables de leur part, que tu m'aurais accusée d'y mettre du mien à mon insu, et de leur prêter des réflexions et des sentiments qu'ils ne pouvaient avoir. En effet, il suffit d'introduire, dans l'expression de leurs idées, un mot qui ne soit pas de leur vocabulaire, pour qu'on se sente porté à révoquer en doute l'idée même émise par

FIG 2.1 : George Sand, *Les Maîtres sonneurs* [1853] (Clichy: Loignon, Dupont et Cie, 1869). Joseph listens to the master piper Père Bastien.

Chapter 2

Conjuring Folk Music: George Sand's *The Master Pipers* (1853)

Katharine Ellis

Recommended Text

George Sand, *The Master Pipers*, trans. Rosemary Lloyd (Oxford: Oxford University Press, 1994). Numbers in brackets refer to this edition.

Keywords

Acousmatic, *Bildungsroman*, difference, folk music, France, music profession, narrators, novel, Romantic virtuoso, society

Prelude

Extract 1

George Sand, *The Master Pipers*, 34–5.

I was heading in that direction, thinking I'd find the path which cut directly through the wood, when I heard the sound of music, which resembled that of bagpipes, but which was so loud it was more like thunder. […] I was chilled to the bone by the sort of fear you can't explain to yourself, because you've no real idea what's caused it. The darkness, the winter fog, all the noises that you hear in the woods, and that are different from the noises of the plains, endless stupid tales you've heard told and that come back to you […]. Mock me if you will. That music, in a place where so few people went, seemed to me the work of the devil. It was too loud to be natural, and above all it was a sad and strange song, that resembled no air known in Christendom. I walked more quickly but then I stopped, amazed at another noise. While the music brayed away on one side, a little bell rang out on the other, and these two sounds came towards me, as if to stop me going either back or forward. I threw myself to the side, doubling up in the bracken […].

Extract 2

Sand, *The Master Pipers*, 263–4.

So saying, she adorned her cap and her blouse with Huriel's flowers, and having put the rest in her room, she was on the point of throwing the other bouquet in the remains of a former ditch that separated the meadow from the little park, but as she reached out for it, since Huriel had refused to insult his rival in that way, the sound of bagpipes could be heard from the thicket that lay close to the little courtyard opposite us, and someone who, evidently, had been hidden close enough to hear and see everything we did and said, played the tune of the three woodcutters that Père Bastien had composed. At first he played it in the form we knew, and then rather differently, and finally he changed it completely, varying the modes and including his own inspiration which was certainly not of a lower standard, and even seemed to sigh and pray in so tender a manner that you couldn't help being moved to pity. Then he played it in a stronger and livelier way, as if it were a song of reproach or command, and Brulette, who'd gone forward and had stopped at the edge of the ditch ready to throw her bouquet into it, but unable to find the heart to do so, leaped back as if frightened by the anger the music revealed. Then Joseph, pushing aside the brush with his feet and shoulders, appeared on the bank of the ditch, his eyes blazing, playing still, and appearing through his playing and his expression to threaten Brulette with deep despair if she didn't abandon the affront she'd intended to inflict on him.

Extract 3

Sand, *The Master Pipers*, 175–6.

Music has two modes that the scholars, or so I've heard tell, call the major mode and the minor mode, and that I myself call the clear mode and the muddy mode; or, if you prefer, the blue-sky mode and the grey-sky mode; or else, the mode of strength and joy, and the mode of sorrow and reverie. You can spend an entire day and still not find all the contrasts that exist between these two modes, any more than you would find a third mode. […] The plains sing in the major mode, and the mountains in the minor mode. If you'd stayed in your own country, you'd still be thinking in the clear, calm mode, and when you return to it, you'll see what advantages a mind like yours can extract from such a mode, for neither is lesser or greater than the other. But, because you felt you were a complete musician, you were tormented when you couldn't hear the minor mode ringing in your ears. Your minstrels and singers have learnt it for form's sake, because songs are like the air that blows everywhere, and carries the seeds of plants from one horizon to the other. But since nature did not make them passionate, deep thinkers, the people of your country make a poor showing in the sad tones, and corrupt them when they use them. That's why you felt your bagpipes were playing out of key.

Extract 4

Sand, *The Master Pipers*, 304–6.

I went first, unable to see where I was putting my feet, feeling the walls, which created a very narrow passage, and where you hardly needed to raise your head to reach the ceiling. We'd been proceeding in this way for some time when there came from below us such a din that you'd have thought forty thunderbolts were rolling through the devil's caves. [...] Joseph was there on his own, eyes free of their blindfold, arms crossed, as calm as I was anxious. He seemed to be listening scornfully to the pandemonium of eighteen bagpipes all brawling together and prolonging the same note in a kind of roar. This madmen's music came from the next-door cavern where the pipers were hiding and where, no doubt, they knew that a strange echo increased the resonance thirty-fold. As for me, who knew nothing about it [...], I first thought that the pipers of Berry, Auvergne and Bourbonnais must all be gathered together there.

The Challenge

In 1853 it was unusual for a group of peasants and forest dwellers to be principal characters in a French novel. It was also unusual for their cultures to be taken seriously as artistic and social phenomena. In Paris, even wealthy provincials were the butt of jokes about backwardness, and peasants usually featured as local color on operatic stages. *The Master Pipers*, by George Sand (1804–76), was first published in thirty-two instalments (evenings) in the national daily newspaper *Le Constitutionnel*. Narrated by a young peasant, Tiennet, it wrapped folk music, artistry, social alienation and socio-musical conflict into a cross-border love story set in the central-French regions of the Berry and the Bourbonnais where Sand had grown up and where she inherited her grandmother's house in the village of Nohant. How, then, does Sand valorize a low-class and denigrated music such as that of the country bagpiper? What is the effect of making Tiennet both narrator and participant in the action? And how does Sand tie music to landscape, sonorous space, difference and community values (both positive and negative)?

Background

Folk music as conventionally understood is passed down within families and communities, from elder to pupil: it is an oral tradition rather than a written one. It usually has no names attached. Ever-changing, it nevertheless gives the impression of always having existed, and its alternative name of "traditional music" – already used in the nineteenth century in France – indicates how closely tied it is to ideas of conservation. In 1853, when George Sand wrote her novel about French country bagpipers, there was no concept of "intangible heritage" on UNESCO lines, and there were very few collections of French folk music in print.

It was, nevertheless, the realization that rural traditions were disappearing (due to railways, economic migration and urban industrial expansion) that prompted the French government to support a project for nationwide folk-music collecting in 1852. It took a decade, though, for its single project-related volume to appear. Neither, in the 1850s, were there leisure clubs for folk music, with bourgeois dancers performing in pristine replicas of regional peasant costume. Les Gâs du Berry, for bagpipers and hurdy-gurdy players, was one of the first (founded 1888). George Sand's son Maurice, who illustrated *The Master Pipers*, was its inaugural honorary president. Sand, then, wrote this and her earlier pastoral novels when country bagpiping was both in decline and undervalued.

Sand sets her novel in the Berry and the Bourbonnais regions – neighboring but contrasting areas of central France clustered around the cathedral towns of Bourges (Berry) and Moulins (Bourbonnais). The rich pastures of Berry, where she presents peasant life as settled and community-oriented, contrast with the Bourbonnais uplands, where her forest-dwellers form a looser, often itinerant, group of seasonal laborers. Six figures animate the plot: from the Berry, the narrator Tiennet, his brother Joseph (Joset in the French original) and his cousin Brulette; and from the Bourbonnais, the mule-driver Huriel, his sister Thérence and their woodcutter father Bastien. Tiennet, Huriel and Joseph all vie for Brulette, and a final double wedding mixes Berry/Bourbonnais pairs. Joseph is left out, destined for brief musical fulfilment but romantic disappointment and an untimely death.

Huriel and his father are guild-certified master pipers who have nevertheless chosen other occupations and so play for love rather than fees. The musical plot is catalyzed when Joseph disappears from his village and, tracked down in the Bourbonnais forests, is found to be studying a "foreign" form of bagpiping with Huriel's father. Counterpointed against this bagpiping trio are the professional members of the Berry guild or brotherhood, led by the elder Carnat. In their trials for licensing as a professional guild member, Carnat's hapless son loses out to Joseph, whose artistic haughtiness promptly incites guild members to revenge. A hazing ritual in the castle dungeons turns into a knife fight when Joseph's friends reveal themselves. Thereafter, in a brief professional career, Joseph alienates his colleagues. At the end of the novel he is discovered drowned in an icy ditch, his broken pipes left strewn on the bank. Suicide? Père Bastien says murder. But all is deniable since everything points towards the legend of the devil claiming a piper who has sold him his soul: by breaking the instrument on the piper's back, sending him mad, and indirectly causing his death by misadventure.

By 1853, Sand had written a whole series of works reflecting the Berry of her childhood. In the first of them, *The Devil's Pool* [*La Mare du diable*] of 1846, she had already included folk-music scenes; but the *Master Pipers* was the first in which music took pride of place. Her art-musical contacts ran deep. In Paris she was at the heart of the Romantic circles of Franz Liszt, Hector Berlioz and Nicolò Paganini – and most famously, Frédéric Chopin was her romantic partner between 1837 and 1847. It is not difficult to see resemblances between Joseph and the poetic, melancholic Chopin, who had died of tuberculosis aged a mere thirty-nine in 1849. The adolescent Joseph, too, struggles with ill health that threatens his artistic ambitions – including coughing blood (92). This unspoken link between art and folk music, underpinned by the idea of a peasant as a *Bildungsroman* protagonist, cements the valorization of peasant culture as an artistic force.[1] In the portrayal of Joseph as a Romantic virtuoso-composer who can express himself freely only through the flute or the bagpipes, Sand poses many of the questions history has asked about composer-geniuses (social alienation, mental-health conditions, self-centeredness and arrogance) but translates them from the cityscape to the depths of the Bourbonnais woods. Tiennet sees Joseph's musical creativity as a series of mistakes; Joseph knows better (40–1, 294).

Attitudes to money are also crucial: Sand erects a Romantic artistic aristocracy in which talent and generosity trump the commercial small-mindedness of a guild of artisan professionals, paid by the dance (75). In so doing Sand both elevates and complicates the image of folk-music practice, dignifying it as music but also acknowledging its reality as a rural trade. As to the narrator: in her preface Sand names him as Étienne Depardieu, whose stories (in dialect) she had listened to as a child; and says she wants to preserve the straightforward manner of his storytelling. She also adds that on artistic questions peasants could utter "sudden insights" that "resemble revelations" (3). Respected as a chronicler of Berry's folk culture, Sand appears frequently in an early history of French folk music (1889) via her novels.[2]

In terms of her artistic connections Sand was a progressive; and contrary to the conservatism that the writing of pastoral novels might imply, she was a radical figure in her personal and social politics. She demanded sexual equality in various ways: she cross-dressed, smoked, abandoned husbands for lovers, and litigated successfully to retain ownership of her property – itself quite a feat in the repressive environment of post-Napoleonic France. As a supporter of social reform, she welcomed the tenets of the 1848 revolution but recoiled against the violence it unleashed. On several levels, including through its battles over music and over types of musical expertise and participation, *The Master*

---

[1] On Joseph as the subject of a *Bildungsroman* or a novel of personal development and self-realization, see David A. Powell, *While the Music Lasts: The Representation of Music in the Works of George Sand* (Lewisburg: Bucknell University Press, 2001) 46–59.

[2] Julien Tiersot, *Histoire de la chanson populaire en France* (Paris: Plon, 1889).

Pipers allegorizes her commitment to non-violent change and to the embrace of social and artistic difference.

Case Study

Especially in its early and closing scenes, Sand evokes bagpiping via the narrative voice of Tiennet/Depardieu and via her own construction of implicit comparisons with the urban and institutionalized music-making that would have been familiar to her readers. As she says in her preface, she is engaged in an act of "translation" (4). Her aim is also social: to allegorize the interaction of three alien worlds – two neighboring French regions (a group of whose inhabitants learn to appreciate each other's differences) and the guild of master pipers, who struggle to accept difference and whose exclusionary rites breed jealousy and violence.

The Power of the Acousmatic

When the piping first starts, it surprises us as readers as much as it surprises Tiennet, lost in the night-time woods, having made a rare foray from his "chicken coop" in the plain to try to find his brother Joseph. He thrashes through high bracken towards what he thinks is a landmark oak tree. [**Extract 1.**] Here is our peasant narrator's first "insight/revelation," one that links three things: a sense of Otherness or difference, music as devilish, and the embedding of bagpipe music into a soundscape that is presented as unsettling because it is acousmatic – i.e., the source of the music is invisible. Tiennet has unknowingly brushed close to the mule-driver Huriel, whose piping is accompanied by the jangling of the bell around the neck of the lead animal in a sizeable herd. That Tiennet feels trapped in the pincer movement of two sound sources, neither of which he can identify, is down to his ignorance of neighboring customs (he knows about sheep-farming, not mule-driving) and peasant superstition (we make of unseen sounds what our imaginations are primed to conjure up, and he thinks he hears the devil at work). But our narrator also references the physical power of sound to define space and to assault both body and mind. The unnatural "thunder" of the bagpipes, together with the approaching bell, cause panic: in his fear, Tiennet jumps deep into the bracken; his heart pounds; he sees stars and spots before his eyes; after the herd has passed, he cannot recall precisely how he reaches the landmark oak tree. Later in the novel, the power of music to possess a human spirit, and the idea that a guild musician must sell his soul to the devil, will return to haunt Joseph. In Tiennet's reaction we are introduced to the visceral power of music, and especially to the menace of a moving sound source closing in, in the dark, on a fearful human. We might even say that sound becomes an antagonist.[3] Certainly, in this brief scene Sand removes any suspicion that her novel will idealize peasant life, or that music will be a mere adornment to the plot.

Difference

Beyond sheer volume, Tiennet's perception of the bagpiping is that it is both "sad" and "strange"; and it is unknown in "Christendom," i.e., in the world Tiennet knows. To Sand's readers, this loaded phrase (using a term, "Christendom," which a nineteenth-century French peasant would find entirely innocent), renders the bagpiping exotic, as though from a land with different mores and customs. In fact, Tiennet is hearing for the first time the bagpiping tradition of the Bourbonnais. For Joseph, who has been secretly learning this bagpiping tradition, and who will come to master it, this element of stylistic difference is addictive; for Tiennet, the shock of that same difference induces terror – it is a sonic indication that he is completely lost. For Sand, we can see it as a symbol of the effort required to embrace, rather than to reject, the Other within France.

As the lives of Tiennet's and Huriel's families progressively intertwine, the stylistic difference of Bourbonnais bagpiping transforms in meaning. Secretly in love with Huriel, whom she has not seen for several months on account of his itinerant work, Brulette hears bagpipe music "on the far side of the water among the oak trees" on the day of her cousin's wedding and is "shaken by it as a leaf is shaken by a gust of wind." She might be described as a "master listener": not only is she convinced that "Neither the pipes nor the tune come from this region," but she correctly identifies the bagpiper as Huriel – whose presence in Berry is once more signaled acousmatically and via his trademark forest environment (210). Finally, in a dramatic scene when Brulette receives "sweetheart" May bouquets from two suitors and prepares to reject one of them, Joseph's acousmatic bagpiping serves as a warning to her that one of those bouquets is his, and that she trifles with it at his (not her) peril. [**Extract 2.**] It is a warning she heeds, once more displaying a sophisticated musical understanding as a listener.

In this, the most sustained description of music in the novel, bagpiping ventriloquizes Joseph's emotions, which he finds so difficult to express in words that he has in earlier scenes been cast (and has cast himself) as "Joey the madman, Joey the innocent, Joey the dullard" (48–9). There are links here with French Romantic literary images from the 1830s that Sand knew intimately: of Beethoven as a taciturn depressive in the stories of Jules Janin, or of Balzac's

---

[3] Musically-animated fear of this kind also characterizes the climactic initiation/hazing ceremony Joseph endures in the castle dungeon (including **Extract 4**). Powell sees this scene as musically superficial because "musical din" (55), rather than music *per se*, is involved. However, linking the dungeon scene with Tiennet's forest experience [**Extract 1**] suggests a more nuanced way to approach Sand's acousmatic soundscapes.

fictional experimentalists, the composer Gambara and the painter Frenhofer, both of whom suffer what we would today call borderline personality disorders.[4] Sand's cliff-hanger, so common in instalmentized novels, ends well, temporarily: the rejected bouquet becomes a garland for Joseph's bagpipes as Brulette saves his dignity by proclaiming his playing superior to Huriel's.

The "sadness" of the music Tiennet describes in his nocturnal panic attack is explained in one of the novel's most famous scenes: Joseph's music lesson with the great woodcutter Père Bastien. This is not, as might be imagined, a lesson on a particular bagpipe tune, but a foray into Western music theory: the contrasting expressivity of the major (Berry) and minor (Bourbonnais) modes. [**Extract 3.**] Interpreting Sand here is complicated. To a postcolonial musician today, the basic premise of the "lesson" is misguided and crass: that there are only two modes in the world, and that they can be categorized as having immanent meaning. Worse, a lesson in conservatoire music theory is implausible as an example of the ways rural musical traditions were handed down. Nevertheless, the formality of the lesson serves a contrasting argument just as well: that Sand is dressing up an oral tradition in theoretical clothing in order to elevate its status among an urban elite readership who might otherwise be dismissive of it: in other words, she might well be treading a fine line between realism and literary evangelism for the folk musics of her region, and potentially, for French folk music more generally.

Moreover, if we turn to a famous history of French folk music written in 1889, we find the precise opposite of Père Bastien's claims about the modal character of Berry's folk music: all the tunes Tiersot gives (and most of them come from Sand herself, via transcriptions by the singer Pauline Viardot) are in modes Tiersot categorizes as "minor." He describes them variously as "dreamy" or "melancholic," a conventional interpretation of minor-mode music. Tiersot even quantifies things: in Viardot's own collection of Berry folk songs, he finds only six melodies in the major mode, as against ten in minor modes.[5] But we should also note how Père Bastien distances himself from the "scholars" and their language of "mode" with the interjection, "or so I've heard tell." A narrator's sleight of hand such as this raises further questions as to Sand's own stance.

---

[4] See Katharine Ellis, "The Uses of Fiction: *contes musicaux* in Schlesinger's *Gazette musicale*, 1834–44," *Revue de musicologie* 90.2 (2004): 37–65. Sand contributed to this fund of musical tales. On Hoffmann's composer Johannes Kreisler, who shares many of Joseph's feelings of alienation from society, who refuses to respect society's hierarchies or niceties, and who treats artistic inferiors with contempt, see his cycle of musical writings entitled *Kreisleriana*, and especially the opening story, "Kapellmeister Johannes Kreisler's Musical Sufferings." *E.T.A. Hoffmann's Musical Writings: Kreisleriana, the Poet and the Composer, Music Criticism*, ed. David Charlton, trans. Martyn Clarke (Cambridge: Cambridge University Press, 1989) 81–7.

[5] Tiersot, *Histoire*, 100–2, 151, 156–8 (tunes and descriptions); 300 and 309 (Viardot's account of the number of major and minor modes in her Berry collection).

She seems to be doing more than "translating": she appears to be leveraging Depardieu's story for her own ends, and we might well question whether the "lesson" is actually her own invention.

The possibility of significant poetic license illustrates how careful we must be in using literature as a way into history. In effect, Sand is creating an inauthentic form of musical difference that can then be used allegorically.[6] Tiersot for one was not fooled: despite his interest in mode and his citing of Sand's novels, he does not mention Père Bastien's music lesson in his *Histoire*. But Sand's urban (and urbane) readers of 1853, following the story in the newspaper *Le Constitutionnel*, would surely have found her binary of major and minor entirely normal. And they might have been interested in the way she uses it as a dynamic symbol, first drawing distinctions between the societies of the Berry (major, plains) and the Bourbonnais (minor, mountains), and then mingling them via musical metaphor and natural simile (seeds blowing across borders).

The lesson that original readers are likely to have seen in *The Master Pipers* is that there is no hierarchy between these modes and their respective musics, and that it is possible to appreciate both. Indeed, through Bastien's reference to the "complete" musician, Sand implies that successfully crossing borders – even on a small-scale level such as between the Berry and the Bourbonnais – is necessary to achieve one's full potential. Whether clothed in musical garb or not, in a France dominated by the centralized official culture of Paris, the idea of crossing internal borders in this way was fairly radical. It is what Joseph does in his mature playing [**Extract 2**], and what the two happy couples and Père Bastien agree to do in the utopian climax of the novel's final page, when they decide to live together but to divide their lives between plain and upland forest (323).[7]

Cacophony, Torture and Violence

None of that mutuality includes the loner Joseph, who can compromise neither musically nor socially. In this *Bildungsroman* crowned by failure rather than by self-realization, his life becomes increasingly extreme. The musical climax of *The Master Pipers* has two instalments, both (unusually) occurring in confined spaces: the public audition scene in the local tavern; and the ensuing initiation scene, where the trials necessary to become a master piper start with

---

[6] Powell, citing the scholar of music and literature Léon Guichard, describes this inversion of modal characteristics as allowing the conventional emotional connotations of the two modes (major, happy; minor, sad) to be aligned with the characteristics of life in the two communities as Sand wishes to project them. Powell, *While the Music Lasts*, 82.

[7] In her editorial preface to *The Master Pipers*, translator Rosemary Lloyd talks of "a slow evolution towards tolerance" (viii) and sees the major and minor of the two regions' inhabitants "fuse" in the two marriages (xix).

intimidation and end in torture. It is here that Sand leverages the idea – implicit in Tiennet's earlier night-time panic – of sound having the power to derange psychologically and to subjugate physically, especially in darkness.

As narrator, Tiennet draws attention to the innocent noise of the tavern scene and the intimidation of the dungeon. In the tavern, even for the competition between Joseph and the younger Carnat, "[s]ilence wasn't demanded, since when bagpipes are played in a room, they're not an instrument that can be drowned out by other noises" (285). And in the novel's first musical encounter he describes a tavern gathering where drunkenness means "everyone singing in their own key and their own measure [tempo], one table saying their refrain beside another table saying their own different refrain, and all that going on at the same time, creating a madman's sabbath noisy enough to split your head" (32). It is benign enough, and Joseph's response is to ignore it with a detachment worthy of E.T.A. Hoffmann's misunderstood composer-genius Johannes Kreisler, and to leave for the Bourbonnais woods and his bagpipe lessons.

In the dungeon scene this same extraordinary detachment enrages the brotherhood, who are already willing Joseph's downfall. Joseph is led in, blindfolded. Tiennet and friends follow covertly, anticipating trouble (and enabling Tiennet to narrate what happens). [**Extract 4.**] His description immerses the reader in the aural assault of cacophonous bagpiping. We too are trapped in a dark, reverberant, subterranean, hellish space. And we know the sonic experience is cacophonous because for Tiennet it is as if the master pipers were each playing one of three regional musics simultaneously, heedless of the differences between them (306). This is not music as art, but noise as weapon. At first the bagpipers are hidden (yet more acousmatic music), later revealed in close-up as performing spectators goading Joseph and the "devil" in a bare-knuckle fight. Yet the fight is rigged: as they all know, and as Tiennet comes to realize, the costume of the "devil" is studded with flaying blades and nails. It is Huriel who calls the brotherhood "torturers," but his attempt to halt the initiation descends into general violence routed only (in a comic sonic twist) by "a plaintive voice [...] in the depths of the prison reciting the mass for the dead" (311). The local friar scatters Joseph's superstitious enemies with acousmatic chanting of the liturgy. Once more, music and sound act as dramatic antagonists. Long before scholars of musical and sonic torture studied the practices at Guantánamo Bay,[8] Sand portrayed a musical hellhole in a prison dungeon as the flip side of a rural idyll, and she used it to warn that the power of music and community alike were vulnerable to abuse precisely because of their potency.

---

[8] Initiated by Suzanne Cusick in her "Music as Torture / Music as Weapon," *Trans: revista transcultural de música* 10 (2006) <https://www.sibetrans.com/trans/articulo/152/music-as-torture-music-as-weapon> [Accessed October 24, 2024].

Conclusion

Sand's *The Master Pipers* attunes readers to the emotional power of music, the sonic power of noise, and the blurred lines between the two. At the same time, her novel allows music to be read symbolically, as an indicator of identity and as a vector for social change. There are nods to autobiographical matters (the plight of the artist) in her presentation of a sickly anti-hero so soon after her split with Chopin; but the main thrust of the novel invites broader readings in which the lowly genre of folk music – pervasive within the text, thematized and even theorized – is elevated to a lofty position as the novel's animating force.

Further Reading

Cohen, Margaret. "Women and Fiction in the Nineteenth Century." *The Cambridge Companion to the French Novel*. Ed. Timothy Unwin. Cambridge: Cambridge University Press, 1997. 54–72.

Datlof, Natalie, Jeanne Fuchs and David A. Powell, eds. *The World of George Sand*. New York: Greenwood Press, 1991.

Finch, Alison. *Women's Writing in Nineteenth-Century France*. Cambridge: Cambridge University Press, 2000.

Kawabata, Maiko. *Paganini, the "Demonic" Virtuoso*. Woodbridge: The Boydell Press, 2013.

Powell, David A. *While the Music Lasts: The Representation of Music in the Works of George Sand*. Lewisburg: Bucknell University Press, 2001.

Reid, Martine. *George Sand*. Trans. Gretchen van Slyke. University Park, Pennsylvania: Penn State University Press, 2018.

Samson, Jim. *Chopin*. Oxford: Oxford University Press, 1996.

Sand, George. *Consuelo*. Trans. Gretchen van Slyke. Pennsylvania: University of Pennsylvania Press, 2010.

———. *Lettres d'un voyageur*. Trans. Sasha Rabinovitch and Patricia Thomson. London: Penguin, 1987.

———. *La Petite Fadette*. Trans. Gretchen van Slyke. Pennsylvania: Penn State University Press, 2017.

CHAPTER 3

Bands of Mercy Music: A Cultural Study of Victorian Animal Welfare Songs for Children

ALISA CLAPP-ITNYRE

Recommended Texts

Sarah J. Eddy, comp., *Songs of Happy Life: For Schools, Homes and Bands of Mercy* (Providence, Rhode Island: Art and Nature Study Publishing, 1897); reproduced by BiblioBazaar, c.2020. Also available at *Internet Archive*, <https://archive.org/details/songsofhappylifeooeddyrich> [Accessed October 24, 2024].

To hear Songs 1 through 4, and other songs of the Bands of Mercy movement, see *Sounding Childhood* (<www.soundingchildhood.org> [Accessed October 24, 2024]). This academic website showcases various genres of children's music of the Victorian era (hymns, school songs, etc.). Most **starred songs** in this chapter are found in "Political Songs: Bands of Mercy" Songs (Part 3). A few ("Woodman, Spare that Tree" and "Dare to do Right") are in "Songs for School and Play" (Part 2).

Keywords

Agrarian, America, animal-welfare movement, Bands of Hope, Bands of Mercy, Bird Days, birds, children's education, nostalgia, periodicals, pets, RSPCA, songs, urban, Victorian Britain

Prelude

Extract 1 / Fig. 3.1

G.W. Martin, "The Helpless Lamb" (no. 7), words S.W. Partridge, *Band of Mercy Advocate* 1.7 (July 1879): 56.

Extract 2 / Fig. 3.2

M.W. Seeley, "A Cry for Liberty," (no. 56), *Songs of Happy Life: For Schools, Homes and Bands of Mercy*, comp. Sarah J. Eddy (Providence, Rhode Island: Art and Nature Study Publishing, 1897) 85.

Extract 3 / Fig. 3.3

L.B. Marshall, "Voice of the Helpless," (no. 65), words Carlotta Perry, *Songs of Happy Life*, comp. Eddy, 95.

Extract 4 / Fig. 3.4–3.5

J.C.O. Redington, "Dare to do Right," (no. 14), *Songs of Happy Life*, comp. Eddy, 24 [**Fig. 3.4**]; William Bradbury, "Dare to do Right," program for the Church of England Temperance Society, Exeter Hall Meeting (April 26, 1898) [**Fig. 3.5**].

Dare To Do Right.

Dare to do right! dare to be true! You have a work that no oth - er can do.

Dare to do Right!

W. B. BRADBURY.

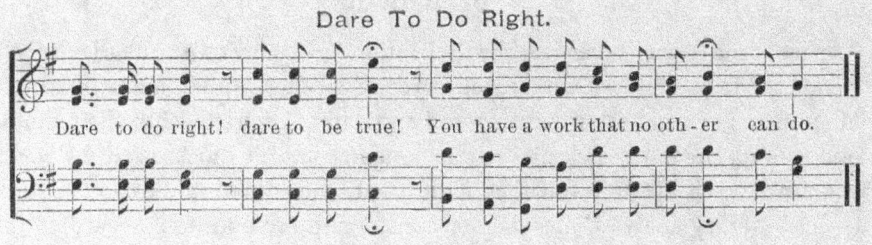

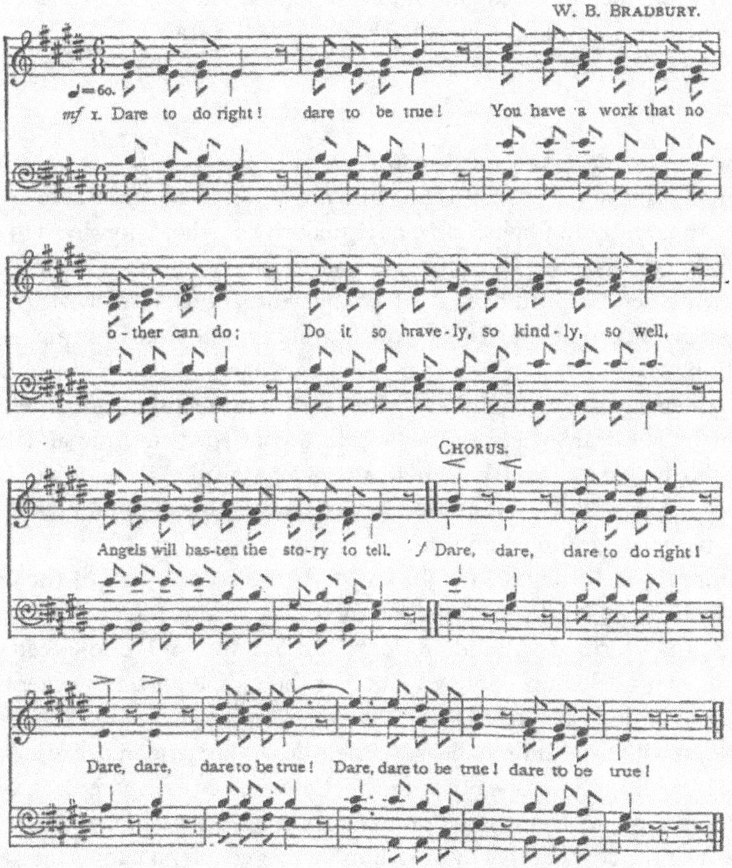

♩=60.
mf 1. Dare to do right! dare to be true! You have a work that no
o - ther can do; Do it so brave - ly, so kind - ly, so well,
Angels will has - ten the sto - ry to tell.
CHORUS.
f Dare, dare, dare to do right!
Dare, dare, dare to be true! Dare, dare to be true! dare to be true!

2.

mf Dare to do right! dare to be true!
p Other men's failures can never save you;
r. Stand by your conscience, your honour, your faith,
Stand like a hero, and battle till death.
f Dare, dare, &c.

3.

mf Dare to do right! dare to be true!
God who created you cares for you too,
Treasures the tears that His faithful ones shed,
Counts and protects every hair of your head.
f Dare, dare, &c.

4.

mf Dare to do right! dare to be true!
Keep the great judgment-seat ever in view.
Look at your life as you'll look at it then,
Scanned by your God before angels and men.
f Dare, dare, &c.

5.

mf Dare to do right! dare to be true!
Jesus, your Saviour, will carry you through;
City and mansion and crown all in sight,
Can you not dare to be true and do right?
f Dare, dare, &c.

The Challenge

As part of the Royal Society for the Prevention of Cruelty to Animals (RSPCA), Bands of Mercy children's organizations sang about a more humane treatment of animals in rural and urban England and, later, America. With their simple poetry and engaging melodies, these songs represent music used for social activism and child empowerment of the era. Using animal studies, music studies and literary analysis, this chapter considers these questions regarding the four songs above: What characterized the treatment of and growing sensitivity to domesticated and wild animals in the Victorian era? How did music and text work together to evoke an animal-welfare aesthetic? How did children participate in music culture and social reform of the era?

Background

It is an often overlooked but incontrovertible fact that the animal-welfare movement came about exactly as England moved from an agrarian to an urban society. Apparently, to English citizens (a majority of whom now lived in cities), animals "served as living, tangible relics of the old agricultural way of life that people, whether removed from the farm by generations or a few years, feared to let slip away completely."[1] In fact, the first successful piece of animal-welfare legislation, Martin's Act of 1822 (after Richard Martin, MP, who introduced it to Parliament) gave farm animals (cattle, sheep) protection from cruelty. Two years later, the Royal Society for the Prevention of Cruelty to Animals (RSPCA) was established in Britain (the American Society for the Prevention of Cruelty to Animals, the ASPCA, was established in 1866) to educate about and regulate animal-usage, beginning with those on farms.

Children were brought into the cause in the second half of the century when, in 1875, philanthropist, temperance activist and RSPCA leader Catherine Smithies formed a "Band of Mercy" for children in Wood Green Grove, England, as modeled on Bands of Hope of the temperance movement.[2] Mrs. M.L. Schaffter described them thus: "Starting with the fact that all such reforms must begin with the children, because their hearts are tender, because they are impressionable, and because they indirectly educate their parents, a Band of Mercy might be justly termed a preparatory class for a Humane Society."[3] So popular was the concept that by 1892, 800 Bands (chapters) had formed around

---

[1] James Turner, *Reckoning with the Beast: Animals, Pain, and Humanity in the Victorian Mind* (Baltimore: Johns Hopkins University Press, 1980) 33.

[2] Bands of Hope formed in 1847 in Leeds, England, to inspire children in the temperance cause, and used songs and recitations in their meetings. For more about both Bands and their music, see Alisa Clapp-Itnyre, *British Hymn Books for Children, 1800–1900: Re-Tuning the History of Childhood* (Farnham: Ashgate, 2016) 196–209.

[3] Quoted in Sarah J. Eddy, *Songs of Happy Life: For Schools, Homes and Bands of Mercy* (Providence, Rhode Island: Art and Nature Study Publishing, 1897) 159.

England.⁴ Further, when taken to America, the movement added over 27,000 chapters by the early twentieth century. Meeting weekly or monthly, a Band meeting centered on storytelling, fact-sharing and singing about the humane treatment of animals. Children would "sign the pledge" and recite it: "*We agree to do all in our power to protect animals from cruel usage, and to promote as far as we can their humane treatment.*"⁵ When compulsory education was instituted (1880 in the UK, 1900 for most in the US), many schools added humane education to their curriculum, establishing Bands of Mercy in schools and, in the US, using these materials in celebrating Arbor Day (est. 1872 by J. Sterling Morton) and Bird Day (est. 1894 by Charles Babcock).

Materials were needed for meetings, schools and home use; such publications included the periodical *The Band of Mercy Advocate*, begun in 1879 by Smithies's son Thomas Bywater Smithies (later taken up by the RSPCA in 1883 and renamed *Band of Mercy*). Each monthly issue contained stories, poetry and beautiful etchings of animals, with a fully scored song on the back cover. The periodical indirectly aligned children and animals in their smallness, voicelessness and passivity, then empowered both through illustrations beautifying smallness, songs giving voice to the voiceless and stories showing heroic actions from both children and animals.⁶ In addition, *Songs of Happy Life* (1897), a book edited by the American Sarah J. Eddy, contained outlines for Bands meetings, advice for school programs, suggestions for Bird Days, essay topics, inspirational quotes and, most importantly, songs. Over 100 songs fell into six categories: "Help and Kindness to All," "Animals," "Bees and Other Insects," "Birds," "Nature and Seasons" and "Liberty, Love, and Peace." Imperative to the success of any Band meeting was the inclusion of music-making, which was probably the most enjoyable activity for children, who were able to engage bodily and sing lustily after sitting during recitations and lessons. But these songs also contained vital messages about the worth of animals and the agency of children to speak for them.

Indeed, the Bands served to raise social and political awareness to the problems facing many animals beyond the agricultural sector by late century: horses and all beasts of burden, untold numbers of stray dogs, and animals in slaughterhouses. The nineteenth century became "the great age of the horse" as horse-racing and hunting by the wealthy expanded, while urban spaces greatly increased the need for horse-drawn vehicles.⁷ Anna Sewell wrote *Black Beauty*

---

⁴ Brian Harrison, *Peaceable Kingdom: Stability and Change in Modern Britain* (Oxford: Clarendon Press, 1982) 129.

⁵ *Band of Mercy Advocate* 1.1 (January 1879): 7; original emphasis.

⁶ See Alisa Clapp-Itnyre, "Advocating for the Least of These: Empowering Children and Animals in *The Band of Mercy Advocate*," *Animals and Their Children in Victorian Culture*, eds Brenda Ayres and Sarah E. Maier (New York: Routledge, 2020) 87–105.

⁷ Elsie B. Michie, "Horses and Sexual/Social Dominance," *Victorian Animal Dreams: Representations of Animals in Victorian Literature and Culture*, eds Deborah

(1877) to attack the inhumane treatment of horses, often worked to death without compunction; she specifically decries the painful use of the bearing rein to keep horses' necks erect. Dogs' homes were established to address the problem of strays: the first opened in London in 1860, and with new, expanded quarters in Battersea by 1871. Nevertheless, "new and improved" methods of euthanasia were commonplace there.[8] As for slaughterhouses, more city inhabitants to feed led to the requisite butchery and bloodshed right inside city limits (such as London's Smithfield Market). In fact, the Vegetarian Society of the United Kingdom was established as early as 1847 to combat the "brutalizing force" of meat-eating, taking inspiration from the American vegetarian Bronson Alcott, father of the author Louisa May Alcott.[9]

The RSPCA would, mid-century, expand into wild-bird protection, both in Britain and America. Birds were being killed in droves, for sport but also for women's hat and clothing fashions. Some species of birds were precariously close to extinction (e.g., egrets) and some had already gone (the dodo). Societies campaigned for a change in sport – bird-watching rather than bird-hunting as advocated in Charles Dixon's *Rural Bird Life* (1880), for example – and in women's fashion, promoted by such women's groups as the Plumage League. In 1870, the Association for the Protection of British Birds was established and, working with the RSPCA, succeeded in getting a series of Wild Birds' Protection Acts passed in the UK (1872, 1876).

By late-century, though, in attempting to fight vivisection (experiments on live animals) and hunting as sport, the RSPCA suddenly found itself working against the educated, the scientists and the wealthy; indeed, even Queen Victoria patronized stag-hunting.[10] As such, they failed. As James Turner concludes, "After the 1870s, the scope of the SPCA work slowly constricted. Contentious issues like field sports and factory farming were avoided in favor of teaching children to be kind to pets and birds and caring for stray dogs and cats."[11] However, I will argue in the next section that children were key in agitating for reform for many animals beyond cats and dogs.

Denenholz Morse and Martin A. Danahay (New York: Routledge, 2007) 145–66.

[8] See Susan Hamilton, "Dogs' Homes and Lethal Chambers, or, What Was it Like to be a Battersea Dog?" *Animals in Victorian Literature and Culture: Contexts for Criticism*, eds Laurence W. Mazzeno and Ronald D. Morrison (London: Palgrave Macmillan, 2017) 83–107.

[9] See the Vegetarian Society of the United Kingdom website at <https://vegsoc.org/who-we-are/history/> [Accessed October 24, 2024]. Ironically, although RSPCA animal activists regulated cruelty in slaughterhouses, they rarely promoted a vegetarian diet. See Jon Gregerson, *Vegetarianism: A History* (Fremont, California: Jain, 1994) 75.

[10] Harrison, *Peaceable Kingdom*, 91.

[11] Turner, *Reckoning with the Beast*, 122.

Case Study

Song was important to Bands of Mercy for entertainment, and it was not lost upon the movement that nature had its own songs, too, especially through birds. As presented in the *Advocate*, human performances were never "equal to those of the blackbird, the thrush, and the nightingale. Our country-side has a finer orchestra, morning and evening in early summer, than can be found in London or Paris. And don't tell us it is wild and uncultivated."[12] In *Songs of Happy Life*, Eddy includes a compilation of "Musical Notes of Birds and Animals" (by W. Gardiner), which uses musical notation to present the songs of the nightingale, robin, canary, lark and thrush, and even the sounds of a kitten and sheep.[13] The Bands especially promoted songs about birds, as children mimicked their singing and gave voice to their sufferings. Out of twelve months' worth of songs in the first volume of the *Advocate*, seven focused on birds, for example, while Eddy's book has an entire section on "Birds": thirty-three songs on "The Constant Dove" (no. 63) and "The Humming-Bird" (no. 75*), for example, but also with didactic messages: "Don't Kill the Birds" (no. 60) and for "The Wounded Curlew" (no. 55). We should recall that the focus on birds became a specific campaign of the RSPCA, so such songs fed into its priorities, especially by late century. The protection of birds was also very relevant to children who, especially in the countryside, would scour bird nests for eggs as a common pastime. Charles Babcock was inspired to organize Bird Day in 1894 because the "love of feather ornamentation so heartlessly persisted in by thousands of our women, and the mania for collecting eggs and killing birds so deeply rooted in our boys, are legacies of barbarism inherited from our savage ancestry."[14] Hence, children sing "Don't Rob the Birds, Boys" (Eddy, no. 68); while "The Voice of the Helpless" (Eddy, no. 65*), to be explored in a moment, even remonstrates, "that little dead bird on your bonnet, / Is it worth the cruel wrong?" (verse 5). These are sharp words of recrimination for the nineteenth-century fashion industry in both England and America, which annually caused the killing of millions of egrets, herons, hummingbirds and many other species.

Of course, both publications feature songs on other humane topics as well. The *Advocate* contains songs lamenting the death of a cat ("Only a Pussy," no. 15, 1880); urging respect for spiders ("The world is surely large enough for you and me," from "The Spider," no. 22, 1880); and the proper nurture of work animals ("Feeding Neddy," no. 28, 1881*). Eddy's *Songs of Happy Life* includes songs of social activism and Christian charity: to "Make the World More Bright" (no. 1), to "Speak Kindly" (no. 16), to "Be Kind to Living Things" (no. 10), to celebrate

---

[12] *Band of Mercy Advocate* 1.6 (June 1879): 43.

[13] Eddy, *Songs of Happy Life*, 188–9.

[14] J. Sterling Morton, quoted by Charles Babcock in his *Bird Day: How to Prepare for It* (New York: Silver, Burdett and Company, 1901) 10. Available at *Project Gutenberg*, <https://www.gutenberg.org/files/21266/21266-h/21266-h.htm> [Accessed October 24, 2024].

nature ("The Morning Light [that] is Breaking," no. 103*), and to admonish ("Woodman, Spare that Tree," no. 90*). Other songs appeal specifically to Bands to "Ring the Bells of Mercy" (no. 22).

Perhaps more impressive are the songs that empower the abilities of children despite their youth and smallness, like "God Bless the Little Children" (Eddy, no. 17*) and "Little Deeds of Kindness" (no. 6*): "How many deeds of kindness / A little child may do, / Although it has so little strength / And little wisdom too!" (verse 4). Children could speak for the voiceless animals. "Open Thy Mouth for the Dumb" (*Band of Mercy* 1885, no. 75) asserts this directly: "Speak out for the dumb and weary, [...] / Stop the lash [...] / Stop the blows that fall" (on beasts of burden). Other songs speak of the strength of the collective, the many voices of children marching for animal welfare in militant fashion "[t]o protect the weak and helpless [...] / With our Bands we'll join all nations" (verses 2, 3 in "Lift Aloft our Banner," Eddy, no. 20*). By engaging them both directly and collectively, the Bands of Mercy urged, through music, children's public participation in one of the most important social-reform movements of the era.[15]

Further, these songs empowered children in some fairly consistent aesthetic ways. For one, all songs have what might be viewed as "simpler" poetry and "lively" tunes: rhymes that are either couplets (two adjacent rhymes) or abcb form (where lines two and four rhyme), usually iambic meter (unstress-stress), and very often in 6/8 time which makes them very danceable (though dance is not specifically assigned). Further, most tunes in Eddy's book are choral SATB (for soprano, alto, tenor and bass) which assumes adult male voices for tenor and bass, although it would be easy enough to use only the top two voices (soprano and alto) for children, or even to have them sing in unison. Many of the songs, such as "Marching 'Round the World" (no. 7*), are written for bodily movement. Some are even participatory, such as "Over in the Meadow" (no. 30: "Lived a mother toad and her little toady one [...] and her little fishes two [etc.]"). Another technique used to appeal to children was that of animal autobiography, not to be confused with animal fantasy where animals act as humans, but rather a genre in which humans attempt to understand the feelings and possible thoughts of real animals.[16] For example, many of *The Advocate*'s songs about birds are told from the perspective of the birds, like "The Sparrows' Petition" in their inaugural issue (song no. 1, 1879). This song is a reminder to city dwellers of the wildlife right outside their windows, as the birds speak to "Kind girls and boys of Chester Square" (London) to "pray give us of your meals to share" (verse 1) during the cold winter months. They further expound, "Hunger and frost are hard to bear" so "Just throw us out a crumb or two" (verse 2).

---

[15] For more about the Bands of Mercy music as empowering child-singers, see Clapp-Itnyre, *British Hymn Books*, 209–25.

[16] See essays in Margo DeMello, ed., *Speaking for Animals: Animal Autobiographical Writing* (New York: Routledge, 2012).

A Close Look at Four Songs

The following discussion applies some of these social and aesthetic concepts to the four songs presented in the opening Prelude. In so doing, we see how poets and composers taught animal empathy to young singers.

In both nostalgic and spiritual ways, "The Helpless Lamb"* [**Extract 1**] invokes a pastoral life that many Victorian children would not have known. The engraving insert establishes the pastoral tone by showcasing a shepherd in Victorian rustic garb with a shepherd's crook and faithful dog surveying a flock of sheep, and a church steeple in the distance registering the Christian parallels with Christ the Good Shepherd. The song itself, with words by S.W. Partridge and music by G.W. Martin, is an interesting mix of amusement and didacticism. The A section begins "moderato and lightly" in the major key of D, then turns to the minor for the B section, making its message more dramatic. The lighter melody of the A section undergirds the helplessness and deficiencies of the lamb: "swiftness, strength, nor sense have you" (verse 1), and "Strength nor cunning you possess" (verse 2). The B section music becomes more determinedly martial, its closed tetrameter couplets sung in unison and then answered in harmony. The first presentation of this section underscores other animals' more auspicious ferocity:

> Lions boast a mighty paw,
> Eagles have a piercing claw;
> Bulls can gore, and dogs can bite;
> You can neither fly nor fight. (verse 1)

The third verse brings the shepherd's protection into view: "At his side you need not fear, / Danger cannot reach you there" with its chorus and emphatic tune finally connecting the message to a child-singer: "I am weak, poor lamb, like you, / Need a guardian shepherd too; / That Good Shepherd, Jesus, need, / Or I shall be weak indeed." Thus, the animal pastoral is ultimately a lesson for children of *their* vulnerability and need for a Good Shepherd, Jesus. It is an example of using animals metaphorically for a human message.[17]

Turning now to **Extract 2**, the song "A Cry for Liberty"* (words anonymous but music by M.W. Seeley) is number 56 of Eddy's *Songs of Happy Life* (1897). It is one of the many Bands of Mercy songs about birds, now from a caged-bird's perspective. It evokes the passionate issue of individual freedom, certainly a

---

[17] Anna Feuerstein argues that animal welfare organizations of the era, like the RSPCA, evinced what she calls "pastoral power" over animals: invoking Christian terms of the "Good Shepherd" protecting His flock, such constructions simultaneously regulated and exploited animals for material benefits (sheep are needed within the economy). See Anna Feuerstein, *The Political Lives of Victorian Animals: Liberal Creatures in Literature and Culture* (Cambridge: Cambridge University Press, 2019) 64–5. Interestingly, Jesus is never presented as the Sacrificial Lamb in this song, which might encourage too much sympathy for the exploited sheep.

charged concept for American listeners who were only decades out from a Civil War (1861–5) which was largely associated with emancipating enslaved people. "O Liberty! sweet Liberty! / I pine and faint for thee! / Fain would I burst my prison bars, / And soar among the free!" intones the bird in the first verse, which could equally be a line from a Spiritual. At the time, it was very popular among children to keep caged birds; thus, this song indicts singers themselves for depriving the bird of his God-given right to be free, for which he yearns: "Then would I mount to azure heights, / And chant my Maker's praise" (verse 4). The human propensity to supply "daily needs" (verse 2), a "silver-sanded floor" (verse 3) and "bars of glitt'ring brass" (verse 3) for animal companions is now soundly, if politely, rejected by the bird-speaker:

> E'en though my little daily needs
> Each morning are supplied,
> A humbler fare were sweeter far
> With fetter'd wing untied. (verse 2)

The lines in rhyming ballad meter (four stresses alternating with three stresses) draw out the poignant argument, while Seely's tune in F major invokes a parlor ballad in its earnestness. Its careful use of tight harmonies (often in thirds) and ascending lines to fit moments of "soar[ing] among the free" appears to be tone-painting to mimic the desired flight of birds. In the chorus, the soprano and alto lines alone repeat the opening tune-phrase to reinforce the theme ("O Liberty, sweet liberty!"). The line continues, the rest of the choir joining and converging on the poignant question, "When wilt thou come to set me free?" Music and text part ways here, dramatically: the query hangs, but the music is more confident, resolving firmly downwards after reaching its highest peak on the action verb "wilt."[18]

Generally speaking, the *Advocate* shared songs that were simple in music and message. Likewise, Eddy's 1897 collection of songs contained similarly simple examples. But the collection's expansiveness also allowed Eddy room to include songs of a more complex nature, like "The Voice of the Helpless" (no. 65*), a ballad by Carlotta Perry [**Extract 3**], which reflects on the various birds of the air which are killed for sport and vanity. In a haunting tune by L.B. Marshall, set in F major, the song tells a poignant, sentimental tale in keeping with other songs of the era.[19] It opens dramatically with "a cry from the forests dim," a "plaintive cry" personified (verse 1), and gradually verse 2 reveals "a woodland tragedy":

---

[18] Similarly, "The Little Maiden and the Little Bird" (Eddy, no. 64*), based on a poem by Lydia Maria Child, consists of a dialogue between a young girl calling, "Little bird! Come to me! / I have a green cage all ready for thee," to which the bird responds, "Nay, little damsel, away I'll fly / To greener fields and warmer sky," directly flouting human protection.

[19] Consider such sentimental ballads as Arthur Sullivan's "The Lost Chord" (1877) and Thomas Moore's "Eveleen's Bower" (1808).

'Tis the cry of the orphan nestlings,
'Tis the wail of a bird that sings
His song of grace in the archer's face,
'Tis the flutter of broken wings.

An archer has killed a mother bird, leaving her nestlings orphans. But by the third verse, true culpability is leveraged on the young girls who might sing this song:

Oh! Lovely, unthinking maiden,
The wing that adorns your hat,
Has the radiance rare, that God placed there,
But I see in place of that,
A mockery pitiful, deep, and sad.

Deepening the guilt, the fourth verse personifies this tragedy as a human one, the song now addressing a human mother who, it suggests, is not unlike a bird mother:

Oh! Mother you clasp your darling,
Close to your loving breast;
Think of that other, that tender mother,
Brooding upon her nest
In the little chirp from field and wood,
Does no sound touch your motherhood? (verse 4)

Worse yet, the human mother has indirectly caused the bird deaths, as shown in the fifth verse when singers speak of "that little dead bird on your bonnet" and "the hummingbird on your velvet dress" (verse 5).

The beseeching, labored melody by Marshall repeats the opening three-note phrase in every line, then gradually builds in intensity as each line climbs higher and higher, peaking in the third line at a point that often emphasizes significant words in the verse: "cry" (verse 2), "sad" (verse 3) and "dress" (verse 5). That third line of text is then repeated, with a new melody and increasingly chromatic harmony, placing the moment of greatest intensity at exactly the same moment ("cry," "sad"), but now giving it diminished harmony, conventionally associated with anguish. Full of pathos, the music allows the young singers to react with crescendos, decrescendos and other musical dynamics to tell their sad tale.

The words of the song are thus placed in the mouths of children for self-examination, but also for the education and incrimination of their own parents. Real-life connections could be made to the egret trade in the American Everglades that came close to wiping out the species (five million birds killed a year), mainly for plumage for women's fashion accessories. Due to such activism as in this song, the Lacey Bird and Game Act of 1900 gave many bird species important protection.[20]

---

[20] See Ken Burns, dir., *National Parks: America's Best Idea* (PBS, 2010). <http://www.pbs.org/nationalparks/parks/everglades/> [Accessed October 24, 2024]. I am using

The final song in this discussion is a marching song: "Dare to do Right."*
[Extract 4.] Inspired by the mid-century "muscular Christianity" movement promoting patriotism and self-discipline, as well as by the American Civil War (whose tunes crossed the ocean in high numbers), composers of such militant songs encouraged singers literally to march into action. This song actually came from the temperance and Bands of Hope repertoire. So, in daring singers to "do right," the song serves as inspiration to both adults and children for a multitude of causes. Given its popularity in both Bands of Mercy and Bands of Hope songbooks, its impassioned confidence in the power of children is notable:

> Dare to do right! dare to be true!
> You have a work that no other can do;
> Do it so bravely, so kindly, so well,
> Angels will hasten the story to tell. (verse 1, Eddy, no.14*)

These are simple words, with a child-like faith in the presence of angels, yet the message is profound. Rather than doubting a child's "strength or sense" as with "The Helpless Lamb," this song challenges the singer to "Stand by your conscience, your honor, your faith, / Stand like a hero and battle till death" (verse 2). When sung by children, these works engender their own self-confidence in following a cause. The third verse evokes a Christian message, of a God who will help the child in these endeavors, in ultimately selfless pastoral care: "God sees your faith and will carry you through; / Keeping His loving help ever in sight, / Can you not dare to be true and do right?" (verse 3). Eddy utilizes a sprightly tune by J.C.O. Redington in her book. **[Fig. 3.4.]** However, another tune, by famed American hymn-composer William B. Bradbury, is made for marching. **[Fig. 3.5.]** The alliterative, robust words "dare" and "do" are punctuated musically with strong eighth notes [quavers] in the verses, then quarter notes [crotchets] in the chorus, further enforced by Bradbury's judicious use of rests. The melody of the chorus is set much higher than the verse, producing an effect intensified when sung by high child-voices even as the words enforce their abilities to "do right." Notably, none of the words focus specifically on doing right for animal welfare, but its inclusion in books such as Eddy's suggest its important work in using music to emotionally inspire both the child-singer and the adult public to fight for the kind treatment of animals.[21]

---

the British, first edition of *Songs of Happy Life*. The second, American edition (1898) replaced "The Voice of the Helpless" with a much more innocuous song, "Marjorie," about a girl enjoying the daisies. This is one of only a few changes made between editions. I suspect the intense, guilt-laden, politically charged message led to this cut.

[21] Erin Johnson-Williams explores the use of drill music to question "performing autonomy and automation," which is also a fair question to ask of marching songs for children. See Erin Johnson-Williams, "Musical Discipline and Victorian Liberal Reform," *Musical Discipline and Victorian Liberal Reform*, ed. Sarah Collins (Cambridge: Cambridge University Press, 2019) 34. As with any music taught to

Children learned songs like the above, then took them out to the larger world as social action; children's voices and child agency were therefore leveraged upon the adult world in an unprecedented manner. Specifically then, Bands of Mercy songs "sing" not only to the humanity of animal welfare, and a collective cause to heal the rural–urban split of society, but also indicate that children themselves may become an important part of social reform.

Further Reading

Clapp-Itnyre, Alisa. "Advocating for the Least of These: Empowering Children and Animals in *The Band of Mercy Advocate.*" *Animals and Their Children in Victorian Culture.* Eds Brenda Ayres and Sarah E. Maier. London: Routledge, 2020. 87–105.

———. *British Hymn Books for Children, 1800-1900: Re-Tuning the History of Childhood.* Farnham: Ashgate, 2016. 196–209.

DeMello, Margo, ed. *Speaking for Animals: Animal Autobiographical Writing.* Routledge Advances in Sociology Series. London: Routledge, 2012.

Farrington, Charlotte. *Hymns for Children, with Opening and Closing Services and Songs and Hymns for Bands of Mercy and of Hope.* London: Sunday School Association, 1894.

Feuerstein, Anna. *The Political Lives of Victorian Animals: Liberal Creatures in Literature and Culture.* Cambridge: Cambridge University Press, 2019.

Flegel, Monica. "'How Does Your Collar Suit Me?' The Human Animal in the RSPCA's *Animal World* and *Band of Mercy*." *Victorian Literature and Culture* 40.1 (2012): 247–62.

Gregerson, Jon. *Vegetarianism: A History.* Fremont, California: Jain, 1994.

Harrison, Brian. *Peaceable Kingdom: Stability and Change in Modern Britain.* Oxford: Clarendon, 1982.

Mazzeno, Laurence W. and Ronald D. Morrison, eds. *Animals in Victorian Literature and Culture: Contexts for Criticism.* London: Palgrave Macmillan, 2017.

Morse, Deborah Denenholz and Martin A. Danahay, eds. *Victorian Animals Dreams: Representations of Animals in Victorian Literature and Culture.* London: Routledge, 2007.

Turner, James. *Reckoning with the Beast: Animals, Pain, and Humanity in the Victorian Mind.* Baltimore: Johns Hopkins University Press, 1980.

---

children for social action, one can question adult intervention to promote a cause using children's voices and physicality. I would argue, however, that the concern for animals underlying Bands of Mercy music must have struck a chord with many of the children singing, thus amplifying their authentic marching to such music.

CHAPTER 4

The Music of the Women's Suffrage Movement

CHRISTOPHER WILEY

Keywords

America, gender, nineteenth century, politics, song, sound recording, twentieth century, Victorian Britain, women's suffrage

Prelude

Extract 1 / Fig. 4.1

Ethel Smyth, *The March of the Women*, words Cicely Hamilton [1910] (London: The Woman's Press; Breitkopf & Härtel, 1911). Edited by Christopher Wiley.

Extract 2

"Plea to Legislators – Men in Law-Halls" (Tune: "Austria"), words Eugénie M. Rayé-Smith, *Equal Suffrage Song Sheaf*, 2nd edn (New York: Eugénie Rayé-Smith, 1912) 15.

Men in law-halls here assembled,
    Hear us now before you pray.
We, who ne'er have shirked, or trembled,
    Duty's mandates to obey,
On your sense of justice leaning,
    Ask of you in Freedom's name
Rights now fraught with potent meaning
    In those laws which here you frame.

See the frail young lives we cherish,
    Of our flesh and blood a part!
Want and wrong decree they perish,
    Bought and sold upon the mart.
Fathers, hear our plea of anguish;
    Would ye see your daughters die?
Let us save e'er more they languish,
    Give us power to heed their cry!

See these hands with labor broken,
    Where we're speeded up for gain;
See these scars, of war the token,
    Battling want too oft in vain!
Have ye tender wives and mothers?
    Would ye see them blighted stand?
Make us heard then with our brothers;
    Make us equals in the land!

Extract 3 / Fig. 4.2

Herman Paley, "She's Good Enough to be Your Baby's Mother and She's Good Enough to Vote with You," words Alfred Bryan (New York: Remick & Co., 1916). Fig. 4.2 shows the opening only.

> No man is greater than his mother,
> No man is half so good!
> No man is better than the wife he loves,
> Her love will guide him,
> Whate'er betide him!
>
> CHORUS
>
> She's good enough to love you and adore you,
> She's good enough to bear your troubles for you;
> And if your tears were falling today,
> Nobody else would kiss them away.
> She's good enough to warm your heart with kisses
> When you are lonesome and blue,
> She's good enough to be your baby's mother
> And she's good enough to vote with you!
>
> Man plunged the world in war and sadness,
> She must protest in vain;
> Let's hope and pray some day we'll hear her say
> "Stop all your madness, I bring you gladness!"
>
> CHORUS

She's Good Enough To Be Your Baby's Mother And She's Good Enough To Vote With You

Song

Lyric by
ALFRED BRYAN

Music by
HERMAN PALEY

152-3

Copyright MCMXV by JEROME H. REMICK & CO., New York & Detroit
Copyright, Canada, MCMXV by Jerome H. Remick & Co.
Propiedad para la Republica Mexicana de Jerome H. Remick & Co., New York y Detroit. Depositada conforme a la ley
Performing rights reserved

Extract 4 / Fig. 4.3

Phil Hanna, words and music, "The Anti-Suffrage Rose" (Boston: Women's Anti-Suffrage Association, 1915). Fig. 4.3 shows the opening only.

> Suffragists say,
> Happen what may
> They'll win the coming fight,
> 'Twixt you and me,
> I don't agree
> We're going to show them who's right!
> Jonquils they wear,
> Cannot compare
> With the Anti-Suffrage Rose,
> Token of love and a gift from above,
> Loveliest flow'r that grows.
>
> CHORUS
>
> Red, Red, Anti-Suffrage Rose
> You're the flow'r that's best of all!
> You're better far, than Jonquils are,
> We are going to prove it in the Fall.
> Sweetest flow'r in all the world,
> Ev'rybody knows,
> You're the emblem of the Anti-Suffrage Cause!
> You lovely, red, red rose!
>
> Work for the "cause,"
> No time to pause,
> Tell all the men you know,
> Why should a few,
> Rule over you?
> Suffrage is ev'ry man's foe.
> Beautiful flower,
> Sign of the hour,
> If the Jonquil wants to fight,
> You cannot fall, you're the Queen of them all,
> Emblem of Truth and Right.
>
> CHORUS

The Anti-Suffrage Rose

Words and Music by
PHIL HANNA

Suf - fra - gists say, —— Hap - pen what may ——
Work for the "cause," —— No time to pause, ——

They'll win the com - - ing fight, ——
Tell all the men you know, ——

'Twixt you and me, —— I don't a - gree ——
Why should a few, —— Rule o - ver you? ——

Copyright 1915 by Phil Hanna

The Challenge

In the later nineteenth and early twentieth centuries, the campaign for women's suffrage gathered increasing momentum on either side of the Atlantic. Art became a key battleground via which the campaigners sought to further their cause, including through the use of many songs. Some added new lyrics to a previously existing melody that would have been familiar to many on both sides of the campaign, while a parallel tradition of newly composed songs also developed. This music would have been sung by advocates for women's suffrage to give voice to their political views, both at large public demonstrations and in more intimate settings. Its popularity was such that a number of anti-suffrage songs developed in response. In England, composer Ethel Smyth wrote *The March of the Women*, adapting an Italian folk melody to which Cicely Hamilton added words; the song soon became the official anthem of the militant Women's Social and Political Union. But how exactly did songs serve the women's suffrage movement? How did their lyrics and music come together to promote a specific political cause? And what did it mean for many of the songs to have appropriated pre-existing music to serve fresh ideological objectives?

Background

The women's suffrage movement, the campaign for women to be given the right to vote in national elections, developed in the course of the long nineteenth century, and may be traced back to antecedents such as Mary Wollstonecraft's *A Vindication of the Rights of Woman* (1792). Milestone events in the establishment of the campaign include, in the US, the first women's rights convention held in Seneca Falls, New York in 1848, and in the UK, the presentation to Parliament of the first mass women's suffrage petition by MP John Stuart Mill in 1866 (although there were English delegates at Seneca Falls as well). National organizations were formed in both countries in the years around 1870. Not only did the campaign have distinct manifestations in different countries, but it was itself not as unified as the umbrella term might suggest. In England, for instance, among the most influential organizations were the National Union of Women's Suffrage Societies (NUWSS), founded in 1897, and the Women's Social and Political Union (WSPU), founded in 1903. The former (who were described as "suffragists") believed that the vote could be won within the bounds of the law through peaceful campaigning, whereas the latter (who are usually referred to more specifically as "suffragettes"), uniting under the motto "deeds not words," considered that more radical and militant action would be necessary to achieve these ends.[1]

---

[1] The term "suffragist" is here used in a general sense to denote advocates of women's suffrage of any sex, whereas "suffragette" (originally a pejorative term) is reserved

Art was one of the ways in which women's suffrage campaigners sought to express their political ideologies and to promote their cause in public. Many were themselves artists to a greater or lesser extent, and the campaign was carefully orchestrated and clearly branded, for instance, with the WSPU choosing the colors of purple, white and green to represent dignity, purity and hope, respectively (NUWSS colors were red, white and green). Campaigners wrote about their experiences in poetry and prose, in private narratives and in accounts published by the press; they created and performed suffrage pageants and short dramas; they held exhibitions; and they distributed postcards and posters by way of propaganda. The arts and crafts movement (which developed in late Victorian Britain and was associated with artists such as William Morris, whose connection with protest song is explored in Chapter 5) was particularly vibrant, bearing witness to a large number of *objets d'art* including embroidery, ribbons, buttons, badges, jewelry and ceramics, to say nothing of the elaborate banners under which the campaigners marched, for instance during public demonstrations.[2] It seemed only natural that the women's suffrage movement would similarly seek to mobilize music as part of its political campaign, to be performed both at large-scale public gatherings such as demonstrations and suffrage meetings, and in the more intimate, amateur setting of one's own home, with guests gathered around the piano.

In the course of the nineteenth century, rich histories developed of political songs being devised by adding new lyrics to existing tunes associated, for instance, with US presidential elections; the American Civil War; or movements such as temperance, abolition and, of course, women's suffrage. Drawing upon existing music served valuable social and political ends. It meant that song sheets could be printed and distributed cheaply, with just the lyrics plus an indication of the tune to which to sing them (although some songbooks nonetheless included the sheet music, even though this was more costly to print), and without the need for their performers – many of whom might not have been musical and likely could not read music notation – to learn new melodies. In doing so, campaigners appropriated music that was fashionable and likely held dear by those whose ideologies they were opposing, and repurposed it for their own ends; some lyrics were even close parodies or paraphrases of the original. This was particularly significant when the music already had political or patriotic associations, such as the tune "America" ("My Country 'tis of Thee,"

---

more specifically for those who adopted a more militant stance in the UK context, including members of the female-only WSPU.
[2] See, for example, Miranda Garrett and Zoë Thomas, eds, *Suffrage and the Arts: Visual Culture, Politics and Enterprise* (London: Bloomsbury, 2019), and Christopher Wiley and Lucy Ella Rose, eds, *Women's Suffrage in Word, Image, Music, Stage and Screen: The Making of a Movement* (London: Routledge, 2021).

more familiar in the UK as the national anthem), used for the women's suffrage song "New America" with lyrics by Elizabeth Boynton Harbert (1891).[3]

Other songs were newly composed expressly for the women's suffrage cause and sparked anti-suffrage ripostes. These repertories were analogous to the then-contemporary parlor song. Though released commercially as sheet music, complete with artwork on the cover that suitably reflected the movement, some were limited in their circulation, being created by local composers and suffrage societies, and sometimes self-published.[4] Nonetheless, other examples of these songs enjoyed a wide distribution, being publicly performed in music halls and theaters (including within plays about suffrage) and thereby enjoying success as popular music, and even, towards the end of the Anglo-American campaign for the vote in the early twentieth century, being recorded and released for phonograph. Generating significant sales of sheet music served as a means of fundraising to support the movement.

The most popular suffrage songs therefore circulated far and wide, and even spread internationally, particularly between America and England; in the former, competitions were held amongst campaigners by way of cultivating additional songs.[5] As Danny O. Crew notes in a modern anthology, examining these songs chronologically yields a snapshot of the ways in which opinions and preoccupations changed across the history of the movement.[6] (Some even reference specific events and people.) The following case study necessarily focuses on a narrower period, the early to mid-1910s, a crucial juncture of the movement's history in the years immediately prior to many women being granted the vote in both the UK and US, in consequence of the Representation of the People Act (1918) and the Nineteenth Amendment (1920), respectively.[7]

---

[3] See "A Guide to this Book" on pages 10–13 for a discussion of another parody of "America."

[4] See Kenneth Florey, "Sheet Music, Songsters and Records," *Women's Suffrage Memorabilia: An Illustrated Historical Study* (Jefferson, North Carolina: McFarland, 2013) 162–72.

[5] See "Music in the Women's Suffrage Movement," *Library of Congress*, <https://www.loc.gov/collections/womens-suffrage-sheet-music/articles-and-essays/music-in-the-womens-suffrage-movement/> [Accessed October 24, 2024].

[6] Danny O. Crew, *Suffragist Sheet Music: An Illustrated Catalogue of Published Music Associated with the Women's Rights and Suffrage Movement in America, 1795–1921, with Complete Lyrics* (Jefferson, North Carolina: McFarland, 2002) 3.

[7] These landmark electoral reforms gave many women the national vote, but certainly not all. The UK Representation of the People Act granted the vote to women over the age of thirty subject to meeting property qualifications (as well as to almost all men over twenty-one, without restrictions), and they did not receive electoral equality until the Equal Franchise Act of 1928. In the US, the Nineteenth Amendment effectively gave the vote predominantly to white women, with various additional barriers that impeded racial minorities (including men, despite the Fourteenth [1868] and Fifteenth [1870] Amendments, as well as Native Americans, even after being formally

In terms of music of the time, one contributor to the women's suffrage movement stands out in particular: Ethel Smyth (1858–1944). One of the leading British classical composers of her generation, Smyth, then in her early fifties, pledged two years' service to the "Votes for Women" campaign in 1910, joining the WSPU following contact with the charismatic head of the organization, Emmeline Pankhurst. The pair became close friends. Much of Smyth's music from the years immediately following is related to her suffrage activity in some way, including her String Quartet in E minor; her chorus, *Hey Nonny No*, her *Three Songs* (one each of which was dedicated to Pankhurst and to her daughter Christabel, also a leading suffragette); her opera, *The Boatswain's Mate* and her three *Songs of Sunrise*.[8] The latter included the songs "Laggard Dawn," which expressed the plight of the suffragettes; "1910," a musical re-enactment of the events of so-called Black Friday of that year; and most famously, *The March of the Women*, which soon became adopted as the official suffragette anthem.

Case Study

The Suffragette Anthem: *The March of the Women* (1910)

Smyth's biographer, Christopher St John, tells us that in composing her song, Smyth adapted a traditional melody from the Abruzzi region of central Italy. The suffragette and writer Cicely Hamilton, co-author (with St John) of the well-known suffrage play *How the Vote was Won* (1909), then wrote words to fit with Smyth's tune. St John notes that Smyth had previously approached John Masefield, G.K. Chesterton and John Galsworthy to undertake this task, but all had declined.[9] Hamilton's poem presents a call to arms for suffragettes, rallying them to march forth in the fight for women's rights, united in the crusade for a better tomorrow – from which, we are told in verse 3, they will prove to be the "victors." The lyrics incorporate repeated allusions to warfare and the campaign against injustice and oppression, referring successively to "freedom," "comrades," "battle," "toil and pain" and "strife," with more subtle allusions including words such as "banner," "duty" and "defiance." As is not uncommon in times of conflict, religion is invoked in support of the cause, with mentions of the "voice of the Lord" at the end of verse 1, and "heaven" and "faith" in verse 2.

Written in 1910 and dedicated to the WSPU, to whom it was formally presented at a meeting in January 1911, the song exists in multiple versions: for SSA,

---

recognized as citizens by the Indian Citizenship Act of 1924) from exercising that right not fully removed until the Voting Rights Act of 1965, extended in 1975 to prevent discrimination against non-English speakers.

[8] See Elizabeth Wood, "Performing Rights: A Sonography of Women's Suffrage," *The Musical Quarterly* 79.4 (Winter 1995): 606–43.

[9] Christopher St John [Christabel Marshall], *Ethel Smyth: A Biography* (London: Longmans, 1959) 151.

SATB (in the main, a duplication of the SSA harmonies, with the tenor line doubling the tune at the octave) and unison voice;[10] and with accompaniment by band, orchestra or piano reduction. Smyth's music uses a near-identical phrase for lines 1–2, 3–4 and 7–8 of the song [**Extract 1**], an AABA musical structure doubtless facilitating the learning of a new piece of music on the part of the average suffragette, since it soon became expected for WSPU members to commit the *March* to memory. Partly for this purpose, it was made available as sheet music and printed on postcards. The repetition was mirrored in Hamilton's rhyming of lines 1 and 3, and lines 2 and 4, of every verse, *the musical form* (AABA) of the whole verse thereby conflicting with *the poetic rhyme pattern* (abab) of its first four lines.[11]

The opening notes of the music, with the long half notes (minims) reiterating the dominant note for the first two syllables of each of lines 1, 3 and 7, enable an emphatic start to successive phrases of the *March*, which in practice often entails the same word repeated ("Shout, shout"; "March, march"; "Strong, strong"; "Hail, hail"; and so on). In literary terms, the extent of the repetition is significant given the limited number of words available in the poem to begin with, and may have been a rhetorical device to maximize the potency of its key sentiments. As to the music, one notable element is the use of the fanfare-like downwards arpeggio on "Cry with the wind" in line 2 (repeated in lines 4 and 8), since fanfares were a feature across Smyth's output, notably in her final opera, *Entente cordiale* (1923–4), and her late oratorio, *The Prison* (1929–30). They would have held a special meaning for Smyth in this context, since she was the daughter of an army officer (as, coincidentally, was Hamilton). The appeal to such militaristic gestures could be seen to represent not just the repurposing of the musical materials of the patriarchy in the service of a campaign against patriarchal control, but more specifically, a sly allusion to Smyth's own familial patriarch, whose opposition to her ambition to pursue a career in music composition she deftly resisted during childhood, as she memorably recounts in her autobiographical writings.

St John suggests that the suffragettes particularly struggled with lines 5 and 6 of the *March*,[12] not because the melody changed at this point, but rather owing to the presence of the flattened seventh accidental at bar 11 (leading to a harmonically awkward return to the song's opening phrase for line 7). It would have been challenging for an untrained singer to locate the correct note, but –

---

[10] SATB refers to the voice types – soprano, alto, tenor and bass – for which choral music is usually scored. SSA, correspondingly, indicates that the music was written for two soprano lines plus alto.

[11] The ordering of new and repeated sections in music is traditionally labelled with capital letters (here, AABA); poetic rhyme schemes are traditionally labelled with lower case (here, abab).

[12] St John, *Ethel Smyth*, 151–2.

given that it is the highest note of the melody, does not belong to the key in question, and with both a *crescendo* and an accent marked in the score – it lends a special emphasis to the syllables with which it is coincident: "call," "voice," "pain" and "hope." The music of line 5 of each verse divides naturally into two halves, both of which adopt the same rhythm and melodic contour, and to which Hamilton likewise responds through internal rhyming, where a word at the caesura rhymes with the end of the line (story/glory; beauty/duty; weary/dreary; reliance/defiance).[13] These internal rhymes work in tandem with end rhymes and with the striking extent of the repetition of words in general, creating a song in which the heavy use of rhyme reinforces both the consonance of its political message, and the (ostensible) cohesion of the suffragette movement itself. Hamilton's lyrics thereby transform Smyth's music from the simple melody of an adapted folk song, to a more satisfying, rallying protest march in which singing is combined with political demonstration and in-step chanting.

As the most famous and widely circulated of many marches composed for the women's suffrage movement across the years, the song was performed in its time at many a rally and suffragette meeting, thus constituting a powerful piece of musical propaganda. But it was also sung to promote solidarity when serving jail sentences together, and for the suffragettes to console one another (and themselves) during deeply challenging times in the campaign, including the periods of hunger striking. There is even a famous (albeit disputed) story of Smyth using her own toothbrush as a makeshift baton with which to conduct the imprisoned suffragettes in the exercise yard while behind bars herself.[14] Nor was its status as the WSPU's official anthem its only association with the movement worldwide. It was known, for instance, to have been sung at a demonstration by the Congressional Union for Woman Suffrage at the Capitol Building in Washington, D.C. on May 9, 1914.

New Words to Existing Music: *Equal Suffrage Song Sheaf* (1912)

Prior to *The March of the Women*, the suffragettes had been using as their anthem a version of *The Marseillaise*, the French national anthem, to which their member Florence Macaulay had written new words. This addition of new lyrics to an existing, well-known melody was a familiar form for popular suffrage songs to take. Several such collections (sometimes called "songsters") were published, particularly in the US. Some had local affiliations, including the *Utah Woman Suffrage Song Book* (1891), which had its origins in local suffrage meetings, and contains multiple references to Utah as well as neighboring

---

[13] A caesura is a mid-line pause, which may or may not be indicated by punctuation.
[14] See Christopher Wiley, "Autobiography and Memoirs," eds Christopher Wiley and Paul Watt, *The Oxford Handbook of Musical Biography and Life-Writing* (Oxford: Oxford University Press, forthcoming).

Wyoming, where (many, but not all) women had already been granted the right to vote in state elections.[15] The slightly later *The Suffrage Song Book* (1909), by Henry W. Roby, was similarly associated with the state of Kansas.[16]

These songs were drawn from a wide variety of sources. Some were folk melodies such as "Auld Lang Syne," or nursery rhymes such as "Three Blind Mice" (set as "Three Blind Men") or "Oh, dear, what can the matter be?"; a few comprised popular tunes from classical music, including the "Bridal Chorus" from Richard Wagner's *Lohengrin*; others were Christian hymns, such as Arthur Sullivan's tune to "Onward Christian Soldiers" or the traditional "OLD HUNDREDTH." Still more were popular songs such as "Yankee Doodle," Patrick Gilmore's "When Johnny Comes Marching Home" or Stephen Foster's "Oh, Susannah"; or patriotic songs such as "The Star-Spangled Banner" or "Rule, Britannia." "Give Ballot to the Mothers," with lyrics by the prominent suffragist Rebecca Naylor Hazard, was sung to the tune of "Marching through Georgia." "John Brown" (also known as "John Brown's Body" and "The Battle Hymn of the Republic," and further discussed in Chapter 5 in relation to workers' songs) was especially popular, given its rousing "Glory, glory, hallelujah!" chorus. Of twenty-eight songs in *The Suffrage Song Book*, eight are set to this tune.

Like "John Brown," a notable number of the melodies selected were those written or popularized around the time of the American Civil War (1861–5), a period during which the women's suffrage movement was also gaining visibility. Some were close textual parodies of the original, such as "Maryland, my Maryland" (which itself uses the tune of "O Tannenbaum"), whose refrain became both "Mary Ann, my Mary Ann" and "Native land, my native land" in different versions – suggesting the expectation of knowledge on the part of those intended to read and perform the songs, not just of the melodies of the original, but also of their words. Throughout the nineteenth century and into the twentieth, racial segregation operated within the US women's suffrage movement, as it did across the nation, with distinct ethnic groups seeking the vote for different reasons and establishing separate organizations through which to campaign for their rights. While the practice of using existing popular tunes as the basis for pro-suffrage songs was not confined to white Americans, further research may yield more detailed knowledge about the ethnicities to whom specific collections were targeted and of the campaigners who made use of them.

---

[15] *Utah Woman Suffrage Song Book* (Salt Lake City: [Utah Woman Suffrage Association], [1891]), available at <https://archive.org/details/utahwomansuffrag00woma/> [Accessed October 24, 2024].

[16] Henry W. Roby, *The Suffrage Song Book: Original Songs, Parodies and Paraphrases, adapted to Popular Melodies* (Topeka: Crane, 1909), available at <https://www.kansasmemory.org/item/204064/> [Accessed October 24, 2024].

One of the most famous collections of such lyrics in the US, the *Equal Suffrage Song Sheaf*, written in its entirety by law professor and suffragist Eugénie Rayé-Smith, appeared in 1912 in its second edition (the first edition, if it was ever published, has not survived).[17] It is dedicated to Rev. Anna Howard Shaw, then the leader of the National American Woman Suffrage Association. Of its twenty-five songs, "Plea to Legislators – Men in Law-Halls" **[Extract 2]** stands out for the multiplicity of resonances of its associated music, being set to the tune "Austria." Explicitly addressed from the outset to men, these verses take the form of an entreaty by women – the unwaveringly dutiful and hard-working women who raise their children – to incorporate equal rights within the laws they are charged with formulating. Consonant with Hamilton's lyrics for *The March of the Women* on the other side of the Atlantic, Rayé-Smith draws upon analogies with wartime in verse 3, where the bodily manifestations of women's arduous labor are compared to "scars," tokens of "war" and (often futile) "Battling."

The chosen melody originated as the *Kaiserhymne* (1796–7), "Gott erhalte Franz den Kaiser" [God Save Emperor Francis] by Joseph Haydn, thereby striking a blow at the very heart of the fiercely male-dominated art form of music composition, and one of its most lauded genres, the string quartet, since it is also used as the theme for the set of variations of the second movement of the composer's "Emperor" Quartet, Op. 76, No. 3 (1797). The quartet's nickname (and the original German-language hymn's first line) reflects that Haydn's tune was written in praise of the then Emperor of the Holy Roman Empire, Francis II; it was still in use in Rayé-Smith's time as the Austrian national anthem, thereby admitting comparison with both "New America" and "The Women's Marseillaise" (even if it was not adopted as the German national anthem until 1922). It was also familiar as the Christian hymn, "Glorious Things of Thee are Spoken." Its appropriation here, as a song appealing to the sense of justice of the male lawmakers to consider women's voices to be heard equally to men's, therefore evokes a spectrum of national, transnational and religious allegiances.

From the Parlor Song to Popular Music: "She's Good Enough to be Your Baby's Mother" (1916)

In parallel with the traditions of adding new words to popular melodies, there developed a separate tradition of composing new music to promote the women's suffrage cause, particularly in the US. The digital archive *Women's Suffrage in Sheet Music*, maintained by the Library of Congress's Music Division, comprises over 200 items associated with women's suffrage (including anti-suffrage

---

[17] Eugénie M. Rayé-Smith, *Equal Suffrage Song Sheaf*, 2nd edn (New York: Rayé-Smith, 1912), available at <https://www.loc.gov/item/2017562122/> [Accessed October 24, 2024].

music) from between 1838 and 1923.[18] While some of these pieces had the status of parlor music, some were recorded and commercially released once the sound-recording industry had become established in the early twentieth century. They even found their way onto the Broadway stage in the Ziegfeld Follies, a series of musical revues that ran from 1907 to the 1930s and were widely admired for their ostentatiously dressed, sometimes risqué, chorus of Ziegfeld Girls. A significant number of pieces – songs such as "The Bloomer's Complaint" (1851) as well as assorted waltzes, polkas and other stylized dances for piano solo – refer explicitly to the garments that were associated with the women's suffrage movement and later also with female cyclists (the song "Eliza Jane" [1895] being a notable example), a mode of transport that gave women unprecedented freedom and independence in society.

"She's Good Enough to be Your Baby's Mother and She's Good Enough to Vote with You" [**Extract 3**] was probably the most popular suffrage song after *The March of the Women*, on the evidence of the number of surviving copies and the several different editions through which it passed.[19] Published late in 1916 (by which point the women's suffrage movement had taken a back seat to the war effort in the United Kingdom, but the United States had not yet formally entered the conflict), it was recorded at the time by vaudeville singer Anna Chandler in an extended version. The historical significance of this recording is evident from its inclusion on Rhino's five-CD compilation box set *R-E-S-P-E-C-T: A Century of Women in Music* in 1999.[20] The song has more recently been covered by acoustic trio Trillium-239 on the album *Rare Isotope* (2019).

Just as Rayé-Smith's "Plea to Legislators" appealed to the (male) lawmakers as people, asking in its third verse whether they had wives and mothers of their own, "She's Good Enough to be Your Baby's Mother" was directed to men on a personal level as the traditional head of the household that typically also included a wife and child. Rather than being cast in the more generalized vein of songs such as *The March of the Women*, then, this one speaks in the second person to address the individual man. It thereby set out the key suffrage argument that the people to whom men were denying the vote were the same people to whom they entrusted the care of their children, yet without giving women the power to influence the world in which that family was nurtured (verse 2 indicating that men were responsible for the "war and sadness" in the

---

[18] See <https://www.loc.gov/collections/womens-suffrage-sheet-music/> [Accessed October 24, 2024].

[19] See Kenneth Florey, "Sheet Music," *Woman Suffrage Memorabilia*, <http://womansuffragememorabilia.com/woman-suffrage-memorabilia/sheet-music/> [Accessed October 24, 2024].

[20] See Neely Tucker, "Suffragists in Song," *Library of Congress Blog*, March 25, 2019, <https://blogs.loc.gov/loc/2019/03/suffragists-in-song/> [Accessed October 24, 2024].

world, a clear allusion to contemporaneous global hostilities). At the same time, it responded to the major anti-suffrage argument that a woman's place was in the home not the voting booth, and that giving women the vote might lead to the abandonment of their domestic duties, prompting (it was supposed) a social revolution of sorts in which men would find themselves needing to assume these roles instead.

While the title of a song often derives either from its first line, or from the first line of the chorus, in this instance the title is taken from the song's *last* line; this rhetorical device ensured that the listener was left with the main message of the song at the end of each presentation of the chorus (which may even earn a special round of applause in performances, such are its powerful political resonances). The interpretation of the words is also greatly aided by the very specific performance instructions in the song, from which we may deduce that unlike the above examples, the lyrics may have been written before the music in this instance. The verse ends with the last line ("Whate'er betide him") being held back prior to the *a tempo* repeated "She's good enough" of the chorus; moreover, attention is drawn to the delivery of the song's title at the end of the chorus through a series of notated directions: "[slower] She's good enough to be your baby's mother [pause on second syllable of "mother"] [back to original tempo] And she's good enough [pause] to vote [pause] with [pause on "with"] you!"[21] Other features of the music give added emphasis to these closing lines, including the tessitura – the song is at its highest during this climactic phrase – and the fact that whereas previous lines of the chorus (including the repeated "She's good enough") commence with an ascending arpeggio, rising from a low note, this one instead starts with a descending one, falling from a high note.

Anti-Suffrage Music: "The Anti-Suffrage Rose" (1915)

Along with the emergence of a significant body of music in support of women's suffrage came a number of songs advancing opposing political views. Anti-suffrage music sometimes looked, on the surface, to advocate for the cause, and only once the irony of the detail of the lyrics was digested did it transpire that its message was differently focused. In some instances, modern commentators even disagree as to whether a given song is sympathetic to women's suffrage or mocking of it.

Early examples of anti-suffrage songs include "Women's Rights" by Kate Horn (1853), written in the wake of the earliest women's rights conventions in the US, and dedicated "Without Permission" to activists Elizabeth Oakes Smith and Amelia Bloomer (the latter an early advocate for the clothing that came to

---

[21] The square brackets above transliterate different types of pauses and other changes of tempo indicated in the sheet music; the original may be consulted at *Library of Congress*, <https://www.loc.gov/resource/mussuffrage.mussuffrage-100123/?sp=5&r=-0.654,-0.019,2.307,1.39,0> [Accessed October 24, 2024].

be named after her). Later instances include "I'm Going to be a Suffragette" with words by D.R. Miller and music by Sandy Engelke (1910), sung from the perspective of the husband whose wife is sympathetic to the suffrage movement, as well as "Mind the baby, I must vote to-day" by E.H. Webb (1914).[22] "Female Suffrage" by George H. Briggs (1867) was dedicated somewhat contemptuously to "Lucy Stone, Susan B. Anthony, Elizabeth Cady Stanton, George Francis Train, and the Advocates of Female Suffrage." "Since my Margarette-become-a-da-suffragette" (1913), composed by Gus Edwards with lyrics by Will D. Cobb, and recorded by Maurice Burkhardt, was simultaneously anti-suffrage and anti-immigration, requiring the singer to affect a mock-Italian accent.

With words and music by Phil Hanna, "The Anti-Suffrage Rose" (1915) **[Extract 4]** followed in the wake of the founding of the National Association Opposed to Woman Suffrage (NAOWS) four years earlier. It was well known in anti-suffrage circles, being recorded at the time in addition to being sold as sheet music, and even being announced in *The New York Times* of August 28, 1915. It was recently included on the album *Shoulder to Shoulder: Centennial Tribute to Women's Suffrage* by the Karrin Allyson Sextet (2019), along with "She's Good Enough to be Your Baby's Mother" and a jazz version of *The March of the Women*.

As Laura Yust notes, none of the several main political arguments against women's suffrage are set out in "The Anti-Suffrage Rose," which seems instead simply to praise the notion of anti-suffragism itself;[23] for the most part, it merely affirms that women will not be successful in winning the vote, and are wrong to seek it, as time will supposedly tell. In that respect it differed markedly from "She's Good Enough to be Your Baby's Mother," which centrally addressed some of the most important pro-suffrage arguments. Nonetheless, the lyrics leave us in no doubt as to the song's political persuasion, particularly lines such as "Suffrage is ev'ry man's foe" (which seems to overlook the significant numbers of men who were in favor of women's suffrage and actively campaigned alongside women).

Dedicated to the Women's Anti-Suffrage Associations (a collective term rather than a specific named organization) and published by the Boston branch, its title alludes to a symbol of the anti-suffrage movement in the US, the red flower (particularly the rose), as contrasted with the color widely adopted

---

[22] Gregory Yerke, "(Anti)Suffragist Sheet Music," *University of Houston Libraries Special Collections Blog*, May 21, 2014, <https://weblogs.lib.uh.edu/speccol/2014/05/21/anti-suffragist-sheet-music/> [Accessed October 22, 2019]. The source in question has been removed and is not archived.

[23] Laura Yust, "Polarizing Political Issues: The Anti-Suffrage Rose," *In the Muse: Performing Arts Blog*, Library of Congress, March 27, 2019, <https://blogs.loc.gov/music/2019/03/polarizing-political-issues-the-anti-suffrage-rose/> [Accessed October 24, 2024].

by the country's supporters of women's suffrage, yellow/gold, and associated flowers including the yellow rose, sunflower and, as in this song, the jonquil. The lyrics praise the rose as the "Loveliest flow'r" and the "Emblem of Truth and Right," which we are told "Cannot compare" to the jonquil; it is surely no accident that the word "rose" in verse 1 is coincident with the highest, longest note of the verse.

While all campaigners for women's right to vote ostensibly worked in the service of a common cause, the women's suffrage movement itself has (as noted) encompassed a wide range of parallel manifestations internationally and across history. The music that underpinned this multi-faceted political movement similarly reflects this diversity and richness: some pieces were indebted to classical music, others to popular song; some appeared as lyrics only, others as sheet music; some were written by women, others by men; some were pro-suffrage, others not; some were given amateur performance at rallies and demonstrations, others were performed professionally and commercially released in early recordings; some were newly composed, others set pre-existing tunes to original words, and still others used no words at all.[24] Scholarly work on the vast, heterogenous body of music associated with the women's suffrage movement, in its many divergent forms across nations and decades, remains in its infancy, and an essay of this scope can hope only to offer brief glimpses into a considerably larger area. Further research will shed greater light on the role played by music in supporting the campaign for votes for women (particularly beyond the Anglo-American frame), how it spread across and between countries, the specific ways in which it was used in different times and places, and its intersections with the music of cognate political movements.

Listening

Karrin Allyson Sextet. *Shoulder to Shoulder: Centennial Tribute to Women's Suffrage*. Entertainment One, 2019.
R-E-S-P-E-C-T: A Century of Women in Music. Rhino, 1999.
Trillium-239, *Rare Isotope*. Trillium-239, 2019.

Further Reading

Crew, Danny O. *Suffragist Sheet Music: An Illustrated Catalogue of Published Music Associated with the Women's Rights and Suffrage Movement in America, 1795–1921, with Complete Lyrics*. Jefferson, North Carolina: McFarland, 2002.

---

[24] Several professional and amateur performances of the songs discussed, as well as digital transfers of historical recordings, are available on standard internet streaming platforms. See also the "Listening" references, below.

Florey, Kenneth. *Women's Suffrage Memorabilia: An Illustrated Historical Study.* Jefferson, North Carolina: McFarland, 2013.

Meacham, Jon, and Tim McGraw. *Songs of America: Patriotism, Protest, and the Music that made a Nation.* New York: Random House, 2019.

Stone, Penny, ed. *The Right to Vote an' a' That.* Edinburgh: Gude Cause, 2009.

Wiley, Christopher. "Ethel Smyth, Suffrage and Surrey: From Frimley Green to Hook Heath, Woking." *Women's History: The Journal of the Women's History Network* 2.11 (Autumn 2018): 11–18.

———, and Lucy Ella Rose, eds. *Women's Suffrage in Word, Image, Music, Stage and Screen: The Making of a Movement.* London: Routledge, 2021.

Wolff, Francie. *Give Ballot to the Mothers: Songs of the Suffragists: A History in Song.* Springfield, Missouri: Denlinger, 1998.

Wood, Elizabeth. "Performing Rights: A Sonography of Women's Suffrage." *The Musical Quarterly* 79.4 (Winter 1995): 606–43.

CHAPTER 5

Song and the Political Body: William Morris

Elizabeth Helsinger

Recommended Texts

William Morris, *A Dream of John Ball* (1886–7, 1888), eds Peter Wright and Florence S. Boos. Subsequent quotations are from the online edition titled "Text of *A Dream of John Ball*," *William Morris Archive*: <https://morris-archive.lib.uiowa.edu/exhibits/show/romances/dreamjohnball> [Accessed October 24, 2024].

Edward Carpenter, ed., *Chants of Labour: A Song Book of the People, with Music* [1888] (London: George Allen & Unwin, 1922). Internet Archive: <https://archive.org/details/chantsoflabours000carp/mode/2up> [Accessed October 24, 2024].

Keywords

Ballad, body, chant, prose romance, rhyme, rhythm, socialism, song, time travel, Victorian Britain

Prelude

Extract 1

From William Morris, Chapter 1, *A Dream of John Ball* (1888).

"Well, friend," said he [Will Green], "thou lookest partly mazed; what tongue hast thou in thine head?"

"A tongue that can tell rhymes," said I.

"So I thought," said he. "Thirstest thou any?"

"Yea, and hunger," said I.

And therewith my hand went into my purse, and came out again with but a few small and thin silver coins with a cross stamped on each, and three pellets in each corner of the cross. The man grinned.

"Aha!" said he, "is it so? Never heed it, mate. It shall be a song for a supper this fair Sunday evening. But first, whose man art thou?"

"No one's man," said I, reddening angrily; "I am my own master."

He grinned again.

"Nay, that's not the custom of England, as one time belike it will be. Methinks thou comest from heaven down, and hast had a high place there too."

He seemed to hesitate a moment, and then leant forward and whispered in my ear: "John the Miller, that ground small, small, small," and stopped and winked at me, and from between my lips without my mind forming any meaning came the words, "The king's son of heaven shall pay for all."

He let his bow fall on to his shoulder, caught my right hand in his and gave it a great grip, while his left hand fell among the gear at his belt, and I could see that he half drew his knife.

"Well, brother," said he, "stand not here hungry in the highway when there is flesh and bread in the Rose yonder. Come on."

And with that he drew me along toward what was clearly a tavern door, outside which men were sitting on a couple of benches and drinking meditatively.

Extract 2

From Morris, Chapter 2, *A Dream of John Ball* (1888).

So such a tale I told them, long familiar to me; but as I told it the words seemed to quicken and grow, so that I knew not the sound of my own voice, and they ran almost into rhyme and measure as I told it; and when I had done there was silence awhile[.] [...]

"Yea," said a third, "hearken a stave of Robin Hood; maybe that shall hasten the coming of one I wot of." And he fell to singing in a clear voice, for he was a young man, and to a sweet wild melody, one of those ballads which in an incomplete and degraded form you have read perhaps. My heart rose high as I heard him, for it was concerning the struggle against tyranny for the freedom of life, how that the wildwood and the heath, despite of wind and weather, were better for a free man than the court and the cheaping-town; of the taking from the rich to give to the poor; of the life of a man doing his own will and not the will of another man commanding him for the commandment's sake. The men all listened eagerly, and at whiles took up as a refrain a couplet at the end of a stanza with their strong and rough, but not unmusical voices.

Extract 3

From Morris, Chapters 2–3, *A Dream of John Ball* (1888).

But here the song dropped suddenly, and one of the men held up his hand as who would say, Hist! Then through the open window came the sound of another song, gradually swelling as though sung by men on the march. This time the melody was a piece of the plain-song of the church[.] [...]

The song still grew nearer and louder, and even as we looked we saw turning the corner through the hedges of the orchards and closes, a good clump of men, more armed, as it would seem, than our villagers, as the low sun flashed back from many points of bright iron and steel. The words of the song could now be heard, and amidst them I could pick out Will Green's late challenge to me and my answer; but as I was bending all my mind to disentangle more words from the music, suddenly from the new white tower behind us clashed out the church bells, harsh and hurried at first, but presently falling into measured chime; and at the first sound of them a great shout went up from us and was echoed by the new-comers, "John Ball hath rung our bell!"

The Challenge

What are the elements of a song – in the words, the music or the performance – that make it a potential force for mobilizing collective political hopes? In 1885, William Morris (1834–96) – poet, artist, socialist – composed verses for songs to be used by the Socialist League of Britain. At the same time, he wrote *A Dream of John Ball* (*ADJB*), a short work of prose fiction that imagines socialist hopes in the Middle Ages as a way to explore possibilities for his own times. Music plays an important role. When Morris's time-traveling narrator awakes one day to find himself in rural England on the eve of the 1381 Peasants' Revolt, he is powerfully moved by the wild melodies of a ballad and the chanting of rebel priest John Ball's marching followers. *ADJB* suggestively describes the effects of music on hearts, minds and bodies; *Chants for Socialists* (*Chants*) puts these lessons to work in the present. How does the singing of an old ballad or the chanting of marchers arouse political feeling? How does Morris build on what he describes in *ADJB* to compose his own *Chants*?

Background

Morris's songs have deep roots in the history of labor protest. The events of 1381 and those of 1885 were firmly sutured in *ADJB* and *Chants*. In the 1850s, Morris had been a young poet, painter and designer in love with medieval art. He hated the shoddy ugliness of modern, mass-manufactured consumer products and was outraged at the miserable lives of those who made them. In 1860 he founded a small business (later Morris and Company) that enlisted artists to contribute designs for simple, well-made household furnishings to demonstrate that it was possible to make beautiful things for everyday use without mindless repetitive labor, long hours, subsistence wages, smoke-darkened skies, polluted waters, urban filth and overcrowding. In his own business Morris fought (not completely successfully) against financial pressures to design expensive goods for a luxury market. He plunged himself into the physical work of dyeing, weaving and printing to improve his employees' experience as well as the firm's products.

By the 1880s, however, Morris became convinced that the aesthetic and social reforms he desired would not be possible without a revolution. In 1885, he wrote *A Dream of John Ball* (*ADJB*), a medieval romance with contemporary political application, to dramatize difficult labor conditions and socialist hopes then and in his own day. He also composed verses for songs to be used by the

Socialist League of Britain. In February 1885, "March of the Workers" – to the tune of "John Brown's Body" – appeared in the second issue of the penny paper Morris edited for the Socialist League, *Commonweal*. *Chants for Socialists*, a penny pamphlet, was published by the *League* in summer 1885: six chants to be sung by large numbers at socialist gatherings. The *Chants*, like *ADJB*, were

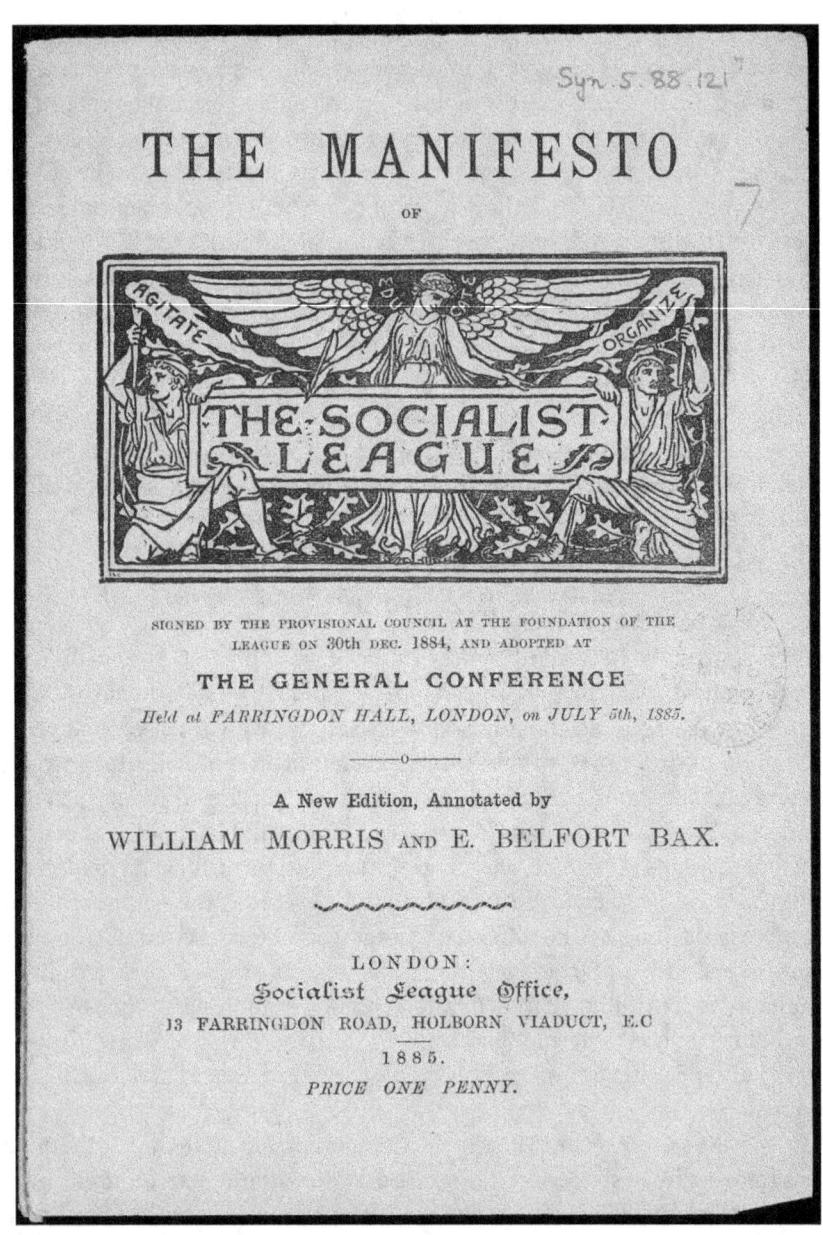

FIG 5.1: "Educate, Agitate, Organize." Walter Crane's design for *The Manifesto of the Socialist League* (London: Socialist League Office, 1885).

intended to awaken workers to the power of collective action, inspiring them with hope for a green England where labor would be pleasure and class distinctions unknown. The motto of the Socialist League was "Educate, Agitate, Organize." [**Fig. 5.1.**] *ADJB* and *Chants* were written to support this three-part program, combining history lessons and accounts of current conditions with the experience of collective political action. Morris provided the words of each chant; Carpenter paired his words with familiar tunes and included them in *Chants of Labour: A Songbook of the People, with Music* (1888, many times republished). [**Fig. 5.2.**] In this form Morris's *Chants* were sung worldwide until well into the twentieth century.

FIG. 5.2: Edward Carpenter, *Chants of Labour*, title-page design by Walter Crane for the first edition (London: George Allen & Unwin, 1888).

ADJB draws on both literary and historical sources to restage the 1381 uprising. Its time-traveling nineteenth-century narrator wakes from a dream in a small English village in Kent in 1381. He encounters its discontented inhabitants in a local tavern, is accepted by them as a wandering "tale-teller," and is moved by their ballads and songs. Many of these villagers, as Morris knew, would have been serfs, a medieval condition of servitude (not race-based) in which those without land were obligated to work for a landlord in return for his protection; the landlord in turn held his lands from the king and owed him military service in time of war. In 1381, the Black Death (bubonic plague) had recently wiped out a third of the population, and those who remained were overworked, hungry and suffering from a burdensome flat-rate poll tax imposed by the king. Not only peasants but many local artisans and village officials were ready to join peasant leader Wat Tyler (1341–81), who called for rising up in protest, burning court records, opening local jails and marching to London to present grievances to the king. Inspired by sermons and verses by the radical priest John Ball, whose arrival in the village is witnessed by *ADJB*'s time-traveling narrator, the villagers join the march to London, seeking a reduction in taxation and an end to the system of unfree labor. Their desires would not be met. Sixteen-year-old Richard II greeted the rebels outside London, at first acceding to their demands. His advisers then assembled military forces and bloodily put down the rebellion.

The idea of the Great Uprising endured in the English imagination, mentioned in medieval and early modern works including poems by Geoffrey Chaucer (*c*.1340s–1400) and John Gower (*c*.1340–1408) and a prose account by Jean Froissart (*c*.1333–*c*.1410). Memories of the Peasants' Revolt nourished a tradition of British egalitarian radicalism in politics, literature and song, invoked during the English civil wars and political upheavals of the seventeenth century and again during later protests against labor and living conditions during the Industrial Revolution. The English Diggers or "True Levellers" (1649–50), for example, were a seventeenth-century radical group who looked back to the Peasants' Revolt in their efforts to found an egalitarian agrarian community by cultivating what had formerly been common (public) land. Their spokesman, Gerard Winstanley (1609–76), composed one of the most famous early English political songs, "The Diggers' Song" or "Stand Up Now."[1] Two centuries later, nineteenth-century poets invoked this tradition to protest industrial labor conditions. Percy Bysshe Shelley (1792–1822), outraged at the massacre of peaceful protesters outside the industrial city of Manchester in 1819, wrote "The Mask of Anarchy" urging oppressed workers to "Rise like lions after slumber"; it was set

---

[1] Words and music: *The Digger Archives*, <https://www.diggers.org/english_diggers.htm> [Accessed October 24, 2024]. A version was recorded by the English group Chumbawamba on their 1988 album, *English Rebel Songs 1381–1914*, <https://genius.com/Chumbawamba-the-diggers-song-lyrics> [Accessed October 24, 2024].

to music in Carpenter's *Chants of Labour* (no. 54), placed just before Morris's concluding "All for the Cause" (no. 55). In the 1840s, when factory workers from the manufacturing cities in the north of England marched to London to present a Charter of their grievances to Parliament, they sang "The Chartist Anthem" by Ebenezer Elliot ("Poet of the People"), number 36 in Carpenter's *Chants*. An American collection, *Songs for Socialists, with Music*, was compiled by Charles H. Kerr and first published in 1901 in Chicago (scene of some of the bloodiest strike-breaking).[2]

Case Study

What makes an effective political song? In *ADJB*, Morris imagines different roles that sound might have played in the 1381 Peasants' Revolt, from rhyming to bellringing to singing and chanting in both sacred and secular settings. We can draw on his representations of these sounds in action to help us understand how he hoped *Chants* might work five centuries later. What lessons did he take from his medieval examples? What specific features of *Chants* furthered his political goals, and how did they do so?

Rhyming and Ringing

ADJB's narrator is possessed of a curious double consciousness: he is at once himself and another, surprised to find he knows what he is not aware of knowing. [**Extract 1.**] In answer to villager Will Green's enigmatic words, uttered with a wink and in a whisper, the narrator replies without thinking with the rhyming second line of what turns out to be a cryptic couplet. These lines served as a password by which the rebel followers of the historical John Ball, known for his radical sermons against serfdom, identified themselves.[3] The musicality of rhythm and rhyme makes the lines memorable. The "grinding" of the miller turning grain into flour (rhythmically emphasized by the repetition of "small, small, small") metaphorically points to the much-resented actions of

---

[2] *Socialist Songs, with Music*, ed. Charles H. Kerr (Chicago: Kerr, 1901); *Internet Archive*, <https://archive.org/details/socialistsongswookerrgoog/2up> [Accessed October 24, 2024]. In the twentieth century, British composer Alan Bush's stirring protest opera *Wat Tyler* (premiered 1953) is based on the events of The Great Uprising (synopsis and commentary at <http://alanbushtrust.org.uk> [Accessed October 24, 2024]).

[3] On Morris's historical sources and for the full text of Ball's verses, see Michael Holzman, "Encouragement and Warning of History: William Morris's *A Dream of John Ball*," *Socialism and the Literary Artistry of William Morris*, eds Florence S. Boos and Carole Silver (Columbia, Missouri: University of Missouri Press, 1990) 98–116. Available at the *William Morris Archive*, <https://morrisarchive.lib.uiowa.edu/items/show/980> [Accessed October 24, 2024]. See also Peter Wright, "*A Dream of John Ball*: Historical Introduction," *William Morris Archive*, <https://morrisarchive.lib.uiowa.edu/items/show/98> [Accessed October 24, 2024].

the king's tax collectors. The answering verse again has a hidden meaning: the King's Son of Heaven is Christ who has promised redemption after death, but it is also his representative, the King of England; the villagers are being urged to take their grievances to him now – to march on London.

The shout [**Extract 3**] that runs round the village and is echoed by the newcomers – "John Ball hath rung our bell" – comes from another example of Ball's gift for condensing argument into memorable, covertly meaningful rhymed verse: "John Ball greeteth you all / And doth to understand he hath rung your bell, / Now with might and right, will and skill, / God speed every dell [deal]."[4] "Ringing your bell" is a reminder of the central role played by church bells in rural settings before the widespread use of clocks and watches, where bells regulated the rhythms of daily life and in an emergency could be used to gather the people together at the village center.[5] (Small bells also punctuated the priest's actions during a church service.) In *ADJB*, someone has rung the church bell, sounding a signal of alarm and calling the villagers to assemble at the market cross where the rebel priest Ball will speak against serfdom and the poll tax.

The frontispiece to *ADJB* [**Fig. 5.3**] incorporates a third example of John Ball's facility with cryptic rhyme: "When Adam delved and Eve span, / Who was then the gentleman?" At the peasants' rendezvous on Blackheath Common outside London, according to Morris's historical sources, Ball preached to the Kentish rebels an open-air sermon in which he began with that rhyming question (spelling modernized):

> When Adam delved and Eve span, Who was then the gentleman? From the beginning all men by nature were created alike, and our bondage or servitude came in by the unjust oppression of naughty men. For if God would have had any bondmen from the beginning, he would have appointed who should be bond, and who free. And therefore I exhort you to consider that now the time is come, appointed to us by God, in which ye may (if ye will) cast off the yoke of bondage, and recover liberty.[6]

The distinctions between "gentleman" (a noble), "yeoman" (a free farmer who owned his own plot of land) and "bondsman" (an unfree laborer or serf who had no land and could not leave the land he tilled, owing his labor and its fruits to a noble landholder) has parallels, *ADJB* suggests, with social distinctions and rising income inequities in Victorian England, sharply separating educated

---

[4] Quoted in Lindsey German and John Rees, *A People's History of London* (London: Verso, 2012) 31.

[5] Alain Corbin, *Village Bells: Sound and Meaning in the Nineteenth-Century French Countryside* (New York: Columbia University Press, 1998).

[6] John Ball, Sermon at Blackheath (June 12, 1381), quoted in Edmund Howes, *The Annales, Or Generall Chronicle of England: Begun First by Maister Iohn Stow, and After Him Continued and Augmented with Matters Forreyne, and Domestique, Ancient and Moderne, Vnto the Ende of His Present Yeere 1631* (London: Meighen, 1631) 293.

persons of property who owned the means of production from those they employed.

Morris's "The Voice of Toil," like Ball's sermon, uses rhythm and rhyme to publicize the injustices of a form of servitude now imposed on nineteenth-century laborers, who often lived and worked (when they could find work) under conditions determined by their employers that were as dehumanizing

FIG. 5.3: "When Adam delved and Eve span, Who was then the gentleman?" Design by Edward Burne-Jones for the first book edition of William Morris's *A Dream of John Ball* (London: Reeves & Turner, 1888).

as that of their forebears just after the Black Death. Ball's rhyming question, "When Adam delved and Eve span, / Who was then the gentleman?", incorporated into Crane's design, affirms, in memorable rhyme, that such distinctions, then or now, are not naturally ordained. Educated and organized, Morris's *Chants* urged, those who labor can together free themselves from the tyrannies of the present system and bring about a more equitable future. The very nature of work, "The Voice of Toil" urges, needs to be changed to engage the minds and imaginations as well as the bodies of laborers and thus restore them to full humanity.

Singing

The narrator of *ADJB* – having identified himself as a "rhymester" and "tale-teller" [**Extract 2**] – is brought along by Will Green to the local tavern to sing for his supper. "Now hearken a tale," he begins, and proceeds to tell the story of one of the old Icelandic sagas, which Morris had recently translated: "As I told it the words seemed to quicken and grow, so that I knew not the sound of my own voice, and they ran almost into rhyme and measure as I told it." Is he speaking or singing? Morris is describing the work of the oral poet that in his dream he finds himself to be.

The narrator's contribution is immediately followed by that of a young man singing a ballad of Robin Hood, the nearly contemporary but already legendary figure of an outlaw who robs the rich and gives to the poor. Like the others in the tavern, the narrator is moved both by the content – a story of a fight against tyranny – and by the sound of the "sweet wild melody" followed by the "strong and rough" voices of listeners joining in the choruses. (Why does Morris describe their voices as "strong but rough"?) Morris is depicting a common feature of medieval village social life: communal song-making and storytelling in a primarily oral culture.

The songs frequently took the form of a ballad. Narrative verses, usually in short rhyming lines, were sung or sometimes recited by one person, regularly punctuated by a group of recurring lines (a refrain) in which others could join. From the late eighteenth century, renewed interest in such older, oral practices of storytelling and song-making was fired by collections of ballads and songs gleaned from old manuscripts (usually recorded without music).[7] The oldest of these collected ballads were thought to go back to the sixteenth century or earlier, but as collectors discovered, similar songs continued to be invented, sung and passed on from singer to singer, sometimes with the help of cheap songbooks (like Morris's penny pamphlet of *Chants*) or broadsheets (single

---

[7] On the ballad and song revival and its influence on Romantic and later poetry, see Steve Newman, *Ballad Collection, Lyric, and the Canon: The Call of the Popular from the Restoration to the New Criticism* (Philadelphia: University of Pennsylvania Press, 2007).

sheets of lyrics sold for less than a penny). Oral practices of making and passing on verses, with or without music, continued even after the coming of print. Such songs were not infrequently political.

Literary poets were intrigued: using local reporters, Walter Scott and Robert Burns in Scotland, Thomas Moore in Ireland and John Clare in England collected such songs, with Clare, Burns and Moore taking note of not only words but music, using musical notation – though this was an imperfect method before the age of the tape recorder, and often resulted in arrangements that over-regularized the music. Poets imitated the rhythmic and verbal simplicity of these songs and ballads, sometimes for ironical and critical purposes, in works like William Blake's *Songs of Innocence and Experience* (1784)[8] and William Wordsworth's and Samuel Taylor Coleridge's *Lyrical Ballads* (1798). Their song and ballad verses, like those collected from traditional and living ballad-singers, did not use the longer lines of eighteenth-century poet Alexander Pope's witty rhymed heroic couplets or William Shakespeare's and John Milton's stately blank verse, preferring shorter rhyming lines with a strong, repeating beat, often arranged in stanzas alternating four- and three-beat rhyming lines with a refrain.

Some of Morris's *Chants* follow this short-lined, rhyming ballad pattern. Others use longer lines in narrative sections (where he is seeking to "educate" his audiences), but these are usually formed by combining several two-, three- or four-beat lines, with the shorter line segments retaining their rhymes, as in "The Voice of Toil." [**Fig. 5.4.**] Like traditional and more recent ballads, they use simple language and structures of incremental repetition (on Sunday, on Monday, etc.), where content can be varied and improvised, shortening or lengthening a song as needed. The *Chants* proceed in familiar patterns tolerant of such omissions or additions. They also repeat words and phrases, creating a musical texture of repeating sounds within verses as well as through a recurring refrain. Like popular writers generally, Morris avoided ambiguous language (but not, as we have seen, hidden meanings that his audiences would recognize) and focused on a few simple ideas and feelings. The tunes to which his chants were sung (when they were not simply chanted) were, like the old ballads themselves, not necessarily harmonically complex, though they might contain at least one harmonic twist or surprise. Morris's *Chants*, like the old ballads when put to political purposes, were intended to forward several goals at once: to entertain, to teach and to encourage participation, thus engaging hearts as well as minds for what Morris called simply "the Cause" ("The Voice of Toil").

---

[8] For performances sung by Beat poet Allen Ginsberg, see *Internet Archive*, <https://archive.org/details/naropa_allen_ginsberg_performing> [Accessed October 24, 2024].

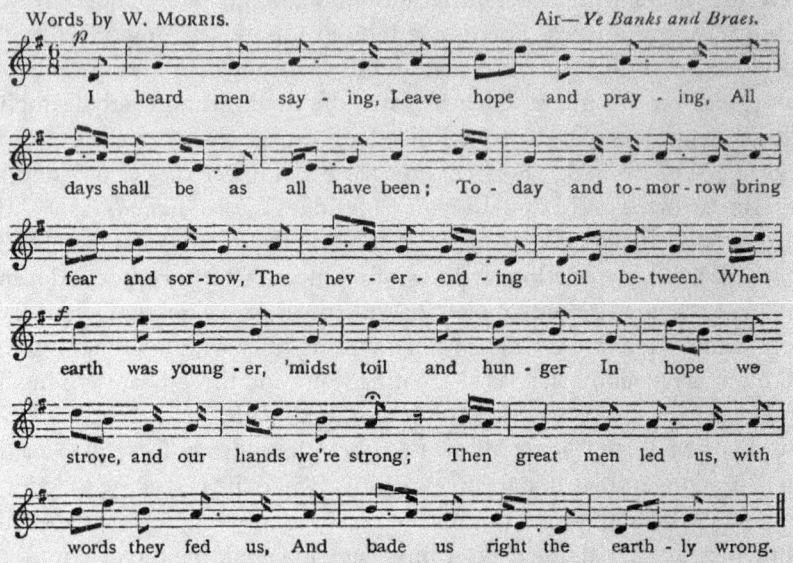

FIG. 5.4: William Morris, "The Voice of Toil," no. 27 in Carpenter, *Chants of Labour*, to the traditional tune "Ye Banks and Braes."

64   *CHANTS OF LABOUR*

2.

Forth they come from grief and torment; on they wend toward health
   and mirth;
All the wide world is their dwelling, every corner of the earth;
Buy them, sell them for thy service! Try the bargain what 'tis worth,
          For the days are marching on.

FIG. 5.5: William Morris, "The March of the Workers," no. 38 in Carpenter, *Chants of Labour*, to the tune of "John Brown's Body."

Chanting and Marching

As the men of the tavern in *ADJB* rush out to join other villagers alerted by the tolling of the church bell, the narrator hears singing – not a melody, exactly, but rather a kind of chant, words intoned monophonically, as they were in the monophonic plainsong used in medieval churches (Gregorian chant is one kind of plainsong). [**Extract 3.**] Church chanting of psalms, prayers and Bible readings, usually by priests or monks, was intended to engage listeners even when they could not understand the language (Latin). The sound of plainsong chanting would have been familiar in fourteenth-century English churches, as it was to Morris who was an enthusiastic participant in the plainsong revival of the 1850s (though he embraced its secular musical and literary possibilities more than its religious ones). But Morris imagined in *ADJB* that what the villagers heard from John Ball's marching followers had a strong regular beat, rhythmically different from medieval plainsong, which was not usually measured (metrical). Morris must have been aware of the difference. Why did he then describe what the villagers heard as a kind of chant?

Morris's own *Chants* also have a very strongly marked, regularly recurring beat, indeed more like a march or a work song in which bodies and minds are timed together to coordinate physical actions. ("Left, left, I had a good job and I left" as an old army marching song has it, with the emphatic "Left" timing the left–right strides of the marchers.) Morris realized that one of the best ways to get others to join the chanting was to use the rhythmic patterning of a song they already knew. For "The March of the Workers" [**Fig. 5.5**], one of his first written chants, he borrowed the rhythmic pattern from "John Brown's Body."[9] Morris later discovered that the friend who had copied out the song's rhythm had made a mistake and the verses do not perfectly fit the tune, but Carpenter used the rhythm and the tune anyway. "The March of the Workers" – like other Morris chants combined with familiar tunes by Carpenter – could then be used to assemble labor protesters and unite them in a shared, rhythmically coordinated activity. *Chants* (and Carpenter's *Chants of Labour*) call nineteenth-century laborers to what Ball, in *ADJB*, called a "fellowship" of action – communal action timed to music.

Morris's words anticipate this use. "The March of the Workers" describes the very action it urges, calling attention to the *sound* of massed voices chanting, the pressure of rising emotions and the cumulative force embodied in the marching singers themselves, even as the song sweeps them along with its rapid, emphatic beats toward release in repeating the triumphant lines of the

---

[9] This tune, named after the abolitionist leader of a slave rebellion and appropriated by Union troops as a marching song in the US Civil War, was refashioned with more uplifting words by abolitionist writer Julia Ward Howe as "The Battle Hymn of the Republic" and has since been re-appropriated by innumerable schoolchildren for their own less reverent purposes.

refrain: "Hark the rolling of the thunder! / Lo the sun! And lo thereunder / Riseth wrath and hope and wonder, / And the host comes marching on." [**Fig. 5.5.**] We know that Morris was particularly sensitive to both mental and bodily effects of strongly rhythmic activities of all kinds, from weaving to reciting verse (in fact, as poetry his verses were sometimes accused of too much rhythmic regularity). When Morris first heard one of his songs sung at a mass meeting with a huge audience joining in, he found the sound physically thrilling (vibrations felt throughout the body) as well as emotionally moving. As the refrain recognizes, however, Morris saw the dangers of moving an audience to wrath as well as the potential for moving them to constructive political action. His songs, like those he describes in *ADJB*, warn of this danger but also embrace the power of chanting, marching and, if necessary (when protest led them into situations where violence was used against them), fighting defensively "shoulder to shoulder." Hope is the final message carried by the rhythmic rhyming of John Ball, and hope is voiced again and again in Morris's chants and Carpenter's songs, hope for a future, as the last words of "The Voice of Toil" announce, of "joy at last for thee and me."

Further Reading

Elliot, Ebenezer. "The Chartist Anthem" (also known as "The People's Anthem"). 1847. Words with music in Edward Carpenter, ed. *Chants of Labour: A Song Book of the People, with Music* [1888]. London: George Allen & Unwin, 1922. No. 36.

Helsinger, Elizabeth. "Telling Time." *Poetry and the Thought of Song in Nineteenth-Century Britain*. Charlottesville: University of Virginia Press, 2015. 149–65.

Holzman, Michael. "The Encouragement and Warning of History: William Morris's *A Dream of John Ball*." *Socialism and the Literary Artistry of William Morris*. Eds Florence S. Boos and Carole Silver. Columbia, Missouri: University of Missouri Press, 1990. 98–116; *Morris Archive*, <https://morris-archive.lib.uiowa.edu/items/show/980> [Accessed October 24, 2024].

Janowitz, Anne F. *Lyric and Labour in the Romantic Tradition*. Cambridge: Cambridge University Press, 1998.

Kerr, Charles H., ed. *Socialist Songs with Music*. Chicago: Kerr, 1901. *Internet Archive*, <https://archive.org/details/socialistsongswookerrgoog/mode/2up> [Accessed October 24, 2024].

Morris, William. *Chants for Socialists*. London: Socialist League Office, 1885. Repub. with additional chants, London: Longmans, Green, 1894. *Marxist Writers*, <https://www.marxists.org/archive/morris/works/1885/chants/poems/index.htm> [Accessed October 24, 2024] and <https://www.marxists.org/archive/morris/works/1894/chants.htm> [Accessed October 24, 2024].

———. *News from Nowhere*. Hammersmith: The William Morris Society, 1890. *William Morris Archive*, <https://morrisarchive.lib.uiowa.edu/exhibits/show/romances/newsfromnowhere> [Accessed October 24, 2024].

Newman, Steve. *Ballad Collection, Lyric, and the Canon: The Call of the Popular from the Restoration to the New Criticism*. Philadelphia: University of Pennsylvania Press, 2007.

Shelley, Percy Bysshe. "Rise Like Lions" from "The Mask of Anarchy" (written 1819 or 1820). Words with music in Edward Carpenter, ed. *Chants of Labour: A Song Book of the People, with Music* [1888]. London: George Allen & Unwin, 1922. No. 54.

———. "Song: Men of England," (written c.1819, first published posthumously in 1839). Words with music in Edward Carpenter, ed. *Chants of Labour: A Song Book of the People, with Music* [1888]. London: George Allen & Unwin, 1922. No. 29.

Waters, Christopher. "Morris's 'Chants' and Socialist Culture." *Socialism and the Literary Artistry of William Morris*. Eds Florence S. Boos and Carole Silver. Columbia, Missouri: University of Missouri Press, 1990. 127–46.

Weiner, Stephanie Kuduk. *Republican Politics and English Poetry, 1789–1874*. Basingstoke: Palgrave Macmillan, 2005.

CHAPTER 6

Understanding Colonial Mission Hymns and Hybridity

Philip Burnett

Keywords

Anglican hymns, colonialism, contact zones, hybridity, missionaries, Jonas Ntsiko, religion, South Africa, translation, isiXhosa

Prelude

Extract 1 / Fig. 6.1

"*Ndiza kuwe wena Mvana*," with the tune ROCKINGHAM, *Amaculo*
(Gwatyu: Ishicilelwe e-"S. Peter's Mission," 1875), no. 96.

Original isiXhosa lyrics	Literal Translation of the lyrics (by the author)
Ndiza kuwe wena Mvana,	I come to you, O Lamb,
Ndingenazwi kupel' eli;	I do not have a word that is enough,
Wandopela, wandifela,	He bled for me, He died for me,
Wandibiza ndize kuwe.	He calls me to come with Him.

Extract 2 / Fig. 6.2

General Hymns.

Hymn 136.

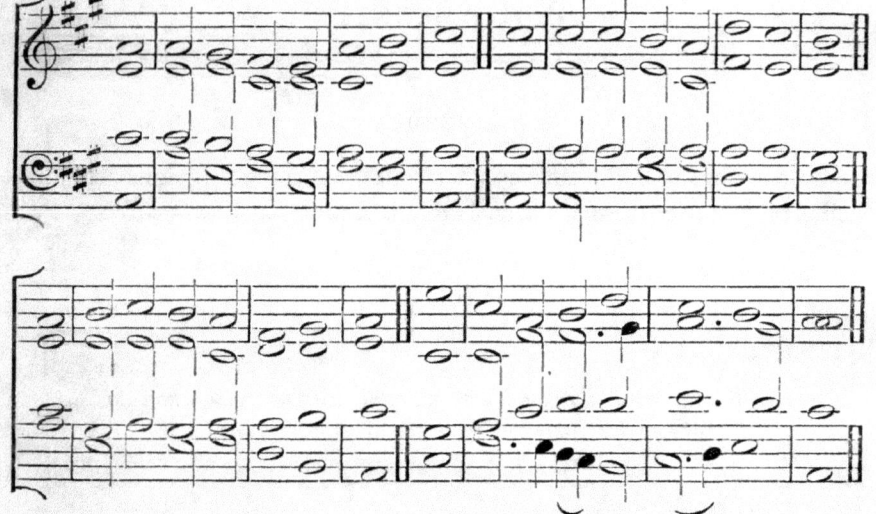

"O be joyful in the Lord, all ye lands."

ALL people that on earth do dwell,
Sing to the Lord with cheerful voice;
Him serve with fear, His praise forth tell,
Come ye before Him and rejoice.

The Lord, ye know, is God indeed:
Without our aid He did us make:
We are His flock, He doth us feed,
And for His sheep He doth us take.

O enter then His gates with praise,
Approach with joy His courts unto;
Praise, laud, and bless His Name always,
For it is seemly so to do.

For why? the Lord our God is good,
His mercy is for ever sure;
His Truth at all times firmly stood,
And shall from age to age endure.

To Father, Son, and Holy Ghost,
The God Whom heaven and earth adore,
From men and from the angel-host
Be praise and glory evermore.

A - men.

"All people that on earth do dwell," with the tune OLD HUNDREDTH,
*Hymns, Ancient and Modern, For use in the Services of the Church,
with Accompanying Tunes* (London: Novello, 1861), no. 136.

Extract 3 / Fig. 6.3a–6.3b

Ukuhanjiswa kwe-Lizwi
51.
Tune 196.

Ap' ilanga lihambayo,
Yen' uYesu 'yakupata,
Eli-Tshawe lezwe lonke,
Zid' inyanga zingabiko.

Bonk' abantu, zonk' ilwimi
Zoluvum' utando lwake :
Namazwana entsanana
Olibong' igama lake.

Yen' elaula litamsanqa
Kuzo zonke ezindawo ;
Nal' ikonxwa likululwa.
Nas' isintu sisindiswa.

Makuvukwe yinto yonke,
Idumis' INkosi yetu ;
Makuvunywe nazingelos'
Uz' umhlaba uti 'Amene'. Amene.

"*Ap'ilanga lihambayo*", *Amaculo* (Gwatyu, 1875), no. 51 [**Fig 6.3a**].

"*Ap'ilanga lihambayo*"/"Jesus shall reign," with the tune St Aidan, *Amaculo* (Gwatyu, 1875), no. 51 [**Fig 6.3b**].

Extract 4

W.R. Stevenson, "Missions, Foreign," *A Dictionary of Hymnology, Setting forth the Origin and History of Christian Hymns of all Ages and Nations*, ed. John Julian (London: Murray, 1892); original emphasis.

[T]he languages and dialects in which Christian hymns in connection with Foreign Missions have been written, or into which they have been translated, are nearly *one hundred and fifty*, and [...] in many of them, several hymn-books of considerable size have been prepared. The list include languages spoken by all the great divisions of the human race, Aryan, Semitic, Turanian; languages in all stages of formation, monosyllabic, as the Burman, agglutinative, as the Tamil and Turkish, inflexional, as the Sanskrit group of Northern India; languages of extreme antiquity, as the Chinese, and of comparatively recent formation, as the Urdú; languages harsh and guttural, as the speech of some African tribes, and soft and mellifluous, as that of the Polynesian islanders. All these by the energy and diligence of Christian missionaries have been mastered, their words have been arranged in tuneful measures, and in them God's praises are now sung, and His "wonderful works" declared. [...] The fact is, that the best hymns of Watts, Doddridge, Cowper, Newton, Wesley, Heber, Lyte, Keble, Bonar, Miss Steele, Miss Havergal, and other English authors, – the best German hymns, – the best hymns of American composition, – are now sung in China and South Africa, in Japan and Syria, among the peoples of India, and in the isles of the Pacific Ocean, – indeed, in almost every place where Protestant missionaries have uplifted the Gospel banner and gathered Christian Churches.

The Challenge

Hymns were sung in many parts of the world, in various languages, because they expressed the Christian missionary movement's desire to Christianize every corner of the globe. Wherever a hymn was taken, it had to be adapted for use in its new context. Christian mission activity often took place in regions where there was British colonial activity, and so hymns became part of a religious and cultural project to re-form Indigenous societies that came to fall under colonial rule. Indigenous people sang hymns, translated English lyrics, and composed tunes. Missionary hymns, therefore, became a meeting point in a complex encounter of different literary worlds. The lyrics and music of hymns can help us to see how religious, textual and musical hybridity unfolds when texts move from one place to another.

Using a case study of hymns translated into isiXhosa (a language spoken in the Eastern Cape region of South Africa) and sung on the Anglican missions of the mid- to late nineteenth century, the challenges are threefold. How do differing views of culture and religion interact in the translation process? What do hymns tell us about the hybrid forms of knowledge production that arose from the meeting of different cultures? What are the implications and challenges of moving hymn texts and how did they create a "contact zone" between colonized and colonizing peoples?

Background

This chapter invites you to think about hybridity by exploring the relationship between hymn-singing, colonialism and nineteenth-century mission work. In its simplest meaning, "hybrid" refers to the way in which two things meet, interact and then produce something new. In other words, it is about mixture, and what results from the process of mixing two, or more, things together. In post/colonial contexts, hybridity has a variety of implications and meanings and is used to refer to the outcomes of the meeting between colonizers and colonized peoples, particularly knowledge. This process begins with an initial encounter, but then often unfolds over a long period of time.

In the field of postcolonial studies, hybridity refers to "the creation of new transcultural forms within the contact zone produced by colonization."[1] Studies of hybridity have developed ways to examine how colonial power fractured identities as the cultures of colonized and colonizer met and interacted with each other.[2] There is no one definition or application of hybridity, and the products vary as they are shaped by the circumstances of a particular situation or location. For instance, Samuel A. Floyd has explored the superimposing of European forms on African religious practices that resulted in genres such as Spirituals.[3] Hybridity can refer to the layering and interaction of influences – musical, cultural, religious – out of which emerges something that is recognizable, yet different and new. The case study that follows examines one instance of how this unfolded on the missions founded in 1854 by Anglican missionaries in the present-day Eastern Cape region of South Africa.[4]

My first experience of translated missionary hymns came in 2008 when I attended a church service in a former mission station in the Eastern Cape. I recognized many of the hymns and understood some of the lyrics as I had

---

[1] For further discussion of this definition, see Bill Ashcroft, Gareth Griffiths and Helen Tiffin, *Post-Colonial Studies: The Key Concepts* (London: Routledge, 2013) 135–9.
[2] Two of the most notable scholars of theories of hybridity are Homi K. Bhabha and Gayatri Spivak.
[3] Samuel A. Floyd, *The Power of Black Music: Interpreting its History from Africa to the United States* (Oxford: Oxford University Press, 1995) 39–44.
[4] There have been several studies of missionary hymns in (former) colonial settings. See contributions in *The Canterbury Dictionary of Hymnology*, eds J.R. Watson and Emma Hornby (Norwich: Canterbury Press, 2018) <https://hymnology.hymnsam.co.uk/> [Accessed October 24, 2024].

learned isiXhosa, but while the hymns were familiar, they were also unfamiliar.[5] Xhosa musical and literary practice had become fused with the British Victorian hymns introduced by Anglican missionaries during the nineteenth century. Since then, local, isiXhosa-speaking people had been singing hymns, translating them and writing new ones so that an effectively new repertoire had emerged.

For centuries the hymn has been an important form of religious expression, but the long nineteenth century saw an extraordinary outpouring across Europe, not least in Britain.[6] One estimate suggests that between 1837 and 1901 approximately 400,000 English hymns were written, and 1,200 separate hymn-book titles published.[7] This was also a period of British imperial and colonial activity, which itself was often preceded, accompanied or followed by missionary activity. The two were related phenomena, because the hymn, like many other British cultural and religious practices, was taken outside Britain and introduced into other parts of the world. The first cultural exposure that Western and non-Western societies had with each other was often through music and it was usually a hymn that facilitated this encounter.[8] It is hardly surprising, then, that in journals (of all denominations), reports abound of hymns that had been translated into Indigenous languages. Hymn-singing came to be the sonic representation of the presence of missionaries: when their congregations could sing hymns, either by reading or from memory, missionaries used this as a sign to show that their work was proceeding. Stories from the mission field even became part of the heritage of particular hymns: in his 1859 history of a famous hymn tune, the Anglican hymn-writer William Henry Havergal (1793–1870) recounted, via the experience of missionary Samuel Marsden, how the missions in Australia began with the singing of "All people that on earth do dwell" to the tune OLD HUNDREDTH. [**Extract 2.**][9]

One of the key reasons why hymns were of use to missionaries is because they were easily portable. To be performed they did not necessarily require instrumental accompaniment. Their musical features were simple, with music

---

[5] I use "isiXhosa" to refer to the language, and "Xhosa" to refer to the people, cultures and customs.
[6] The classic study is J.R. Watson, *The English Hymn: A Critical and Historical Study* (Oxford: Oxford University Press, 1997).
[7] Ian Bradley, *Abide with Me: The World of Victorian Hymns* (London: SCM Press, 1997) 4; and Jeffrey Richards, *Imperialism and Music* (Manchester: Manchester University Press, 2001) 368.
[8] Bruno Nettl, *The Western Impact on World Music: Change, Adaptation, and Survival* (New York: Schirmer, 1985) 7.
[9] W.H. Havergal, *A History of the Old Hundredth Psalm Tune, With Specimens* (London: Sampson and Low, 1857) 48. It is a British convention to give names to hymn tunes in order to identify them.

repeated to usually strophic lyrics.¹⁰ The melodies tended to have a range of no more than an octave and moved mostly by step while also keeping to simple harmony. As singing was a cultural practice common to both missionary and Indigenous cultures, hymns often had a mutual appeal which provided a meeting point. **Extract 4** above also shows us that missionaries devoted tremendous amounts of time to translating, printing and teaching hymns. Protestant Christianity, certainly as it has been practiced in Western Europe for centuries, is text-based and requires literacy. For missionaries it was imperative that their texts were available in translation. The texts of Christianity (the Bible, hymns, prayers) were seen as providing the basis for civilization, and so being able to read these texts was the route towards grace. In **Extract 4**, the writer assumes that translation, and in particular the number of translated texts produced, means that "Gospel faith" had been established in the countries and regions he lists. To understand hybridity requires asking whether this was really the case, and whether the message of the missionaries was transmitted as intended. **Extract 3b** also shows us that the impression was created that hymns were being successfully transferred into their new contexts. The printed hymn in **Extract 3b** looks like a faithful reproduction of British hymn books.

However, colonial presence, whatever form it took, both disturbed and disrupted Indigenous culture and thought. At the same time, the response of Indigenous people to colonial presence often questioned and disrupted the ways of the colonizer and gave rise to local practices and ways of being. A key feature of colonial encounters was the struggle for authority over signs and symbols, and an indication of these struggles is to be found in the altered shape and forms that texts – literary, musical, official, to name a few – took on. This is because it was through texts that power was not only conveyed, but also undermined, resisted and subverted. As a result there emerged altered or new states of being or self, both of individuals and of types of expressions like hymns. Hybridity, in many ways, challenges the claims made to the universality of form and meaning found in texts.

Case Study

This section discusses two missionary hymn texts [**Extracts 1 and 3**] by Jonas Ntsiko (1850–1918), a Xhosa convert to Christianity. The exact date of the composition of these hymns is not known, but the texts first appeared in printed form in the 1873 and 1875 editions of the Anglican-Xhosa mission hymnal known as *Amaculo*.¹¹ These two texts suggest both the ways in which hymns were adapted for the mission field and the kinds of changes that hymns

---

[10] "Strophic" means that every verse of lyrics is sung to the same music.
[11] The title *Amaculo* translates literally as "songs," and was the isiXhosa word chosen by Christian missionaries of all denominations to denote hymns.

underwent as they took on life outside Britain and Europe. They also serve as examples of the ways in which hybridity in missionary texts came about through the agency of local Indigenous converts. Ntsiko's exact place and date of birth are unknown, although he is thought to have converted to Christianity in his teenage years, sometime in the 1860s. In the 1870s he went to England to study at St Augustine's Missionary College in Canterbury, where he would have gained first-hand experience of metropole culture, religious and otherwise. After completing his training, he returned to the Eastern Cape, where he worked as a catechist before being ordained as a deacon in 1873. He was one of the first Xhosas to be admitted to Anglican Holy Orders. Later in life, he became disillusioned with Christianity and worked as a courtroom interpreter.

Ntsiko's own biography helps to shed light on how hybridity emerges. His response to Christianity, like so many converts around the world, came from his background and his linguistic skills, and it would seem natural that he would craft his understanding of Christianity through the frameworks of his own background. We could call this "overlaying," and it is one of the beginnings of hybridity, because it is how different understandings become grafted onto each other to produce new results and formulations.

An Original (to existing music): "*Ndiza kuwe*" [Extract 1]

In "*Ndiza kuwe*" [Extract 1], Ntsiko's lyrics offer a meditation on the nature of a sinner's life and the fulfilment that can be found in accepting the teachings of Christ. The hymn's lyrics comprise four quatrains (four verses each of four lines). Save for the language, "*Ndiza kuwe*" resembles a hymn such as one might find in a Victorian hymnal of the time. But what differentiates this example is the colonial-historical moment when this hymn was created.

To begin with, the hymn is addressed to the Lamb of God, a title for Jesus used in St John's Gospel. In Christian teachings, the Lamb of God refers to the sacrifice Christ made by dying on the cross in order for humankind to have redemption. It was not an unusual choice for a hymn's subject matter, and Ntsiko's opening verse closely resembles the first verse of "Just as I am, without one plea," a popular Victorian hymn:

> Just as I am, without one plea,
> But that thy blood was shed for me,
> And that thou bidd'st me come to thee,
> O Lamb of God, I come.[12]

Each verse begins by addressing "Mvana," the Lamb. Beyond reference to Christ, the Lamb as the symbol of sacrificial offering was an established trope

---

[12] The full text of the hymn is available online at "Just as I am, without one plea," Hymnary.org. <https://hymnary.org/text/just_as_i_am_without_one_plea> [Accessed October 24, 2024].

in Christian scripture. For example, Genesis 22 tells the story of how God instructed Abraham to offer his son Isaac as a sacrifice, and in Exodus 12, God commanded the enslaved Israelites to paint the blood of the lamb slaughtered and eaten for the Passover meal over their door lintels in order to protect themselves from the Angel of Death as it passed over Egypt. In this hymn the singer would in most cases have been a convert, and singing the hymn became a way of offering their life to God as a sacrifice.

How well would the "average" convert have understood the associations between "the Lamb," sacrifice and Jesus Christ? Ntsiko's translations give us some insight because he inhabited the spaces of two languages. This duality helps create the text's hybridity: that of the Indigenous religious self which, when met with newly introduced Christian understandings, was challenged and changed.

The notion and practice of sacrifice was present in pre-Christian Xhosa religion. Xhosa religion was monotheistic, but communication to the Xhosa God, known as *u-Dali* (the Creator) was seen to take place through the Ancestors whose agency was believed to exert influence over the world. Thus, as sacrifices were made to the Ancestors, the idea of intercession (which is central to Christian theologies of the Saints) was a familiar concept for those who had previously practiced Xhosa religion even if practice and comprehension differed between missionaries and converts.

The same could be said of propitiatory sacrifice to deities. The association of the sacrifice of animals to assuage a deity would not have been unfamiliar to those raised in pre-Christian Xhosa religious practices.[13] Animal sacrifices, or *i-Dini*, to propitiate the Ancestors, who were believed to exert influence over phenomena in the world, were offered as an attempt to bring about relief from hardships such as sickness or drought.[14] In Anglican Christianity, sacrifice was symbolic; in Xhosa culture it was real. Missionaries often expressed shock when they encountered such Indigenous rituals, a response too complicated to unpack fully here. However, the disconnect illustrates a key point about hybridity, which is to understand the disruptive affect that Indigenous practices had on the colonizers themselves and, importantly, the results of the encounter. It might have been fine for sacrifice to be alluded to in a Victorian

[13] On Xhosa religion and deities, see Janet Hodgson, *The God of the Xhosa* (Cape Town: Oxford University Press, 1982) 101–3.

[14] For contemporary descriptions and accounts of such ceremonies and rituals, see Albert Kropf, *A Kaffir-English Dictionary* ([Lovedale]: Lovedale Mission Press, 1899) 76–7; and John Henderson Soga, *The Ama-Xosa: Life and Customs* (Lovedale: Lovedale Press, 1932) 146–8. Soga's work is attributed as the first systematic attempt at a written history and ethnography of the Xhosa people. The word *Kaffir* was used in the nineteenth century to refer to isiXhosa. In South Africa today it is considered a derogatory and insulting term and is used here only because it was in the original title of the work cited.

hymn in English, but missionaries could not fully comprehend the frameworks through which Indigenous people thought about sacrifice, because they were so removed from the experience of *actual* sacrifice.

In addition to content and imagery, the meter of the lyrics and its relationship to the music is also an indication of a change and overlaying of practices. The lyrics are written in trochaic tetrameter. This means that each line consists of four trochees – a metrical unit comprising a long or stressed syllable followed by a short or unstressed syllable. For example,

/	u	/	u	/	u	/	u
Ndi-	za	ku-	we,	We-	na	Mva-	na

where / is a stressed syllable, u is an unstressed syllable, and each pair of / and u makes up a metrical unit or foot.

In the hymn book in which this hymn was printed, only the lyrics were provided (see the next extract for an example). Numbers printed next to the text suggested a suitable tune from *Hymns Ancient and Modern*, which was the most widely used Anglican hymn book in Britain at the time. It is likely that most mission converts learned hymn tunes by ear. It was also common for missionaries to print texts alone because music printed in staff notation required specialized print types. We do not know, however, which tune Ntsiko's text would have been sung to in the early years of its existence. Only "L.M." ["Long Meter"] was printed next to the text.[15]

"Long Meter" is the most common meter used for English-language hymns. Each line has four units of iambs (iambs are weak–strong pairs), for a total of eight syllables. Tunes in "Long Meter" will fit most easily to an 8.8.8.8. text by starting on an anacrusis, or upbeat, to follow the unstressed/stressed pattern of the syllable pairs. But as we saw above, Ntsiko's text is trochaic, probably chosen because isiXhosa is a penult language: the second-to-last syllable of each word is usually stressed. isiXhosa is also a tonal language, meaning that pitch and stress are used to determine the lexical and grammatical meaning of a word. Iambs are closer to English speech rhythms, whereas trochees are closer to those of isiXhosa. Here, we can see how two different approaches to meter had to be brought together, and that they reflected the reality of the place where the hymn was created. The reflection of place in forms of expression is a key characteristic of hybridity and one that we shall return to later.

It is not known whether Ntsiko wrote this text with a particular tune in mind, but we do know that tunes were recommended. The earliest of these

---

[15] "Meter" here is a misnomer because it refers to the number of syllables rather than the number of units (of stress and unstress). Nevertheless, hymn tunes are classified according to "meter" in order to help with finding alternative tunes, and this is why hymn books, such as *Hymns Ancient and Modern*, contain a metrical index.

was ROCKINGHAM, which was also used for other hymns in the 1875 book, suggesting that it must have been well known. ROCKINGHAM was, however, a problematic tune in this instance because it begins with an upbeat that conflicts with the trochees of the text, as **Extract 1** shows.

The tune itself had other meanings and associations as it was commonly sung to the English text, "When I survey the wondrous cross," which deals with Christ's crucifixion. Ntsiko's text likewise deals with sacrifice, suggesting that he might have chosen this tune for his lyrics, and that using ROCKINGHAM might have amplified this message. Perhaps he was asking a lot of his fellow converts: while music could amplify the message of the lyrics, it could do so only within a community that shared the tune's symbolic meanings. When, however, the music was transferred into the mission field, where many people would not have been aware of these shared meanings, a gap was opened for new meanings to be inserted.

A Translation: Ap'ilanga lihambayo/"Jesus shall reign" [Extract 3]

The first case study examined an original hymn text written by Ntsiko in which he used poetic license to reframe Christian concepts. But how did he deal with transferring into isiXhosa the imagery expressed in pre-existing English texts? Illustrated in **Fig. 6.3a** is a Ntsiko translation of English lyrics. The original English text of "Jesus shall reign" by Isaac Watts (1674–1748), a Nonconformist minister, first appeared in 1719 in a collection entitled *The Psalms of David*. It was a paraphrase of Psalm 72, a text attributed to King Solomon.[16] In the first line of the hymn, Watts made direct reference to verse 17 of the psalm: "his Name shall remain under the sun among the posterities: which shall be blessed through him; and all the heathen shall praise him."

The hymn's text and tune are rich in missionary allusions which suggest the types of message that missionaries wished to impart. Watts's refashioning of the psalm from a Jewish into a Christian text highlighted the relationship between the texts of the Old Testament which found fulfilment in the New Testament, a progression marked by the salvation brought by Jesus Christ, and the ultimate goal of missionary conversion.[17] In *Hymns Ancient and Modern*, the text appeared with a subtitle taken from the Book of Revelation 11.15: "The kingdoms of this world are become the kingdoms of our LORD and of His

---

[16] For a full biographical sketch of Watts see Alan Gaunt, "Isaac Watts," *The Canterbury Dictionary of Hymnology*, <https://hymnology.hymnsam.co.uk/i/isaac-watts?q=Isaac%20Watts> [Accessed October 24, 2024]. See also J.R. Watson, *An Annotated Anthology of Hymns* (Oxford: Oxford University Press, 2002) 121–46.

[17] Alan Gaunt, "Jesus shall reign where'er the sun," *The Canterbury Dictionary of Hymnology*, <https://hymnology.hymnsam.co.uk/j/jesus-shall-reign-where%E2%80%99er-the-sun> [Accessed October 24, 2024].

CHRIST; and He shall reign for ever and ever." The subject matter of Watts's text and the *Hymns Ancient and Modern* subtitle both indicate the text's application in the mission field: it evoked the proclamation of the seventh angel related in Revelation that a time shall come when all kingdoms will be under Christ's rule. There was a strong directive, then, in this hymn, which informed the imperialism of the missionary project.

The hymn's tune reinforced the various webs of cultural and religious meaning surrounding the missionary message of the lyrics. The tune British Anglicans used to sing this hymn was St Aidan, composed by W.H. Monk (1823–89). [**Fig. 6.3b.**] The tune was named after Aidan of Lindisfarne, the seventh-century Irish missionary attributed with restoring Christianity to Northumbria. To those conversant with these meanings, this was an apposite name for a tune written for a text in which mission and evangelism were key themes. When encountered by anyone else, fresh interpretations and significance could be layered on top of any pre-existing meanings, or could displace them.

How, then, was this hymn, with all its associated cultural and religious meaning, refashioned for the mission field? As we have seen, innovation was possible on a poetic level, and the figurative language used by Ntsiko in his translations and original texts indicates that he made attempts to develop new local idioms to which Xhosa converts could relate. For example, in verse 1 of the hymn he uses the word "Tshawe" for Jesus Christ. In Xhosa culture *Tshawe* was a term used to refer to someone of high birth, such as a prince or an aristocrat.[18] Another noticeable feature of Ntsiko's translation of this verse is that he does not mention the kingdom referred to in the English version. This keeps the focus on the person of Jesus Christ and provides a new application of the pre-Christian concept of "*Tshawe*," reforging it as a Christian term.

Ntsiko's version remained faithful to many of the hymn's technical features in its English form. He retained the 8.8.8.8 "Long Meter," and this meant that the tune ST AIDAN could also be retained:

/	u	/	u	/	u	/	u
Ap'	i-	la-	nga	li-	Ham-	ba-	yo

However, the detailed interaction between the shape of the isiXhosa lyrics (reliant on tonal inflection for meaning) and the tune is important to consider. Like many Western European hymn tunes, ST AIDAN has a tendency to fall at the ends of phrases, while spoken isiXhosa tends to rise. Hence the meters of isiXhosa and English are the opposite of each other. This has implications for translated hymn texts, for even a literal translation can be altered if the tune to which it is sung does not follow the same tonal patterns. For instance, spoken "zingabiko" would rise in tone towards the end, but the tune at that point falls.

---

[18] See Kropf, *Dictionary*, 402.

The same happens at "lihambayo" and "lonke." It may not alter the meaning in every case, but rather it could be described as akin to producing a hybrid sound, like a person speaking a foreign language and mispronouncing a particular vowel sound or emphasizing different syllables.

There are also discrepancies between the penult stresses of isiXhosa and the strong and weak beats of the tune, which do not, for the most part, coincide. The exception is at the beginning of each line where the penult syllable coincides with a strong beat ("Ap-," "Yen" and "Zid" are written so that their final syllable elides into the next word, a feature of spoken isiXhosa). But there are other moments when this does not happen, for example, "lan" of "langa" where a strong syllable in the text occurs on a weak beat.

Conclusion

To illustrate the double-bind resulting from the hybridity of hymns, it might be helpful to imagine an encounter with them through the eyes and ears of an Indigenous convert, on the one hand, and a first-language English-speaker on the other. For the convert, here was their language in an unfamiliar poetic form, using familiar imagery but applied to a different referent, or deity. The native English-speaker might have recognized the tune, and therefore identified the hymn, but the language would have been unfamiliar, leading to a blurred encounter with the hymn. For both groups this would have been a destabilizing experience – an important outcome of hybridity's process, which occurs when the self is split by the confrontation with something at once familiar, yet also unfamiliar.

As we have seen, concepts like "sacrifice" were shared between Indigenous and missionary cultures. Despite the common presence of a signifier, in each culture it had specific meanings and associations, meaning that signifiers could become open to differing interpretations and understandings. Similarly, tune was a musical phenomenon common to both cultures, yet there were differences in the shape, use and function of melody. Both words and tune became hybrid in the sense that they were viewed differently, while also being fused as the Indigenous and missionary worlds met. And this had a wide range of consequences for individuals, texts and cultural practices, all of which became present in and reflective of their colonial reality. Through the process of hybridity came a sense of separation and removal from origins and essence that characterized colonial space.

Further Reading

Agawu, Kofi. "Tonality as a Colonizing Force in Africa." *Audible Empire: Music, Global Politics, Critique*. Eds Ronald Radano and Tejumola Olaniyan. Durham, North Carolina: Duke University Press, 2016. 334–55.

Ashcroft, Bill, Gareth Griffiths and Helen Tiffin. *The Empire Writes Back: Theory and Practice in Post-Colonial Literatures*. London: Routledge, 2002.

Bhabha, Homi K. "Of Mimicry and Man: The Ambivalence of Colonial Discourse." *Tensions of Empire: Colonial Cultures in a Bourgeois World*. Eds Frederick Cooper and Ann Laura Stoler. Berkeley: University of California Press, 1997. 152–62.

Floyd, Samuel. *The Power of Black Music: Interpreting its History from Africa to the United States*. New York: Oxford University Press, 1995.

Hadi Waseluhlangeni [*pseud*. Jonas Ntsiko]. *Collected Writings (1873–1916)*. Eds Jeff Opland and Pamela Maseko, with a Foreword by Marguerite Poland. Pietermaritzburg: University of KwaZulu-Natal Press, 2023.

Irving, David R.M. *Colonial Counterpoint: Music in Early Modern Manila*. Oxford: Oxford University Press, 2010.

Lim, Swee Hong. "Postcolonial Congregational Song." *Hymns and Hymnody: Historical and Theological Introductions*. Eds Mark A. Lamport, Benjamin K. Forrest and Vernon M. Wheley. Vol. 3. Eugene, Oregon: Cascade Books, 2019. 238–54.

Olwage, Grant. "John Knox Bokwe, Colonial Composer: Tales about Race and Music." *Journal of the Royal Musical Association* 131:1 (2006): 1–37.

Webb, Michael. "Heart, Spirit and Understanding: Protestant Hymnody as an Agent of Transformation in Melanesia, 1840s–1940s." *The Journal of Pacific History* 50:3 (2015): 275–303.

Weliver, Phyllis. "Tom-Toms, Dream-Fugues and Poppy-Juice: East Meets West in Nineteenth-Century Fiction." *Music and Orientalism in the British Empire, 1780s–1940s: Portrayal of the East*. Eds Bennett Zon and Martin Clayton. Aldershot: Ashgate, 2007. 257–74.

Whitla, Becca. *Liberation, (De)Coloniality, and Liturgical Practices: Flipping the Song Bird*. Basingstoke: Palgrave Macmillan, 2020.

CHAPTER 7

Representing Non-Western Music: Robert Louis Stevenson in Kiribati

Emma Sutton

Recommended Text

Robert Louis Stevenson, *In the South Seas*, ed. Neil Rennie (London: Penguin, 1998). Numbers in brackets refer to this edition.

Keywords

Anthropology, colonialism, ethnomusicology, Indigenous music, Kiribati, non-fiction, non-Western music, Oceania, Pacific music, Scotland, travel writing, Victorian

Prelude

Extract

Robert Louis Stevenson, *In the South Seas*, 189–90.

Chapter VI
The Five Days' Festival

Thursday, July 25 [1889]. – The street was this day much enlivened by the presence of the men from Little Makin; they average taller than Butaritarians, and, being on a holiday, went wreathed with yellow leaves and gorgeous in vivid colours. They are said to be more savage, and to be proud of the distinction. Indeed, it seemed to us they swaggered in the town, like plaided Highlanders upon the streets of Inverness, conscious of barbaric virtues.

In the afternoon the summer parlour was observed to be packed with people; others standing outside and stooping to peer under the eaves, like children at home about a circus. It was the Makin company, rehearsing for the day of competition. Karaiti [the Makin High Chief] sat in the front row close to the singers, where we were summoned (I suppose in honour of Queen Victoria) to join him. A strong breathless heat reigned under the iron roof, and the air was heavy with the scent of wreaths. The singers, with fine mats about their loins, cocoa-nut feathers set in rings upon their fingers, and their heads crowned with yellow leaves, sat on the floor by companies. A varying number of soloists stood up for different songs; and these bore the chief part in the music. But the full force of the companies, even when not singing, contributed continuously to the effect, and marked the ictus of the measure, mimicking, grimacing, casting up their heads and eyes, fluttering the feathers on their fingers, clapping hands, or beating (loud as a kettle-drum) on the left breast; the time was exquisite, the music barbarous, but full of conscious art. I noted some devices constantly employed. A sudden change would be introduced (I think of key) with no break of the measure, but emphasised by a sudden dramatic heightening of the voice and a swinging, general gesticulation. The voices of the soloists would begin far apart in a rude discord, and gradually draw together to a unison; which, when they had reached, they were joined and drowned by the full chorus. The ordinary, hurried, barking, unmelodious movement of the voices would at times be broken and glorified by a psalm-like strain of melody, often well constructed, or seeming so by contrast. There was much variety of measure, and towards the end of each piece, when the fun became fast and furious, a recourse to this figure –

It is difficult to conceive what fire and devilry they get into these hammering finales; all go together, voices, hands, eyes, leaves, and fluttering finger-rings; the chorus swings to the eye, the song throbs on the ear; the faces are convulsed with enthusiasm and effort.

Presently the troop stood up in a body, the drums forming a half-circle for the soloists, who were sometimes five or even more in number. The songs that followed were highly dramatic; though I had none to give me any explanation, I would at times make out some shadowy but decisive outline of a plot; and I was continually reminded of certain quarrelsome concerted scenes in grand operas at home; just so the single voices issue from and fall again into the general volume; just so do the performers separate and crowd together, brandish the raised hand, and roll the eye to heaven – or the gallery. Already this is beyond the Thespian model; the art of this people is already past the embryo; song, dance, drums, quartette and solo – it is the drama full developed although still in miniature. Of all so-called dancing in the South Seas, that which I saw in Butaritari stands easily the first. The *hula*, as it may be viewed by the speedy globe-trotter in Honolulu, is surely the most dull of man's inventions, and the spectator yawns under its length as at a college lecture or a parliamentary debate. But the Gilbert Island dance leads on the mind; it thrills, rouses, subjugates; it has the essence of all art, an unexplored imminent significance. Where so many are engaged, and where all must make (at a given moment) the same swift, elaborate, and often arbitrary movement, the toil of rehearsal is of course extreme. But they begin as children. A child and a man may often be seen together in a *maniap'* [*maneaba*, an open-sided meeting house]: the man sings and gesticulates, the child stands before him with streaming tears and tremulously copies him in act and sound; it is the Gilbert Island artist learning (as all artists must) his art in sorrow.

The Challenge

This case study examines a passage of descriptive prose about Kiribati (Gilbertese) music and dance by Scottish writer Robert Louis Stevenson from his posthumously published travel book/ethnographic study *In the South Seas* (1896). Stevenson – a self-taught amateur composer – lived and traveled widely in Oceania between 1888 and 1894. During that time, he studied Pacific cultures and frequently made music (informally and at ceremonial occasions) with Pacific Islanders; he also wrote a handful of musical compositions influenced by Indigenous Pacific musical idioms.

The background places Stevenson's writing within its immediate geopolitical context: the widespread annexation of Pacific Islands by Euro-American powers in the 1880s and 1890s and, specifically, the role of music in assertions of Indigenous Pacific and Western cultural authority by Pacific Islanders and colonial powers. The case study uses Stevenson's prose to explore formal and political questions raised by European writers' attempts to represent or evoke non-Western music in language. The challenges are thus: How does the passage explore the difficulties of representing, in language, music from an unfamiliar culture? How does the passage negotiate Eurocentric cultural hierarchies, such as those between "traditional" and acculturated music? And how does Kiribati music put Western definitions of "music" under pressure?

Background

In the South Seas is based on the journals Stevenson (1850–94) kept during three cruises with family members in Oceania between 1888 and 1890, and on letters published in American and British newspapers.[1] Stevenson variously described this uncompleted work, which would later be posthumously selected and edited by his friend Sidney Colvin, as "a very singular book of travels" but one which aspired to anthropological and historical authority – it would be,

---

[1] Stevenson's travels were primarily in Polynesia and Micronesia though he briefly visited Melanesia; I use Stevenson's terms to denote geographical regions, but acknowledge – as Epeli Hau'ofa argued in his seminal essay – that the term Oceania is now preferred. "Our Sea of Islands," *A New Oceania: Rediscovering Our Sea of Islands*, eds Vijay Naidu, Eric Waddell and Epeli Hau'ofa (Suva: University of the South Pacific, 1993) 8 and 16, note.

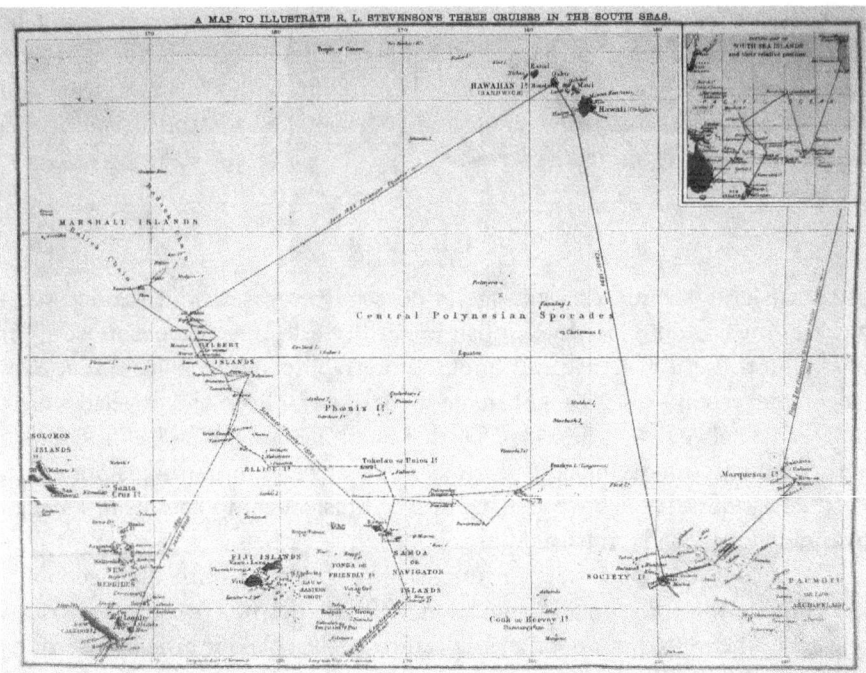

Fig. 7.1: "A Map to Illustrate R.L. Stevenson's Three Cruises in the South Seas." Prefatory illustration to Robert Louis Stevenson, *In the South Seas: Being an Account of Experiences and Observations in the Marquesas, Paumotus and Gilbert Islands in the Course of Two Cruises on the Yacht "Casco" (1888) and the Schooner "Equator" (1889)* (New York: Charles Scribner's Sons, 1896).

he hoped, "*the* big book" on the region.[2] The book was poorly received, in part due to tensions between these genres, and between Stevenson's desire to write an anthropological study and readers' desire for adventure novels like *Treasure Island* that had made his reputation.[3]

In the South Seas – like his fiction, essays and poetry of this period – includes several long accounts of musical performances and numerous passing references to European and Indigenous Pacific music. Stevenson conducted extensive research for the book (reading history, anthropology and fiction about the region and visiting over forty islands), studied Pacific languages (gaining fluency in several) and collected Tahitian "songs and legends" on which

---

[2] Bradford A. Booth and Ernest Mehew, eds, *The Letters of Robert Louis Stevenson*, 8 vols (New Haven: Yale University Press, 1994–5) 6: 312 and 401; original emphasis. Hereafter, *Letters*.

[3] See Vanessa Smith, *Literary Culture and the Pacific: Nineteenth-Century Textual Encounters* (Cambridge: Cambridge University Press, 1998) 101–35.

he planned a chapter.⁴ Music facilitated Stevenson's social relationships with Pacific Islanders: he carried small instruments such as penny whistles for gift exchange, he frequently made music with Islanders, and his family collected instruments. He was close to several distinguished practitioners and patrons of Pacific music including King David Kalākaua and his sister Queen Lili'uokalani, the last monarch of the Hawai'ian Kingdom, who was an accomplished composer of more than 160 *mele* [songs]. Stevenson relished the prestige of song and oratory in many Pacific cultures, observing how "the Samoan coins a fresh song for every trifling incident" (27). Songs were written about and presented to Stevenson and his family, and he reciprocated by writing and reciting poems (frequently ballads, a genre intrinsically connected to song) for and about individuals including Tem Binoka, High Chief of Abemama in Kiribati.⁵

When Stevenson and his family settled in Sāmoa in 1890, he mimicked some Sāmoan cultural practices, including: calling the household to daily prayers with the *foa foa* [conch-shell trumpet]; singing "missionary" hymns in Sāmoan that were set to "wild and warlike" "ancient [Sāmoan] tunes";⁶ and performing poetry and song with guests and hosts at occasions such as feasts or village visits. Stevenson had a piano at his Sāmoan home, played the flageolet (a woodwind instrument resembling a recorder) in domestic ensembles and when traveling, and imported sheet music of classical repertoire. Stevenson's compositions were written for domestic performance: they include arrangements of folk song (especially Scottish song), Schubert *Lieder* [art song], and classical chamber works. Later compositions were influenced by Indigenous Oceanic musical idioms. For all its exceptional aspects, Stevenson's case highlights the extensive movement of European musical culture around the globe in the late nineteenth century, when instruments and printed and memorized music traveled with colonial administrators, servicemen, missionaries, anthropologists, tourists and traders. Western and Indigenous music informed social networks and personal relationships, including those between Stevenson and individual Pacific Islanders – relationships which were unusually intimate and mutually respectful for the period. But music was also prominent in overtly political public events such as religious and military ceremony in colonized sites and areas of colonial contact, whether used as a tool of colonization (as was often the case with hymnody, such as that promoted by the London Missionary Society) or to celebrate and assert the value of Indigenous Pacific cultures (as in the Hawai'ian monarchs' sponsorship of *hula*). Music was intrinsic to innumerable

---

⁴ *Letters*, 6: 239 and 336.
⁵ For examples, see Stevenson's *Ballads* (1890) and *Songs of Travel* (1896).
⁶ Fanny Stevenson, Prefatory Note, *Prayers Written at Vailima*, by Robert Louis Stevenson (London: Chatto & Windus, 1916) ix. Available at *Project Gutenberg*, <https://www.gutenberg.org/files/616/616-h/616-h.htm> [Accessed October 24, 2024].

cross-cultural encounters in this period, playing a vital role in both colonialism and anti-colonialism.

Stevenson's travels exactly coincided with the annexation of Pacific Islands, including Hawai'i, by Euro-American powers; in his literary works and political writings he was an outspoken critic of colonialism and a prominent advocate of Indigenous self-rule. It is important to acknowledge that paternalistic values typical of the period are apparent at points in his writings and in his behavior, but his exceptional support for Indigenous individuals, communities and political autonomy was publicly acknowledged by Sāmoans, Tongans and other Islanders during his life and at his death.[7] For Stevenson, music exemplified the devastating wider loss of customary Indigenous Pacific cultures under Western influence: in the Marquesas, he laments, "the dance languishes, the songs are forgotten [...] The whole body of Marquesan poetry and music was being suffered to die out with a single dispirited generation" (27). During the nineteenth century, introduced instruments such as the *ukulele* plus formal elements from hymnody (originally brought by missionaries), sea shanties and marching-band repertoire were rapidly adopted and adapted by Pacific Islanders for their own purposes within vernacular terms, creating "acculturated" or "syncretic" musical genres and cultures. Like many contemporary Western writers and scholars, Stevenson privileged, even fetishized, "traditional" (i.e., non-acculturated) musical cultures: his disparaging reference to contemporary *hula* that "may be viewed by the speedy globe-trotter in Honolulu" implies, for example, that this syncretic *hula* is – to Stevenson – a degraded form of customary Hawai'ian culture influenced by global tourism.[8] This period also marks the development of ethnomusicology, when formal studies of non-Western music were first undertaken, and when there was a global trade in "exotic" instruments and in visual images of non-Western musicians.

Case Study

The Prelude above describes a *te rei* [practice] for a *kaunikai* [a Kiribati formalized competition of music and dance] on the island of Butaritari in 1889. This was the first of Stevenson's two visits to the Kiribati atolls (known at the time as the Gilbert Islands) when he stayed at islands including Butaritari (the "Europeanized" "commercial centre of the group" [168]) and Abemama (for

---

[7] For differing perspectives, see Ann C. Colley, *Robert Louis Stevenson and the Colonial Imagination* (Aldershot: Ashgate, 2004); and Joseph Farrell, *Robert Louis Stevenson in Samoa* (London: MacLehose, 2017).

[8] On "syncretic" *hula*, see James Revell Carr, *Hawaiian Music in Motion: Mariners, Missionaries, and Minstrels* (Urbana: University of Illinois Press, 2014).

several weeks). Little Makin is two miles north of Butaritari.⁹ *Kaunikai* utilize displays of singing and dancing skills to transmit Kiribati *kainikamaen* [ritual knowledge], reinforcing kinship and social hierarchies. Pre-colonial *kaunikai* "could be a replacement, complement or prelude to actual warfare";¹⁰ by the time of Stevenson's visit, *kaunikai* retained their importance as rituals curating kinship and customary knowledge. The performances described here followed several days of disorder fueled by a lifting of the *tapu* [ban] on alcohol in Butaritari for a "feast": Stevenson states that the wife of a local trade-store manager introduced Stevenson to the Butaritarian "king" as "an intimate personal friend of Queen Victoria's" ("soon promoted to be her son") for his protection (171, 181). Following this account of the Makin *te rei*, Stevenson describes the *kaunikai* three days later: performing companies from Kuma village and Little Makin are positioned at one end of the *maneaba*, facing the companies from Butaritari and nearby villages at the other end; orderly alternation of performances collapses into fractious interruptions of each other's song and dance.

I begin by asking two generic questions: who are the implied readers of the **Extract** and who is the narrator (as distinct from the author)? These questions are especially pressing when a text represents a culture unfamiliar to the author or readers, and when one culture or cultural group implicitly or explicitly asserts superiority over the other. It is vital to consider who claims the authority to represent others and on what basis they claim that authority. Examining the narrative voice and implied readership also makes it possible to ascertain what genre of writing this is and its claim to narrative "truth." The analysis then turns to questions specific to literary representations of music.

Narrative Voice, Implied Readers and Textual Authority

Stevenson makes clear from the outset of the **Extract** that it is addressed to Western – perhaps specifically British or, even more specifically, Scottish – readers "at home." The passage employs elements of "scene setting" to introduce the event, its participants, venue, climate and so on: such accounts of musical performances were stock elements of travel writing and anthropology of the period. The narrator's urbane amusement, curiosity and enthusiasm, and the use of similes referencing material recognizable to his readers ("like children at home about a circus"), also suggests their position as an observer encountering

---

[9] The island of Butaritari was sometimes known as "Makin" in the late nineteenth and twentieth centuries; what is today known as Makin was sometimes known as "Little Makin." I thank Mary (Lisa) Lawson Burke for drawing that point to my attention; see also, Carla Manfredi, *Robert Louis Stevenson's Pacific Impressions: Photography and Travel Writing, 1888–1894* (Basingstoke: Palgrave Macmillan, 2018) 138, note.

[10] Petra Autio, "Hard Custom, Hard Dance: Social Organisation, (Un)Differentiation and Notions of Power in a Tabiteuean Community, Southern Kiribati," diss., University of Helsinki, 2010, 201, cited in Manfredi, *Robert Louis Stevenson's Pacific Impressions*, 139.

a novel experience. This status is apparent too in the extensive use of European terms to describe the music and performers, from "soloists" to "quartette." The narrator (in this case, apparently identical with Stevenson himself) thus acts as a mediator, "translating" the material: he uses the incongruous Western term "summer parlour," for example, to describe the meeting house before introducing the Kiribati term *maniap'*. This strategy presupposes the unfamiliarity of this subject matter to the readers; Stevenson makes clear that it is relatively unfamiliar to him, too.

Stevenson's narrative voice is vivacious but aware of its limited knowledge, introducing the "Makin company" with the phrases "they are said" and "it seemed to us." When the "troop" all stand, he confesses he "had none to give me any explanation" of the "highly dramatic" "songs," acknowledging that his account is subjective, arrived at without culturally specific knowledge. His observation that "I would at times make out some shadowy but decisive outline of a plot" similarly draws attention to his intermittent, strained comprehension of what he sees and hears. Unlike the assured narrative voice typically found in ethnomusicological studies, the narrator's voice here is tentative, drawing in the reader by making the narrator's personality and their identity as a relatively inexperienced tourist or traveler explicit in the text. Stevenson's recognition that his observations may be erroneous or incomplete is sustained through the passage, which makes little claim to musical expertise. The vocabulary in which he describes the practice is, for example, mostly non-specialist, at times even imprecise: when he writes that a "sudden change would be introduced (I think of key)" he avoids overstating his musical knowledge and comprehension. It is just possible that Stevenson's hesitancy about the word "key" signals his knowledge of the influence of Western tonal music on pre-colonial microtonal Pacific musical cultures, just as his reference to "psalm-like" melodic sections may register the influence of hymnody. But, more important for our purposes is that the narrator's vocabulary implies he is addressing a wide readership which itself lacked specialist knowledge of Micronesian or Western music – readers not unlike Stevenson himself, a self-taught amateur, whose grasp of composition was limited.[11] However, a couple of details such as the inclusion of musical notation indicate that Stevenson assumes his readers will have at least some musical training, and we should remember that music was an almost ubiquitous element of domestic and formal education for British girls and boys in the nineteenth century.

---

[11] Stevenson habitually understated his own abilities as an instrumentalist and composer for comic effect (e.g., *Letters*, 5: 385 and 278); nonetheless, examination of his manuscript scores confirms his ability was limited.

Comparisons and Cultural Value

Stevenson's representation of Kiribati music relies on conspicuously incongruous comparisons and oxymorons, particularly those that attempt to unsettle ideas about cultural refinement and "primitivism." This is evident from the outset when he introduces the performers from Little Makin by comparing them to "plaided Highlanders" "proud" of their "barbaric virtues"; the Makins' apparent "primitivism" is represented as an admirable quality shared with Western, specifically Scottish, readers and subjects. The word "barbaric" is clearly intended as a term of approval rooted in Stevenson's admiration for and celebration of Highland culture in his writing. Elsewhere in the book Stevenson elaborates on the affinities he perceives between Scots (especially Highlanders) and Pacific Islanders, noting linguistic similarities, a shared love of song and narrative, and common experiences of the loss of traditional cultures under colonialism. These repeated comparisons are intended to augment his anti-colonial argument: evoking the English Clearances of the Scottish Highlands (c.1750–1860), he identifies parallels between English colonialism within the British Isles and globally. Stevenson's comparison of Pacific Islanders and Scots was not unique in the nineteenth and early twentieth centuries, but this is not to imply, of course, that it is an unproblematic rhetorical strategy.[12] Although still reiterating concepts of the "savage" and the "civilized," Stevenson's account makes sustained attempts to challenge Eurocentric, hierarchical dichotomies. Paradoxically describing Kiribati "music" as "barbarous, but full of conscious art," he counters apparently negative references to "fire and devilry" and "barking, unmelodious" voices with repeated admiration of more lyrical sections and of the overall artistry and effects of the performance which "leads on the mind; it thrills, rouses, subjugates." Though a word such as "barking" may suggest that Stevenson perceives this as simply sound or even noise (terms that many Western contemporaries applied to non-Western music), he insists that *kaunikai* be recognized in the aesthetically and culturally prestigious terms of "music" and "art." Here and elsewhere, he resists the common Western mind/body dichotomy which, in contemporary writings on music, was often used to characterize non-Western music as more physical or "primitive" in its creation and effects than "rational" Western music. Stevenson's attempt to separate the Kiribati performers from negative associations with physicality shows some strain, however, and is complicated by his emphasis on the visceral effects of Kiribati music which "thrills, rouses [and] subjugates" even while it stimulates the "mind."

---

[12] See Graham Tulloch, "Stevenson and Islands: Scotland and the South Pacific," *Robert Louis Stevenson Reconsidered: New Critical Perspectives*, ed. William B. Jones, Jr (Jefferson, North Carolina: McFarland, 2003) 68–84.

Stevenson's account also resists the racialized hierarchies of instruments, styles, formal elements and genres common in nineteenth-century writing about music. "Rhythm," for example, was associated with the sensual and irrational (and, by this logic, with non-Western peoples) in comparison to harmony, associated with intellectual accomplishment. Similarly, drums were perceived as almost culturally ubiquitous and as less "developed" than the keyboard and orchestral instruments associated with prestigious Western genres of music.[13] Despite emphasizing the percussive and rhythmic qualities of *kaunikai*, and its physicality – the performers are "convulsed with enthusiasm and effort" – Stevenson emphasizes the artistry of the performers and of *kaunikai* itself, the "conscious" effort necessary to learn and perform it, and its powerful "effect" on I-Kiribati (the native people of Kiribati) and Western audiences alike. Moreover, his representation of a Kiribati child "learning [...] his art in sorrow" recalls tropes that were common in biographical representations of the childhoods of canonical Western composers such as Bach.[14] This example of the widespread Victorian belief that suffering was necessary for the creation of great art may additionally have encouraged Stevenson's readers to recognize the Islanders' practice as high art.

The complexities and limits of this comparative strategy become particularly clear in Stevenson's extended comparison of Kiribati music and dance to opera or lyric drama. Observing the choreography, gestures and vocal interjections of the standing "troop" he notes that he was "continually reminded" of an operatic crowd scene, concluding: "Already this is beyond the Thespian model; the art of this people is already past the embryo; song, dance, drums, quartette and solo – it is the drama fully developed although still in miniature." By referring to the sixth-century BC singer-actor Thespis, recognized by Aristotle and others as introducing innovations that led to the development of Greek tragedy, Stevenson evokes a developmental model of opera and drama as progressing (perhaps even evolving) over time from its classical "embryo." Developmental narratives about music history were common in nineteenth-century musicology and wider cultural debate,[15] the "evolution" of opera from Greek tragedy playing an important part in Wagner's writings, for example. One difficulty that arises from this imagery, though, is that it implies that earlier instantiations of an artform are "primitive" (note the racialized connotations) and inferior in comparison to their "mature" forms. However, Stevenson's argument explicitly rebuts this implication: he insists that Kiribati musical drama is "fully

---

[13] See further Bennett Zon, *Music and Metaphor in Nineteenth-Century British Musicology* (Aldershot: Ashgate, 2000).

[14] See Christopher Mark Wiley, "Re-writing Composers' Lives: Critical Historiography and Musical Biography," diss., Royal Holloway, University of London, 2008, 2 vols, especially 1: 36–87 and 2: 2–6.

[15] See Zon, *Music and Metaphor, passim*.

developed" (implying it is equal to the "developed" form of opera) yet differs from "grand opera" in scale (it is "still in miniature," like Thespian tragedy). Carla Manfredi rightly notes that Stevenson's "miniaturizing discourse" repeatedly infantilizes and trivializes Kiribati individuals and (political) culture; thus there seems some tension between his imagery and his argument.[16] However, Stevenson's developmental metaphor also implicitly rejects racist contemporary accounts that depicted non-Western cultures as archaic or immutable: his insistence that Kiribati performance is "beyond" "embryonic" Greek drama hints that this Indigenous artform may share some qualities with Thespian drama but has surpassed it through change.

Stevenson's comparisons raise a number of questions about Anglophone representations of non-Western (musical) cultures in writing. By using musical and other terms familiar to his implied readers, Stevenson "translates" another culture into readily understood language while acknowledging that such translation is inevitably incomplete and potentially inaccurate. Some may see Stevenson's comparative rhetorical strategies as trivializing or exoticizing Kiribati culture; others may see them as acknowledging with humility his limited comprehension and cultural knowledge. We should note that the incongruous comparisons rely on the unlikeness, as well as the similarities, of the two things being compared: their very incongruity implies that Pacific music is fundamentally different from European music. Stevenson's wife Fanny Van de Grift Stevenson in fact makes exactly the same point in her diary, which Stevenson quotes in this passage. She states: "The music itself was as complex as our own, though constructed on an entirely different basis" (191). In one pithy sentence, Fanny entirely dismisses the Western idea of "universal" musical hierarchies, a foundational concept of Western musicology that was innately racist and Eurocentric (and, in some cases, deployed to valorize the musical culture of one specific nation).[17] Like Stevenson's emphasis on the "conscious" art of the performers, Fanny's emphasis on the complexity of Kiribati art also asserts the cultural value of *kaunikai* and rejects hierarchical models of Western and non-European musical cultures. Fanny's statement implies profound cultural difference; Stevenson's unexpected comparisons also foreground as well as apparently minimize cultural difference, suggesting that a culture can only be (partially) understood within the language and conceptual terms available to

---

[16] Carla Manfredi, *Robert Louis Stevenson's Pacific Impressions: Photography and Travel Writing, 1888–1894* (London: Palgrave Macmillan, 2018) 140.

[17] Such values are evident in, to pick one contemporary example, the activities of Britain's Associated Board of the Royal Schools of Music, which began operations in colonial sites in the 1890s at the behest of South African expatriates; these activities were, Erin Johnson-Williams argues, a form of musical colonialism. See "The Examiner and the Evangelist: Authorities of Music and Empire, *c.*1894," *Journal of the Royal Musical Association* 145.2 (2020): 317–50.

the observer/listener. Yet even as the Stevensons recognize cultural difference, Stevenson also asserts humanist similarities between cultures: he insists that Kiribati performance "has the essence of all art" and qualities common to "all artists." Thus, while he acknowledges cultural difference, he rejects Eurocentric cultural hierarchies that would privilege Western over non-Western music – a comparativist perspective unusual in the period.

What is "Music"?

In this passage cited in the **Extract**, Stevenson deploys a variety of terms to describe what he hears and sees. The word "music" coexists with "drama," "opera," "songs" and "so-called dance." While *kaunikai* is often classified by ethnomusicologists and others as "dance," it is notable that Stevenson gives as much attention to the vocal and percussive sounds as to movement. His variety of terms suggests several points: it draws attention to the fact that the performance comprises not only discrete musical units (what he calls "songs"), organized sound more widely ("music," which may include sounds such as slapping), but also other artforms. The proliferation of terms suggests that definitions of "music" are culturally specific and that Western understandings of this term do not correlate to the social role or conception of these practices in Kiribati culture. Thus, Stevenson's attempt to describe Kiribati "music" puts Western definitions of the term under pressure. This implication is anticipated in the chapter title, which may evoke a musical or other cultural festival (the Three Choirs Festival, the Bayreuth Festival); a holiday or festivity; or a religious or spiritual event (the latter perhaps closest to the ritual function of *kaunikai* in Kiribati custom). It is perhaps tempting to argue that, by attending to many non-acoustic elements of this event (such as setting and audience response), Stevenson is attempting to represent the cultural function of the performance, of which music is only one part. He may perceive that Eurocentric and formalist conceptions of music as an autonomous artwork – put simply, just "the notes" – provide inappropriate analytic and narrative tools for representing non-Western performance; his approach may be seen as anticipating recent critical attention to the cultural practice of music.[18]

However, the desire of Stevenson's party to photograph the dancers after the *kaunikai* by asking them to repeat parts of the performance reveals, as Manfredi argues, their failure to understand the cultural significance or context of *kaunikai*: Stevenson's party appears to perceive it as reproducible entertainment (one Western conception of music) rather than as a ritual. The photographs, taken by Stevenson's step-son-in-law Joe Strong, were intended as possible illustrations for Stevenson's book; as such they again evoke the prevalence of tourism and exoticizing narratives in Western representations of

---

[18] See, for example, Christopher Small, *Musicking: The Meanings of Performing and Listening* (Hanover, New Hampshire: University Press of New England, 1998).

and encounters with Oceania. (Joe Strong himself, for example, was manager of the "South Sea Exhibit" at the 1893 Chicago World Fair.) In Manfredi's authoritative account, the Kiribati subjects "resist" the trivializing perspectives of the Stevenson family: she argues that the photographs of smiling Kiribati observers suggest that the Stevensons have now become "an entertaining, perhaps even ridiculous, spectacle" to their Pacific observers.[19] Whether we, as individual readers, conclude that these diverse written and visual records of *kaunikai* are ultimately exoticizing or underpinned by respect and empathy, they exemplify the linguistic, conceptual, technological and social difficulties and limitations of attempting to represent an unfamiliar musical culture in language.

Listening

Archive of Māori and Pacific Sound: <https://www.library.auckland.ac.nz/about-us/collections/special-collections/amps> [Accessed October 24, 2024].

Further Reading

Burke, Mary Lawson. "The Evolution of Performance Tradition in Kiribati." *Traditionalism and Modernity in the Music and Dance of Oceania: Essays in honour of Barbara B. Smith*. Eds Don Niles and Helen Reeves Lawrence. Sydney: Sydney University Press, 2001.

Irving, David R.M. *Colonial Counterpoint: Music in Early Modern Manila*. Oxford: Oxford University Press, 2010.

Manfredi, Carla. *Robert Louis Stevenson's Pacific Impressions: Photography and Travel Writing, 1888–1894*. London: Palgrave Macmillan, 2018.

Radano, Ronald and Tejumola Olaniyan, eds. *Audible Empire: Music, Global Politics, Critique*. Durham, North Carolina: Duke University Press, 2016.

Stevenson, Fanny van der Grift. *The Cruise of the Janet Nicol Among the South Sea Islands*. Ed. Roslyn Jolly. Seattle: Washington University Press, 2006.

Stevenson, Robert Louis. *South Sea Tales*. Ed. Roslyn Jolly. New York: Oxford University Press, 2008.

Sutton, Emma. "Whitman and Stevenson: Singing the Nation from Scotland to Sāmoa via Ohio and Hawai'i." *Song Beyond the Nation*. Eds Philip Ross Bullock and Laura Tunbridge. Oxford: British Academy/Oxford University Press, 2021. 254–68.

---

[19] Manfredi, *Robert Louis Stevenson's Pacific Impressions*, 144.

CHAPTER 8

Musical Encounters at the Louisiana Lakeside in Charles Jobey's "Le lac Cathahoula" (1856/1861)

Charlotte Bentley

Recommended Text

Charles Jobey, "Le lac Cathahoula" [1856], *L'Amour d'une blanche* (Paris: Jung-Treuttel, 1861). Available (in French only) at *Bibliothèque nationale de France: Gallica*, <https://gallica.bnf.fr/ark:/12148/bpt6k1415880r> [Accessed November 1, 2024].

Keywords

American Civil War, Creole, fiction, folk song, improviser, Louisiana, nature, nineteenth-century Black America, oboe, opera, Otherness, Paris, power, race, short story, song, the sublime, travel writing

Prelude

Extract 1

Charles Jobey, "Le lac Cathahoula," 261–3; translation mine.

[*This is a song that an enslaved man named Harris is asked to sing to a white audience, among whom is his enslaver, Zénon Judice. The song deals with an incident in which enslaved people are invited to a ball held by a white man, Mr Préval. Préval does not have permission to hold a ball for enslaved people, and the white authorities shut it down and give very different punishments to the enslaved attendees and the white host. When Harris finishes singing his song, his white enslaver remarks on the performance, making comments about slavery that are shocking from a modern perspective. These comments will be discussed more fully in the "Background" section of this chapter. The footnote outlines my choices regarding sensitive terminology.*][1]

---

[1] This chapter engages with nineteenth-century racial terminology; various terms (as well as my translations of them) deserve a few words of explanation. The term *mulâtre* (the English equivalent of which is "mulatto," which I use in my translations) is one of

After emptying his glass, Harris adopted the attitude of a man strumming a guitar and sang the following verses, which he improvised without hiatus or hesitation, like Eugène de Pradel:

Mouché Préval,	Mister Préval
Li donné grand bal,	Gave a grand ball.
Li fait nègues payé.	He made nègues pay
Pou sauté un pé.	To dance a little.
Li donné soupé,	He gave dinner,
Pou nègues régalé.	So the nègues feasted.
So vié la musique,	His old music
Té baye la colique.	Gave them stomach ache.
Mouché Préval,	Mister Préval
Té capitaine bal,	Was captain of the ball,
So cocher Louis,	His coachman Louis
Té maîte crémoni.	Was master of ceremonies.
Ala ain bourrique,	Then a donkey
Tendé la musique,	Heard the music,
Li vini valsé,	He came to waltz,
Com quand li cabré.	Like when he rears up on his hind legs.
Yavé des néguesses,	There were nèguesses
Belles com yé maîtresses,	Dressed up like their mistresses,
Yé té volé bel bel,	They stole beautiful things
Dans l'ormoir mamzel.	From Mademoiselle's wardrobe.

---

a plethora of terms that were used at that time to refer to people with mixed European and African ancestry. Meanwhile, the French word *nègre* (*négresse* in the feminine form) and its Louisiana Creole counterparts *nègue*/*nèguesse* were regularly used in the antebellum period to refer to people of African descent, and they frequently, as in the extracts below, carried the resonance of "enslaved person." While these terms were widely used in the nineteenth century, their continued use in French expressions in the more recent past has prompted criticism and debate, because of their associations with slavery and racism more broadly. Their appearance in the extracts below reflects nineteenth-century meanings and usages, but I have avoided giving a literal translation in my English versions, instead choosing to reflect the resonance of "enslaved person." In keeping with much recent work on race, I have avoided the use of the term "slave" in my own words, instead using "enslaved person" to reflect both the humanity of the individuals held in bondage and to acknowledge that their bondage was not an essential fact of their being, but rather a state in which they were kept. In my translation of the two extracts below, however, I do sometimes use the word "slave": this is to reflect the way in which the author of those nineteenth-century sources would have conceived of the people about whom he wrote. Decisions about capitalization and race follow MLA style which capitalizes Black when it refers to African Americans.

Blanc et pi noir,	White and Black alike,
Yé dansé bamboula,	They danced the *bamboula*,
Vous pas jamais voir,	You've never seen
Un plus grand gala.	A bigger gala.

[*In the next 11 stanzas, Harris's song describes how the white enslavers realize later in the evening that their clothes and the people whom they held in bondage are missing (and that their money had been stolen to pay the entrance fee to the ball). The local jailer hurries to put an end to the party. The enslaved attendees are imprisoned overnight and whipped, and Mr Préval is fined $100 for holding the event without authorization. The final stanza explains that Mr Préval vows never again to hold a ball without a permit and decides to go hunting instead. The narrative continues:*]

The *nègre*'s [enslaved man's] improvisation was a great success with the theater company; each one paid his compliments [to Harris], but Zénon interrupted this concert of eulogies.

"That's enough, that's enough," he said brusquely, "Harris, although he's a good subject, resembles all those of his race: if we were to let them, those fellows would eat from our hands. They know very well how to compensate themselves through naïve, often witty satire of the slavery in which we are forced to keep them. Who, then, will deliver us from slavery and the slaves, without us losing our fortunes and perhaps our lives!?"

Extract 2

Jobey, "Le lac Cathahoula," 269–72; translation mine.

[*Joseph Vallière, Welsch, Ulysse and Bailly are all white, male, European-born members of the French opera company. Vallière is the theater's oboist, while Ulysse and Bailly are singers.*]

We heard the trembling of the foliage, the sighs of the flowers, from which the breeze brought us perfumed kisses; the plaintive note of the mockingbird, calling his absent mate to the nest, the rapid flight of a flock of water birds, whose whistling wings brushed the surface of the lake; the softened voice of the ocelot, coming from the depths of the forest; the plaintive sounds of caimans, tormented by amorous ardor; and finally those thousand noises that rise from the earth like a farewell concert and serve as an accompaniment to the triumphal march of the sun, receding to light up another hemisphere.

Only one among us dared to mix his voice with this grand symphony of nature. Vallière murmured some plaintive notes on his oboe, that the echo from the opposite bank repeated with a surprising purity and sonorousness. Vallière was familiar with the qualities of this marvelous echo, having tried it out several times when coming to Catahoula. He then made it repeat, phrase by phrase and note by note, a charming Breton melody; it was the naïve response of a child of Armorica [Brittany] to the request full of tenderness and rustic love that her fiancé addressed to her.

Vallière had chosen his moment well to make most of us, who nevertheless heard him every day in the theater, experience emotions that were until then unknown to us. It is not in the concert hall, in the theater, by the light of chandeliers, nor in front of ladies adorned with lace and diamonds that one must hear the oboe; it is at the calm and red hour of dusk, beside a lake, in the shadow of woods, in the midst of the peaceful sanctuary of nature. Vallière finished with the "*air du sommeil*" ["sleep aria"] from Auber's *La Muette* [*de Portici*]. [...]

Besides the pleasure that Vallière had just caused us, he had suggested to most of us a wholly natural idea.

"Let's sing the prayer from *La Muette*," we cried on all sides, "Let's sing the prayer from *La Muette*; Mr Welsch, you lead it!"

"I would be delighted," replied Welsch, "but on one condition. It's that those who sing out of tune, or do not know their part well, should be silent; I further demand that all the performers pay much more attention to the performance dynamics than if we were in the theater."

"What's the point?" said Mademoiselle Maria, "No one is listening to us?"

"What's the point, you ask, Mademoiselle?" replied Welsch severely, "Simply that no one here has asked us or forced us to sing, and that it would be better to be silent than to come and trouble the sublime harmony of these solitudes with our discordant sounds. [...] *taceat* for all those who do not feel capable of making art for art's sake. Attention, all: we will strike together. One, two, three, four; begin!"

And the vaults of the virgin forest resounded, for the first and likely the last time, with this beautiful prayer from *La Muette*, of which the singing, so simple, so broad, begins with a *pianissimo*, resembling a breath of a breeze, and finishes with an energetic fermata, whose echo returned to us like distant thunder.

Turning around, when the prayer was finished, we beheld behind us, on their knees on the sand, the sailor, *le nègre* [the slave] and *le mulâtre* [the mulatto], who were praying to God!

The following day, at daybreak, the artists set off for Saint-Martinville. On arriving, several of them were struck down with yellow fever; eight days later, the earth received the mortal remains of Joseph Vallière, Ulysse and Bailly.

The Challenge

In Charles Jobey's short story, "Le lac Cathahoula," first published in 1856, musical performances provide an unusually vivid insight into issues of race, cultural encounter and colonial legacy in the mid-nineteenth century. More unusually still, the tale addresses these issues from the unlikely perspective of a group of opera singers and theater musicians working in New Orleans. With the aid of local guides of various ethnicities, they undertake a summer trip to rural Louisiana to escape the intense heat of the city, and the "friction" caused by the Europeans' encounters with racial Others in an exotic natural setting is played out in scenes of musical performance. Three challenges arise: How does the narrator deepen his characterization of the enslaved man, Harris, by describing his musical performance? What cultural significance does the fictional work ascribe to opera in the tale's closing scene, and what does this reveal about the relationships between the European visitors and their local guides? How does the narrator encourage the reader to reflect on these relationships through his evocation of the sounds of the exotic natural environment?

Background

Born in Rouen, Charles Jobey (1813–77) spent the years 1834–40 as a bassoonist in the orchestra of New Orleans's French theater, the Théâtre d'Orléans. When he returned to France, he turned to writing: his short stories and poems appeared frequently in Parisian newspapers and magazines, and he was the founder and editor-in-chief of several newspapers in provincial France. He published a novel and a collection of short stories in Paris in the early 1860s, as well as an unusual guide to hunting and preparing game, which combined practical advice with recipes and poetry.

"Le lac Cathahoula" was based on the author's own experiences in Louisiana in the 1830s, and at times the narrator's voice aligns with Jobey's own: the narrator, like Jobey, is a musician who shares Jobey's interests in hunting, shooting and fishing. The plot follows a group of opera singers and orchestral musicians – many of whom are fictionalized versions of Jobey's New Orleans colleagues – as they set out to explore rural Louisiana during a summer excursion away from the city. Outbreaks of cholera and yellow fever (as the unfortunate deaths of three musicians at the end of **Extract 2** indicate) were common during the hot and humid summer months, so the theaters usually closed, and the contracted performers were free to leave the city in search of healthier climes.

The story describes the Europeans' experiences as they travel between the small town of Saint-Martinville and Catahoula Lake, roughly eleven miles away. While the women and children set off by road, the narrator and some of the men take a more adventurous route, picking their way through dense woodland on horseback, and encountering bears, wild bulls and alligators. Their local guides – the landowner Zénon Judice; Harris, a man he holds in bondage; a formerly enslaved man named Jean-Louis, and his servant, an old French sailor called Lucien – struggle to keep them safe. Finally, with the more energetic field sports completed (Catahoula's environs were a rich source of fish and game), a series of musical performances at the lakeside [**Extracts 1 and 2**] brings the story to its conclusion.

Jobey published the tale four times between 1856 and 1861, and the extracts here are taken from the 1861 version, which appeared in *L'Amour d'une blanche* [The Love of a White Woman], a collection of Jobey's short stories.[2] The earlier three instances, nearly identical, were serialized in newspapers and magazines in Paris (the *Journal pour tous*, 1856) and in Louisiana (*La Loge de l'Opéra*, 1856–7 and *Le Villageois de Marksville*, 1857–8, this latter under the title "Souvenirs de la Louisiane").

At the end of **Extract 1**, Zénon Judice expresses his concerns – phrased in terms that strike a modern reader as shockingly racist – that enslaved people are no more than tame(d) creatures unable to look after or think for themselves, and that abolition might be impossible without bloodshed. A little earlier in the story, the narrator condemns slavery outright, exclaiming: "May the shame of this monstrosity fall upon the Christians of the nineteenth century, who have the infamy of maintaining slavery" (215). These observations appear in the Parisian versions (1856 and 1861) but are absent from those published in Louisiana. Whether Jobey decided to remove them, or whether his editors made the decision on his behalf, remains unknown, but their absence from the Louisiana publications reveals just how sensitive a subject the future of slavery had become in the state by the late 1850s. In January 1861, Louisiana seceded from the United States and joined the Confederate States, in protest against the election of Abraham Lincoln as president and the Republican party's moves to prevent the further expansion of the institution of slavery. New Orleans was a major center of the slave trade within the United States at the time, and Louisiana's economy during the period depended in significant part on the labor of enslaved African and African-descended people to sow and harvest the sugar cane and cotton of which it was a major global producer. Many white Louisianans saw chattel slavery as essential to the future prosperity of their state, and the state's secession was a way for them to express their anger at threats to that system.

Jobey himself, to the extent that we can uncover his views from his writings, supported abolition. Nonetheless, his words can also suggest an underlying paternalism towards African-descended people, and on occasion he makes essentializing comments about his characters' behaviors and about customs that he sees as being racially determined. Some of his European readers would likely have shared both attitudes. France had first abolished slavery in all its colonies in February 1794, but Napoleon reintroduced it in 1802. In 1815, Napoleon himself outlawed the trading of slaves, but slavery as a whole was finally

---

[2] The collection takes its title from its opening story. Jobey's decision to use *L'Amour d'une blanche* as the umbrella title makes it a complement to his Paris novel of 1860, *L'Amour d'un nègre* [The Love of an Enslaved Man], which was also inspired by his experiences in Louisiana, and which critiques the way an enslaved man is treated by the woman who holds him in bondage.

abolished only in 1848. The phenomenal European success of the novel *Uncle Tom's Cabin* (1852) by the American author Harriet Beecher Stowe further reinforced anti-slavery sentiments among the French reading public. The earliest French translations (of excerpts) appeared in 1853, alongside several French-language stage adaptations.[3] Anyone reading Jobey's "Le lac Cathahoula" in 1861 would almost certainly have had their perspectives shaped – either consciously or unconsciously – by this earlier work.

Jobey's story sits somewhere between travel memoir and exotic fiction, i.e., literature that focuses on its protagonists' encounters with unfamiliar surroundings, people and cultures (all of which are described in colorful and sometimes hyperbolic terms) and their responses to those encounters.[4] "Le lac Cathahoula" exposes some of the most fundamental tensions of the nineteenth-century world, and the fact that it does so through evoking musical performances is highly revealing.

Case Study

In Jobey's short story, musical performances enable processes of cultural translation, helping French readers understand the nuances of the interactions taking place in the unfamiliar environment of rural Louisiana. For readers in Louisiana (not Jobey's original readership), the environment the narrator describes would have been more familiar in some respects, but its presentation through the perspective and experiences of a group of European visitors may have created something of a distancing effect. Nowadays, the narrative invites us to think more about the role that sound and music might have played in people's experiences of travel and cultural contact in the nineteenth century, and the ways literature reveals that role for us.

The difficulties of interpreting a fictional work like this are manifold: the portrayal of racial and cultural encounter is never straightforward, and Jobey's story invites multiple, and sometimes contradictory, readings. What is more, some of the opinions characters express and some of the language Jobey uses

---

[3] Emily Sahakian, "Eliza's French Fathers: Race, Gender, and Transatlantic Paternalism in French Stage Adaptations of Uncle Tom's Cabin, 1853," *Uncle Tom's Cabins: The Transnational History of America's Most Mutable Book*, eds Tracy C. Davis and Stefka Mihaylova (Ann Arbor: University of Michigan Press, 2018) 81–115.

[4] Jennifer Yee defines exotic literature broadly as "literature taking as its subject a culturally and geographically distant place and people," when considering the work of French authors across the nineteenth century. *Exotic Subversions in Nineteenth-Century French Fiction* (London: Legenda, 2008) 1. Given that Jobey's "Le lac Cathahoula" was published in both Paris and Louisiana (although its primary readership, like that of Jobey's other writings, was French), I have offered a more expanded definition here, which focuses more on stylistic and plot features than on setting alone.

are uncomfortable and even shocking from our perspective as modern readers, and it is particularly important to position them carefully in their historical and cultural context in order to understand the complexities of the past.

Harris's Song

On the surface, the song Harris sings reaffirms the social status quo. [**Extract 1.**] Mr Préval's subversive attempt to hold a ball for enslaved people is swiftly stopped, and both he and the attendees are punished (albeit to very different degrees). However, there are alternative possible meanings in this song, where white authority figures (like Préval) are ridiculed for their naïve or superficial attempts to improve the lives of enslaved people in New Orleans. The simplistic aabb rhyme scheme and, in the original-language text, the almost relentless succession of short, five-syllable lines, underscore a satirical treatment of the subject: Préval's paternalistic assumption that he can override the racial divisions of nineteenth-century New Orleans and bring unfree Black people and free white people together to dance the *bamboula* – for his own financial gain – are punctured first by the arrival of the jailer and then by the fine he receives for his pains.[5] Préval's pride is wounded, but the Black dancers receive a far harsher punishment: they are sent to jail overnight and then whipped ("Yé méné yé tous, / Dans la calabous; / Lendemain matin, / Yé fouetté yé bien.") ["They led them all / to the jail; / The next morning, / they whipped them well"] (lines 33–6). There is, then, a tragicomic element to this song in the way that it dwells on Préval's hurt feelings, thereby highlighting how insubstantial they seem when juxtaposed with the enslaved people's more serious punishments. This characteristic is underscored by the "singsong" feel created by the short lines and the resulting proximity of the rhymes. Préval's decision to go hunting also contributes to the social commentary, as it is possible to interpret it either as a typical frivolous pursuit of the wealthy classes or as a total *volte face*, as he replaces his efforts to bring about harmony and to enhance the lives of unfree people, with attention to a pastime that involves killing living creatures.

Unlike most of Jobey's story, the song is in Louisiana Creole, a language that developed in the eighteenth century predominantly through contact between French speakers and speakers of a variety of African languages. While Jobey's European performers and most of the other characters speak in French, nearly all of Harris's contributions are in Louisiana Creole. Including the language thus adds superficial local color, perhaps comparable to attempts by English-language authors to evoke dialects spoken by African and African-descended English-speakers in the United States at this time. While some of these uses

---

[5] The *bamboula* is a dance (named after the drum that accompanies it) of African origin. It came to New Orleans via Saint-Domingue (modern-day Haiti), and in the first half of the nineteenth century enslaved people could often be seen dancing it on Sundays at the city's Congo Square.

were intended to be accurate portrayals of Black speech (Mark Twain emphasizes that this was his aim in the author's note to *Huckleberry Finn* [1884], for instance),[6] other uses, such as those for the blackface minstrel stage, were created for supposed comic effect, to make the character speaking the words seem less cultured or less intelligent than speakers of "standard" English.

That Jobey was adopting a similar approach here is one possibility for us to consider, but there is another layer of complexity. In the mid-1850s, there was not the same established history of white francophone authors transcribing or evoking Louisiana Creole as there was of English-language writers evoking Black English. Indeed, Jobey's is one of the earliest (surviving) instances of an author, whether European or Louisianan, transcribing Louisiana Creole in their literature.[7] Perhaps Jobey included it as an ethnographic detail, rather than a superficial attempt to make Harris appear comic.

The use of Louisiana Creole also helps to nuance the relationship between Harris and the white European performers. On the one hand, Harris's use of Creole emphasizes the difference in social standing between the enslaved character and the white Europeans: New Orleans readers would have regarded Louisiana Creole as a low-status language in comparison with French, and Parisian readers would have perceived it as alien and exotic. But the dynamics of the relationship are again more complex: Harris has a degree of agency, which is shown through the way he speaks and sings in his own language. Because there is no direct translation of Harris's words for the French readership, the reader must infer the meaning of Harris's speech from the way that Zénon Judice (who understands Louisiana Creole) responds to him, or from the narrator's occasional weaving in of an explanation. By leaving Harris's words untranslated, then, the narrator recreates the European performers' experience: of being outsiders who, unlike Zénon Judice and the other Louisianan characters, do not fully understand him.

Improvisation

The narrator asserts several times that Harris's song is an improvisation, and he likens him to Eugène de Pradel, a French verse improviser of the first half of the nineteenth century. Harris's improvisatory skill clearly impresses the assembled Europeans, who praise his quick poetic mind. There was a vogue for musico-poetic improvisation across genres and registers in Europe in the early nineteenth century, inspired by older traditions of the Italian *improvisatori* (improvising poet-musicians who emerged in the fourteenth century). Aside from their actual performances in theaters, lecture halls and other venues in

---

[6] Mark Twain, "Explanatory," *Adventures of Huckleberry Finn* (1884), ed. Emory Elliott (Reprint, Oxford: Oxford University Press, 2008) 2.

[7] See D.A. Kress, Margaret E. Mahoney and Rebecca Skelton, eds, *Anthologie de poésie louisianaise du XIXe siècle* (Shreveport: Éditions Tintamarre, 2010) 242.

nineteenth-century Europe, improvisators feature in novels and other forms of printed literature from the period. They include the protagonists of Germaine de Staël's *Corinne* (1807) and Hans Christian Andersen's *Improvisatoren* (1835). Owing to the widespread popularity of these and other works (*Corinne* was written in French and Andersen's *Improvisatoren* was translated into French in 1847), the poetic improviser would have been a familiar literary figure to readers on both sides of the Atlantic.

But more than just being an improvisation, the narrator positions Harris's song as akin to a folk song: while the meaning of the song may have escaped its listeners on account of language, or ambiguity, or both, the presentation of a spontaneous performance in a rural, outdoor setting, would have called to mind the presentation of folk traditions in other nineteenth-century literature, such as George Sand's *Les Maîtres sonneurs* [*The Master Pipers*] (1853), the subject of Chapter 2 in this coursebook. Through this performance and the Europeans' overly gushing response to it, the narrator idealizes Harris's talent, giving him a role known from literature of the time as the *bon nègre*:[8] he is a sort of Black, enslaved counterpart to Rousseau's "noble savage," which had become a familiar trope in contemporary tales of encounter between white men and Native Americans in similar forest settings.[9] Evoking the "noble savage" here underscores another irony: in Rousseau's formulation, the "noble savage" is happy because, unlike "civilized" man, he does not have the concept of private property. Harris, by contrast, is only too aware that his life is constrained by white definitions of property, as contemporary society considers him to *belong* to Zénon Judice.

As a European's idealized vision of an unfree man of the period, Harris remains intriguingly Other: this moment of musical and poetic outpouring from an African-descended man in the wilderness seems to nod to but also refigure earlier tropes of colonial encounter, such as François-Réné de Chateaubriand's reminiscences of seeing members of the Iroquois Confederacy (Haudenosaunee) dancing to a version of the tune "Madelon Friquet" (*Voyage en Amérique*, 1827) or Alexis de Tocqueville's surprise meeting with a Métis (Bois-Brulé) man who could sing French songs (*Quinze jours au désert*, written 1831, published 1861).[10] These encounters with Indigenous North Americans

---

[8] Jennifer Yee uses "bon nègre" to signify the figure of the cultivated Black (often enslaved) male in her discussions of Victor Hugo's *Bug-Jargal* (1826) in *Exotic Subversions* (46).

[9] For more on the evolution of the "noble savage" concept, see Ter Ellingson, *The Myth of the Noble Savage* (Berkeley: University of California Press, 2001).

[10] For more on these encounters, see Ruth E. Rosenberg, *Music, Travel, and Imperial Encounter in 19th-Century France* (London: Routledge, 2015) 81–3 and 94–6. In both encounters, there is not just a cultural meeting with an Other, but also an encounter with the legacy of an earlier European "*mission civilisatrice*" ["civilizing mission"]. The comparison with Pradel hints at a similar situation in Jobey's novel.

would undoubtedly have been recognizable literary "types" for Parisian readers of the period, and they would have provided a familiar frame of reference alongside the more unfamiliar aspects of Harris's characterization, such as his use of Louisiana Creole.

Although the narrator calls Harris an improviser, his song is in fact a real one, known in nineteenth-century New Orleans: William H. Coleman mentioned it in his *Historical Sketchbook and Guide to New Orleans and Environs* of 1885; it appeared in an article by George Washington Cable in *The Century Magazine* (along with a fragment of notated melody) in February 1886; and it was discussed in the *Daily Picayune* of March 4, 1900, along with a full transcription of the text. Therefore, passing the song off as an improvisation constitutes poetic license; the narrator's insistence that Harris is improvising suggests that it is the apparent spontaneity of his poetic skill that is the key factor in the European performers' enthusiastic response and idealization of him as *bon nègre* within the short story.

Through this emphasis on Harris's ability to improvise a song, Jobey's story draws a contrast with the specifically musical performances that follow (Vallière's oboe playing and the opera performance in **Extract 2**). Although the story's elements of musical exchange narrow somewhat the socio-cultural gap between the enslaved man and the Europeans, the detailed focus on poetry (for Harris) and music (for the Europeans) serves to emphasize the distance between them, while also undermining any Rousseau-inspired preconceptions the reader might have about associating "text" with "sophistication" and "music" with "natural states."

Sounds of the Natural World

The environment in which Harris's and the Europeans' musical performances take place plays a vital role in creating their impact in the final pages of "Le lac Cathahoula" [**Extract 2**]. Particularly interesting is that the natural world is evoked through an emphasis on its sonic qualities, rather than its visual ones (travel writing usually emphasizes visual modes of understanding other places and people).[11] The narrator highlights the sounds of the natural world: the "sighs of the flowers," "the plaintive note of the mockingbird," the "whistling wings" of the flocking water birds, "the softened voice of the ocelot" and "the plaintive sounds of the caimans." The effect of this focus on soundscapes is twofold: on the one hand, the shift away from the visual highlights the contrast between the Europeans' familiar urban environment and the unfamiliar natural world in which they currently find themselves, thus exoticizing the Louisiana setting for Parisian readers and also driving home the distance between the rural setting and the experience of city life for readers in New Orleans. On

---

[11] See Bernard McGrane, *Beyond Anthropology: Society and the Other* (New York: Columbia University Press, 1989) 116.

the other, the focus on the sonic perhaps subverts the reader's expectations of what exactly "the exotic" means in this story: while certain visual tropes served as descriptive shorthand for the exotic in nineteenth-century literature (e.g., bright colors and styles of dress), sound dominates in this scene, emphasized by alliteration and onomatopoeia in the original, such as "le frémissement du feuillage" ("trembling foliage") or "les soupirs des fleurs" ("the sighs of the flowers").

How, then, to interpret the sounds of the natural world here? Are they simply a marker of the exotic Other, or are there other ways to understand them? The narrator and characters invoke the concept of the sublime at various points. When the European performers are about to sing, Monsieur Welsch demands that they must not "trouble the sublime harmony of the natural world" with a bad performance. The narrator writes of the "grand symphony of nature" (musicalizing the sounds of the natural world) and contrasts the "sublime harmony" of the forest with the humans' potentially "discordant" sounds. And yet at other times, the "softened" and "plaintive" sounds suggest a pleasurable beauty rather than an awe-inspiring sublimity.

Opera

The story's evocation of the natural soundscape and its obvious importance makes sense when put into the context of the final musical performance of the tale, when the Europeans perform the prayer from Act 3 of French composer Daniel Auber's *grand opéra*, *La Muette de Portici* (1828), which Jobey and his colleagues regularly performed in New Orleans during the 1830s.

Particularly noteworthy is the way the narrator portrays the interaction between the natural world and the musicians' performances. Nature, as presented here, is responsive to the humans' performances: when the oboist Vallière performs, the narrator says that he "made it [the natural world] repeat, phrase by phrase and note by note, a charming Breton melody." One way to read this would be to suggest that Vallière enjoys being in harmony with nature, but the fact that the narrator states that the oboist *makes* it repeat the phrase suggests, perhaps, that he wishes to harness the power of nature for his own gratification or gain. The fact that it is the oboist who calls to and takes pleasure in the response of the natural world also plays on tropes of the oboe as a pastoral instrument, as evoked in the "Scene in the Fields" of Hector Berlioz's *Symphonie fantastique* (1830), which opens with a *cor anglais* and oboe duet between two distant shepherds. While Vallière's harnessing of the natural environment mainly serves to create an enhanced aesthetic effect for him as the performer and for his listeners, the idea of his making the environment serve him also hints perhaps at the dynamics of European settler colonialism, which value the environment of the colonized locale to the extent that it serves the colonists' purposes.

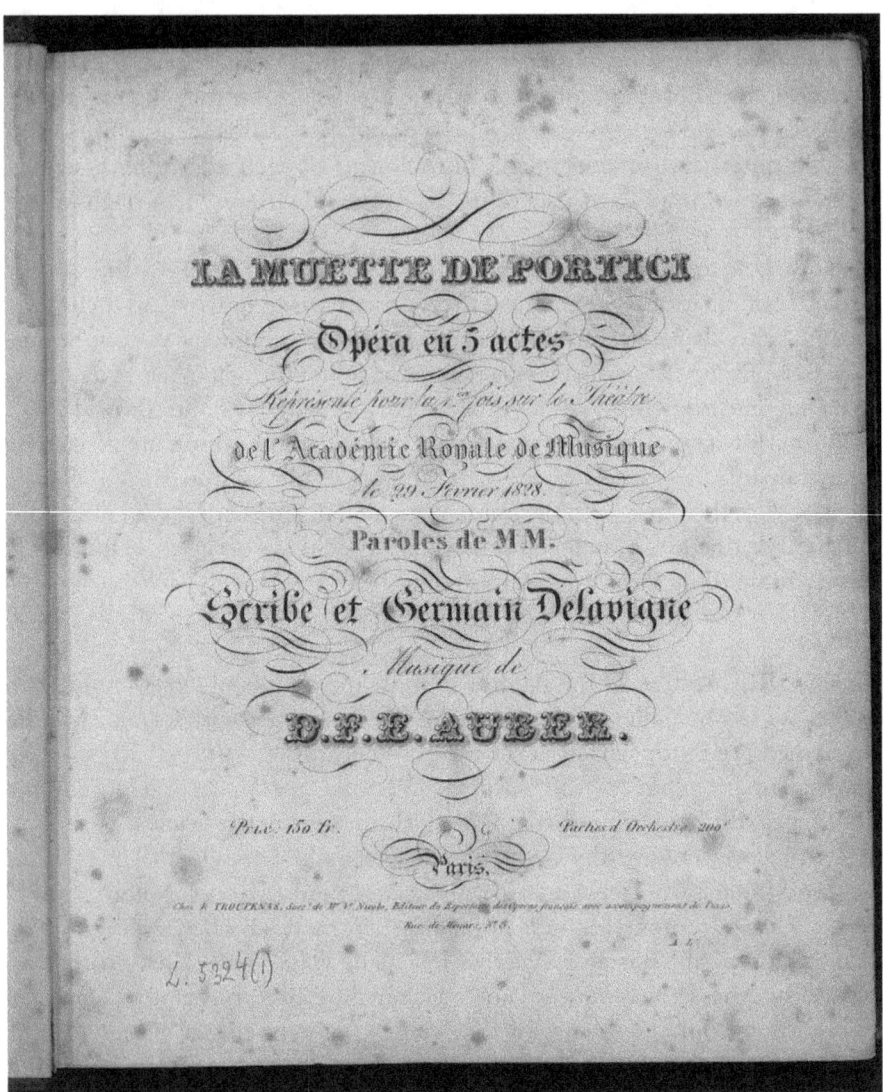

Fig. 8.1: Daniel-Esprit Auber, *La Muette de Portici*, title page from the first edition of the vocal score (Paris: E. Troupenas, [1828]).

The impact of the operatic performance, however, is even more significant: when Vallière plays, it is only the "opposite bank" that returns his melody; but when the troupe sings together, "the vaults of the virgin forest resounded" in response, suggesting the involvement of the entire surrounding environment. The opera performance also has a striking spiritual and physical impact on Harris, Jean-Louis and Lucien (the other servant characters in the story), whom it moves to prayer ("we beheld behind us, on their knees on the sand, the sailor, the enslaved man and the mixed-race man, who were praying to God!" [**Extract**

2]). For a moment, French music takes on the role of a universal music, moving all who hear it, whatever their social status or cultural background.

This element of power is particularly significant, since opera had long served a colonizing function beyond Europe: opera houses were built in colonized locales as a marker of imperial might (and, indeed, of colonists' nostalgia for home), and opera was often seen as a mark of "civilization." At first glance, opera seems here to be a marker both of the urban and the alien, out of place in the woodland environment. However, Jobey subtly alters the power dynamics when he describes how the natural world responds: the sounds are not simply echoed back, but are also adapted by the landscape, resembling first "the breath of a breeze" and then "distant thunder." The landscape, then, has the last word, as it amplifies the final notes of the troupe's performance into a more sublime form.

The cultural work of opera in this story, then, seems to be to represent the moment of cultural contact, where something familiarly European meets something Other; but the power dynamics of that encounter are by no means straightforward or fixed. One way to interpret the role of opera in this scene might be as a potentially uncomfortable reminder to Parisian readers that their culture, powerful though it could be in new environments, was not insulated from the influence of those environments. In other words, the process of cultural encounter could shape both European culture and Europeans' perceptions of it. But there are certainly other potential ways of reading the final scene of "Le lac Cathahoula" and opera's role within it.

Listening

Auber, Daniel-François-Esprit. "Prière: Saint bienheureux" (Act 3), from *La Muette de Portici*, Diego Torre, Oscar de la Torre, Angelina Ruzzafante, Wiard Witholt, *et al.*, Dessau Anhalt Theater Chorus, Anhaltische Philharmonie Dessau, Antony Hermus. CPO Recordings, 2011.

Further Reading

Agnew, Vanessa. *Enlightenment Orpheus: The Power of Music in Other Worlds.* New York: Oxford University Press, 2008.

Bentley, Charlotte. "Between the Frontier and the French Quarter: Operatic Travel Writing and Nineteenth-Century New Orleans." *Operatic Geographies: The Place of Opera and the Opera House.* Ed. Suzanne Aspden. Chicago: Chicago University Press, 2018. 105–18.

———. *New Orleans and the Creation of Transatlantic Opera, 1819–1859.* Chicago: University of Chicago Press, 2022.

Ellingson, Ter. *The Myth of the Noble Savage.* Berkeley: University of California Press, 2001.

Kadish, Doris Y. and Françoise Massardier-Kenney, eds. *Translating Slavery: Gender and Race in French Women's Writing, 1783–1823*. Kent, Ohio: Kent State University Press, 1994.

Pratt, Mary Louise. *Imperial Eyes: Travel Writing and Transculturation*. 2nd edn. London: Routledge, 2008.

Rosenberg, Ruth E. "Among Compatriots and Savages: The Music of France's Lost Empire." *The Musical Quarterly* 95.1 (2012): 36–70.

———. *Music, Travel, and Imperial Encounter in 19th-Century France: Musical Apprehensions*. London: Routledge, 2015.

Yee, Jennifer. *Exotic Subversions in Nineteenth-Century French Fiction*. London: Legenda, 2008.

CHAPTER 9

Critical Dislocations: Champfleury's *Richard Wagner* (1860)

Jeremy Coleman

Recommended Text

Champfleury, *Richard Wagner* (Paris: Librairie Nouvelle [A. Bourdilliat et Cie.], 1860). This chapter uses with permission the translation by Palomba Paves-Yashinsky contained in "*Richard Wagner* and *After the Battle*: Champfleury," *19th-Century Music* 13.1 (Summer 1989): 20–5. Subsequent citations refer to this edition and are given parenthetically.

Keywords

Concert performance, exile, intermediality, listener, music criticism, nonfiction, operatic excerpts, prose poems, realism, reception history, Second-Empire Paris, Richard Wagner

Prelude

Extract 1

Champfleury, *Richard Wagner*, 20–1; emphasis original.

Richard Wagner! I rediscover this name lodged in a corner of my memory by an academic critic, M. Fétis père of Brussels in Brabant, Van Fetis [*sic*], a bookworm, a critic without influence, a scrapbook biographer, who wrote somewhere that Wagner "was the *Courbet* of music."

As you can imagine, it was an insult in the mind of the Flemish man which led me to reflect at length. What would be a Courbet in music? That is what I searched for with difficulty. The great painter, assailed and insulted for so long by *dandies* of unimportant newspapers, is an artist who is remarkable above all for the power of his brush.

One can cut out a portion from each of his canvasses [*sic*], and it remains a painting; but as the French are mediocre connoisseurs of painting and as they are drawn above all to *subject*, to *wit*, and to *prettiness*, Courbet could not be understood.

At the same time, the accusation of *realism* was combined with jealous efforts to impede the master's development, and the word *realism* was thought of in the same way as the appellation *music of the future*, with which Richard Wagner's music was decked ironically.

I will speak later of the title *music of the future*, which Wagner's adversaries used for a long time as a club to beat him with; but journalists' clubs are only the clubs of tight-rope walkers, made of printed cloth, stuffed with straw.

Should we not first thank the professional critics who consistently miss the mark? First they stop the strong man's advance, damage his chances, throw spokes in his wheels, dig ruts to overturn his cart, erect worm-eaten barricades behind which they stand trembling, armed with old syringes filled with ink. Suddenly, after having regained his strength, after months of weakness, the artist stands up, proud, strong, with conviction. With a single glance he routs the mediocre, the jealous, the impotent, the useless, and the pale ink-splatterers, and he trods triumphantly down the path on which an enthusiastic crowd awaits him.

Extract 2

Champfleury, *Richard Wagner*, 22.

From the first bars of the overture, the woeful critics, who misled the public in a spirit of hostile denigration and through jealous impotence, understood that they could only flee, because Richard Wagner was being applauded by the trembling crowd, which recognizes the Beautiful and the True, and which felt moved to the core of its being by the musical waves newly revealed by a navigator.

Lack of melodies, said the critics.

Each fragment from each opera of Wagner is nothing but a vast melody, resembling the spectacle of the sea.

What kind of person, upon seeing the heaving ocean or the blue Mediterranean, would wish to build there a small, white house with green shutters?

Once immersed in the waves of sovereign harmony to which Wagner holds the secret, would not only an idiot ask for a little tune from the *Fanchonnette*?

Wagner's music transports me to remote times when alone, in a small Normandy village, stretched out among the broom-trees on the bluff, I looked at the sea, always beautiful and always new, defying boredom and inspiring lofty thoughts.

There is a religious side to Wagner's work, the religious feeling experienced while silently crossing a dense forest. It is then that the passions of civilization fall away one by one: the spirit leaves its little cardboard box where everyone habitually encloses it before going out in the evening, to a performance, in society; it becomes pure, expands before one's eyes, breathes contentedly and seems to soar to the very top of tall trees.

These are not merely turns of phrase.

But how can one render, except through sensory analogies, the mystical language of intoxicating sounds?

Extract 3

Champfleury, *Richard Wagner*, 23–4.

The task of speaking about sharps, flats, tonalities, ascending modulations, chromaticism, etc., should be left to the critics; what remains for me to say is more interesting.

The fragment from the *Holy Grail* [he means the Act 1 Prelude to *Lohengrin*] is among those which struck me the most, by its religious mysticism and the highest quivering of the violins, at the same time, clear and transparent like crystal. The orchestra gradually becomes more animated and arrives at a kind of radiant apotheosis, golden like the sun, which transports the listener to unknown worlds.

I was given the program of the concert just before it was sent to press. It is useful to quote the *Holy Grail* fragment, taken from *Lohengrin*: [quotation omitted] [*Wagner's program note to the Act 1 Prelude describes the angelic descent of the Grail from heaven to earth.*]

Let those who have a poetic spirit reread these lines and deck them with melodies, and they will be able to have an imaginary idea of the profound musical feeling of the Holy Grail.

The Challenge

In January 1860, the exiled German composer and dramatist Richard Wagner (1813–83) presented the first of three Paris concerts to promote his music. In reaction to largely anti-Wagnerian commentary in the Paris press, novelist and art critic Jules François Felix Fleury-Husson (1821–89), better known by his pen name Champfleury, enthusiastically defended Wagner's music, at that point still relatively unknown in France except via concert excerpts. Champfleury's pamphlet entitled *Richard Wagner* (1860) is at once a concert review and a polemical intervention in a public debate about aesthetics and politics. Yet it may also be read for its literary value and for what it suggests about the manifold relationships between music and literature, and between different artistic media (intermediality). The reader is thus invited to consider various questions. How important is it to understand the context of the so-called Wagner debate in reading Champfleury's nonfictional prose? How do Champfleury's formal and stylistic devices relate to Wagner's concert music and to Champfleury's experience of it? What is the role of experience, imagination and media in the task of aesthetic criticism more generally? And finally, how might we assess the historical and literary significance of Champfleury's remarkable pamphlet, especially as a historical precursor to pan-European literary Wagnerism?

Background

Wagner's impact on literature during the second half of the nineteenth century – and extending well into the twentieth – rendered him a phenomenon. During his lifetime he became one of the few composers to have an -ism appended to his name. Indeed, *Wagnérisme* (the French-language spelling is indicative) has been identified as an essentially literary phenomenon, despite the breadth of Wagner's influence on virtually all artistic fields. By the early 1850s Wagner had become a figure of intense interest for writers and intellectuals, not just for professional music critics.

To engage with Champfleury's contribution to the discussion, it is important to know something of Wagner's own background and reception. As late as 1860, Wagner's music was only rarely heard outside of German states, and what was performed was predominantly in the form of concert extracts. Hence, many of Wagner's Francophone commentators during the 1850s had minimal, if any, direct experience of his stage works. Instead, critics drew on his radical prose writings (such as *The Artwork of the Future* and *Opera and Drama*), the libretti or poems to his operas, and Franz Liszt's still more influential journalistic articles on Wagner's "Romantic" operas *Tannhäuser* and *Lohengrin*.[1] For his Francophone commentators, the music by Wagner they actually heard paled in comparison to the composer's seemingly high-flown claims about the "artwork of the future," and the gap between the two was a target for ridicule.

---

[1] Franz Liszt, *Lohengrin et Tannhaüser* [sic] *de Richard Wagner/Lohengrin und Tannhäuser von Richard Wagner* (Leipzig: F.A. Brockhaus, 1851).

CRITICAL DISLOCATIONS: CHAMPFLEURY'S *RICHARD WAGNER* (1860)

FIG. 9.1: Photographic portrait of Richard Wagner by Pierre Petit, 1861.

The 1860 Paris concerts had been intended as a promotional exercise towards a Paris production of Wagner's newly published drama *Tristan und Isolde*. Up to this point Wagner had been living as a political refugee from German states since his participation in the suppressed Dresden Uprising of May 1849. In the end, *Tannhäuser* was selected and ultimately presented in March 1861 at the Salle Le Peletier (home to the Paris Opéra) in French translation and with expanded scenes including a ballet. Around 1860, critical opinion about Wagner in the French press was becoming ever more polarized. But already in the early 1850s, the Belgian critic François-Joseph Fétis came out against Wagner's ideas in a series of seven articles published in the leading Parisian music periodical, and as Champfleury himself made plain, it was Fétis's invective that inspired Champfleury to rally to Wagner's defense.² Champfleury had been a supporter of Wagner since the latter's arrival in Paris in 1859 and was a regular visitor at Wagner's Wednesday soirées. He had declared his promise to "place [his] pen at [Wagner's] service" to defend the composer against any critical assaults at the 1860 concerts.³ In the event, he was true to his word.

What of Champfleury's previous experience of writing on music? The 1860 pamphlet on Wagner was a rare foray for Champfleury into music criticism, but music had been part of his literary activities in other ways. Besides being a competent amateur musician, he took an interest in the short stories and musical writings of the German novelist, critic and composer E.T.A. Hoffmann, going as far as to translate some of them into French.⁴ Reflecting his interest in rural peasant culture, he wrote extensively on the subject of French folk songs (*chansons populaires*),⁵ while several of his stories center on a musical object, for example "Grandeur et Décadence d'une Serinette" ["The Rise and Fall of a Serinette"] (1847) charts the social fortunes of a mechanical instrument.⁶

Notwithstanding his notable output as a novelist during the 1840s and 1850s, it was above all as an art critic and art historian that Champfleury made his name. He had been a prominent advocate of realism in both literature and painting, a term which gained currency in the wake of the 1848 Revolution especially around the artist Gustave Courbet, whom Champfleury championed in various writings. While realism in art and in literature – to give a broad definition – denoted an aesthetic position that claimed to represent reality regardless of prevailing aesthetic ideals of beauty, such as in the depiction of rural poverty, a key feature of Champfleury's realism was the concept of writerly "sincerity" [*sincérité*]: an open, honest rapport with the reader. In other words, the author's subjective response to the subject matter was for Champfleury

---

² François-Joseph Fétis, "Richard Wagner," *Revue et Gazette musicale de Paris* 19.23–32 (June 6 to August 8, 1852): 185–259; and Fétis, "Lettres aux compositeurs dramatiques," *Revue et Gazette musicale de Paris* 20.47–52 (November 20 to December 25, 1853): 403–46 and 21.2 (January 9, 1854): 9–12.

³ Quotation from Champfleury's 1861 sequel *After the Battle*, trans. Paves-Yashinsky in "*Richard Wagner* and *After the Battle*: Champfleury," *19th-Century Music* 13.1 (Summer 1989): 25.

⁴ Champfleury, "Hoffmann musicien," *Revue et Gazette musicale de Paris* 20.46–9 (November 13 to December 4, 1853): 395–423; and Champfleury, "Le Poëte et le Compositeur," *Revue et Gazette musicale de Paris* 21.23–8 (June 4 to July 9, 1854): 183–225.

⁵ Champfleury had written a pair of articles on French folk song in 1851, and in 1860 he contributed commentary to a book of folk songs collected and arranged with piano accompaniment by Jean-Baptiste Weckerlin.

⁶ A "serinette" is a kind of high-pitched barrel organ, so called because it was used to teach tunes to canaries (after the French for canary, *serin*). Champfleury, "Grandeur et Décadence d'une Serinette," *Pauvre trompette: Fantaisies de printemps* (Paris: Martinon, 1847) 47–106.

already enough to deem a work realist. The connections between artforms that Champfleury suggests in his Wagner pamphlet (literature, music, painting) raise questions of intermediality, that is, the possible translations of an affect or an idea between different artistic media. The entire Wagnerian literary discourse functioned as a site for discussion about such ideas as synesthesia[7] and the synthesis of the arts. Champfleury's comparisons between artforms thus anticipate developments (Symbolism, Aestheticism, Decadence, to name a few) both in French- and English-language fiction and criticism in the second half of the century.[8]

Case Study

Towards the start of the pamphlet [**Extract 1**], Champfleury relates some of the prejudices about Wagner that had been circulating in the Parisian press for the last decade. This includes Fétis's alleged criticism of Wagner as "the *Courbet* of music." In fact, it seems that Champfleury had unwittingly invented this quotation.[9] Nonetheless, the point remains that Champfleury had been a champion of Courbet and promoted him as a realist in defiance of the critical establishment during the 1850s. Now Champfleury found himself defending Wagner *against* comparison with Courbet as a realist.[10] On the one hand, this apparent change of position has to do with how he saw the essential differences between visual art and music; on the other, it reflects the ways in which "realist" could be deployed more as a vague term of insult than as a critically meaningful label.[11]

Champfleury apparently had difficulty imagining what a Courbet in music might be, although he later dismisses "*imitative music*" as an example of musical realism "in the worst sense of the word." If "*realism* in music" is "the monstrous overflowing of one art into another, the tainted mixture, as ambiguous

---

[7] The term generally refers to the physiological condition involving the experience of intersensory connections, such as when a person's response to hearing music is to see color.

[8] See, for example, Emma Sutton, *Aubrey Beardsley and British Wagnerism in the 1890s* (Oxford: Oxford University Press, 2002).

[9] Fétis mentions Courbet only once in his 1852–4 articles on Wagner. Fétis, "Lettres aux compositeurs dramatiques," *Revue et Gazette musicale de Paris* (November 20, 1853): 404. There is an allusion to Wagner in the same article (405), but Wagner is not identified by name ("l'auteur d'une nouvelle réforme qui préoccupe en ce moment l'Allemagne" [the author of a new [operatic] reform that has become a *cause célèbre* in Germany]). With thanks to Adeline Heck for help with this translation.

[10] Champfleury first mentioned Wagner in a letter to George Sand on Courbet, published in the journal *L'Artiste* (1855) and reprinted in his book *Le Réalisme* (Paris: Michel Lévy, 1857).

[11] See Jane Fulcher, "Wagner as Democrat and Realist in France," *Stanford French Review* (Spring 1981): 97–106; and James Garratt, "Inventing Realism: Dahlhaus, Geck, and the Unities of Discourse," *Music & Letters* 84.3 (August 2003): 456–68, especially 462.

as a bunch of grapes grafted onto a pear tree," he concludes that "Wagner in no way belongs to this school" (22–3; original emphasis). He disparages another phrase that Wagner's French critics had used against him: *la musique de l'avenir* [the music of the future]. And in response to yet another accusation from the anti-Wagner camp, he writes: "Lack of melodies, said the critics. Each fragment from each opera of Wagner is nothing but a vast melody, resembling the spectacle of the sea." [**Extract 2.**] As these examples suggest, it helps to know something of the (local) discursive context into which Champfleury's text was a deliberate intervention and rebuttal.

The last quotation is an example of Champfleury's use of figurative language, especially simile ("resembling the spectacle of the sea"). Comparisons associated with the sea recur at various points, to the extent that this repeated use of sea-related words (a lexical group) provides a cohesive strategy. For example, Champfleury refers to "musical waves newly revealed by a navigator," "the heaving ocean or the blue Mediterranean," "waves of sovereign harmony" [**Extract 2**], all of which make comparisons between Wagner's music and the sea. Champfleury avoids the term motif, let alone the Wagnerian term leitmotif,[12] but it could be argued that the repeated use of sea images provides a structural strategy in an analogous way to the function of recurring motifs in a musical form. Champfleury also uses imagery of the forest, connecting his interest in folklore and the bucolic with images in German Romanticism, allowing him to position Wagner's music as an escape from bourgeois convention ("the spirit leaves its little cardboard box [...] and seems to soar to the very top of tall trees"). At the same time, the idealist imagery of nature seems to distract from the socio-political concerns of Wagner's entire project and his concern with "revolution" (whether in politics or in art), an aspect of Wagner's self-presentation that Champfleury for the most part elides.

With such literary techniques, Champfleury's review stands out from most music criticism and analysis of the time (such as that of Fétis), which focused more on objective, technical features. Champfleury was clearly aware of the different discursive registers for writing about music and about listening: "I do not intend to furnish a conventional analysis of each of these fragments, but rather the sum of sensations which I received from the whole" (22); and later: "The task of speaking about sharps, flats, tonalities, ascending modulations, chromaticism, etc., should be left to the critics; what remains for me to say is more interesting" (23). This difference in literary approach also marks a shift from the analyst to the listener, and indeed from the professional critic to the

---

[12] Leitmotif: "A term used to identify the most important thematic materials in Wagner's later works which are associated with events, objects, feelings, and characters and which recur in varied forms, bringing an evolutionary continuity to the drama." Arnold Whittall, "Leitmotiv," *The Cambridge Wagner Encyclopedia* (Cambridge: Cambridge University Press, 2013) 245.

amateur. And yet the phrase "the sum of sensations which I received from the whole" implies that his experience of Wagner's concert music went beyond mere listening, as we shall see in more detail below.

"These are not merely turns of phrase," Champfleury comments immediately after the forest scene. "But how can one render, except through sensory analogies, the mystical language of intoxicating sounds?" [**Extract 2.**] If the "mystical language of intoxicating sounds" refers to Wagner's music, Champfleury admits that those sounds – or rather their subjective effect – need to be somehow translated via "sensory analogies." Compared with the sonorous poetry of French Symbolism which would follow within a decade or two, the apparent need to render musical sounds and feelings using analogy implies a certain violence of translation, specifically "intersemiotic translation" to adopt Roman Jakobson's term for "an interpretation of verbal signs by means of signs of nonverbal sign systems."[13]

Champfleury's entire pamphlet aims to do just this, to convey something of his experience of Wagner's concert music while at the same time denoting the limits, and the artifice, of such description. He repeatedly foregrounds his own ignorance, memory lapses and musical dilettantism, to establish a frank rapport with the reader and to register the *sincérité*, the genuineness, of his response. Champfleury's pamphlet took up the task of music criticism in a subjective, sometimes openly autobiographical manner, which he expresses more as a prose poem than a technical analysis. He also makes use throughout of the first-person voice – a feature that Charles Baudelaire openly adopted and discussed at the opening to his own 1861 article on Wagner's concerts, also titled "Richard Wagner," and soon thereafter expanded and republished as "Richard Wagner and *Tannhäuser* in Paris."[14]

Fragments

Champfleury referred to Wagner's concert excerpts consistently as "fragments," using the standard French term. [**Extracts 1–3.**] The program consisted of orchestral numbers, many of them with chorus, from Wagner's operas *Der fliegende Holländer*, *Tannhäuser*, *Lohengrin* and the Act 1 Prelude to his new work *Tristan und Isolde*.[15] Formally like the object it describes, Champfleury's

---

[13] Roman Jakobson, "On Linguistic Aspects of Translation," *Translation*, ed. R.A. Brower (Cambridge, Massachusetts: Harvard University Press, 1959) 233.
[14] Charles Baudelaire, "Richard Wagner," *Revue européenne* (April 1, 1861): 460–85. For an English translation of the expanded version of the article, see Baudelaire, "Richard Wagner and *Tannhäuser* in Paris," *The Painter of Modern Life and Other Essays*, trans. and ed. Jonathan Mayne (London: Phaidon, 1964) 111–46.
[15] For an insight, listen to *Wagner: Orchestral Highlights from Operas*, The Slovak Philharmonic Orchestra, Michael Halász, Naxos, 1988. This album features many of the same orchestral pieces as were included in the Paris concert program on January

pamphlet is presented as a series of short sections of text, each one separated by a horizontal dash.[16] Some of these textual chunks are as short as a single sentence, and it is for this reason – and the fact that frequently each sentence takes a new line – that the pamphlet may be described as a prose poem; it plays with lineation. The genre of prose poem was famously used by Baudelaire, but also by Champfleury himself in other writings, and even in his manifesto *Le Réalisme* which resembles the publication of *Richard Wagner* in terms of layout.[17] Yet the text's organization as a loose collection of partially dislocated thoughts can also be understood in the context of German literary Romanticism according to which the "fragment" (related to, but distinct from, the rhetorical device of aphorism) held critical and philosophical value as a form in its own right not only in literature, but also across the arts.[18]

The analogy between music and painting ("One can cut out a portion from each of [Courbet's] canvasses [*sic*], and it remains a painting" [20]), which was after all Champfleury's critical milieu, helps to make the point that Wagner's concert numbers stand sufficiently well on their own, independent from their original dramatic context. This is what Liszt had argued in the expanded, book version of his article on *Tannhäuser*. But in contrast to the high register or diction (formality) of Liszt's paean, Champfleury resorts to the somewhat violent image of "tearing" to describe Wagner's concert extracts: "The three current concerts which will be given in succession are only pages torn from great poems already familiar" (25). In another version of the same image, the author admits that he is familiar with "neither the subject of [Wagner's] operas nor the splendid fabric which clothes them" and that he has seen only "bits of this fabric." Champfleury continues: "It seems as if a fragment of medieval tapestry suddenly falls before my eyes" (23). Here the image of the tapestry fragment is being equated to the extraction of a piece from a larger whole, although the image of tearing or ripping is less obvious. At the same time

---

25, 1860 (such as the *Lohengrin* Act 1 Prelude). It is something like an equivalent to the nineteenth-century concert of operatic excerpts.

[16] The use of lines between sections is present in the original 1860 French-language publication and is retained in Paves-Yashinsky's English translation.

[17] Sara Pappas describes Champfleury's *Le Réalisme* as a "loose collection of letters, primary sources, and essays with a reticent preface and no conclusion" and as a "scattered edifice." Sara Pappas, "The Lessons of Champfleury," *Nineteenth-Century French Studies* 42.1–2 (Fall–Winter 2013–14): 64. For background on prose poetry, see Steven Monte, *Invisible Fences: Prose Poetry as a Genre in French and American Literature* (Lincoln: University of Nebraska Press, 2000) 59–60.

[18] For a philosophical study of German Romantic literature, particularly the Jena Set, see Philippe Lacoue-Labarthe and Jean-Luc Nancy, *The Literary Absolute: The Theory of Literature in German Romanticism*, trans. Philip Barnard and Cheryl Lester (Albany: State University of New York Press, 1988). On the influence of the Romantic fragment on composers of the early nineteenth century, see Charles Rosen, *The Romantic Generation* (Cambridge, Massachusetts: Harvard University Press, 1995).

the image represents for Champfleury the enchanting theatrical scenography ("the splendid fabric which clothes [the subject of Wagner's operas]") that had been omitted in the concert performance and at which the titles and program merely hinted.

Curiously, Champfleury draws upon the same imagery (the tearing of fabric, the fragment from a larger artwork) to characterize the anti-Wagner protests voiced by a handful of critics in the foyer during the interval: "There were few enough to be counted, and they spoke with the grimaces and anger of monkeys who, being shown a beautiful fabric, would tear it into a thousand pieces" (23). Thus, the same image is used within a few paragraphs for positive and negative ends. One explanation is that Champfleury was aware of the practical necessity of concert presentation given Wagner's circumstances (being a political exile among other things). But the description of Wagner's music as a beautiful piece of tapestry emphasizes the self-sufficiency of these concert extracts from the larger whole. On a different level of extraction, Wagner himself liked to present the poems to his dramas, for example *Der Ring des Nibelungen*, as texts for reading and recitation in their own right.[19]

The diffuseness of Champfleury's text – passages of uneven length which refuse seamless connection – is also a formal device that conveys the sheer immediacy that apparently characterized his experience of Wagner's music. That experience relied on a mode of concert presentation whereby Wagner's operatic fragments were not only extracted from a larger whole, but also divested of their true theatrical and dramatic context. The absence of theater by no means stunted Champfleury's poetic imagination, but on the contrary left open a metaphorical space, by turns discursive and psychological, in which his imagination could take flight. The breathless urgency of his prose poetry, seemingly in tension with the absence of a "total" theatrical artwork, actually emerges from his escape, instead, into imaginary encounters and autobiographical reveries – aspects that would forever characterize French literary Wagnerism.

Immediacy

To pursue further ideas of immediacy and presence, what might we make of Champfleury's allusions to nineteenth-century mass media and technology? With the image of the new electric telegraph and its military deployment, Champfleury satirizes reactionary, anti-Wagnerian fear-mongering ("telegraphs carrying the commands of the conductor to other assistant conductors in other halls and to the cellar and to the attic" [22]), and views live performances as a testing ground for composers ("the electric shivers which run through an entire audience" [25]). In a more serious sense, Champfleury's opening comments on

---

[19] Richard Wagner, *The Ring of the Nibelung*, trans. and ed. John Deathridge (London: Penguin, 2018) xvi–xx.

his own literary outpourings allude to ideas of almost mesmeric presence: he was "impatient to cry out the truth, and unable to escape the tyranny of the thought which sends to my mind complete sentences about the work of Richard Wagner and which dictates the quivering lines that follow, scarcely allowing time for my pen to trace them" (20). This striking image suggests something of automatic writing, even anticipating the interpretation of that idea by the surrealists. So overwhelming is Wagner's music, for Champfleury, that it converts spontaneously into written language, hence the immediate translation from one medium to another which almost bypasses rational thought or causal mechanism, as if under a magical spell of pure thought and feeling.

According to Paves-Yashinsky, translator of Champfleury's pamphlet, the pamphlet "records Champfleury's spontaneous and unrestrained enthusiasm for the music of Wagner."[20] But how "spontaneous and unrestrained" was it really? "At the Théâtre des Italiens, I refused to read the libretto," he declares: "above all, I was thirsty for *music*; the *drama* would have distracted me. A concert is not a theatrical performance; the true musicians know no other language than the language of sound, and the printed word has no business in front of an orchestra" (23; original emphasis). Yet he does not conceal the fact elsewhere that his experience and interpretation of Wagner's concert music had been informed by literary texts of various kinds, providing a useful anchor amidst a potentially disorientating musical experience. For instance, Champfleury quotes from Wagner's program note to the *Lohengrin* Act 1 Prelude,[21] commenting: "Let those who have a poetic spirit reread these lines and deck them with melodies, and they will be able to have an imaginary idea of the profound musical feeling of the Holy Grail." [**Extract 3.**] The composer's program note in turn brought the Brothers Grimm fairy tales to the mind of Champfleury, who proceeds to quote from the Grimm tale "Lohengrin de Brabant" in French translation.[22]

As these and further examples suggest, Champfleury's music criticism blends together sensory impressions from different media, not merely to compensate for the absence of theatrical performance, but also to help him articulate thoughts and feelings that emerged as if spontaneously from the experience of musical listening. There is something ambiguous and unresolved – or perhaps consciously playful – in Champfleury's hesitation between a kind of pure, immediate experience of Wagner's music and a literary translation of that

---

[20] Champfleury, trans. Paves-Yashinsky, "*Richard Wagner* and *After the Battle*: Champfleury," 19.

[21] See [Richard Wagner], *Concert de Richard Wagner* (Paris: Aubusson et Kugelmann, 1860) 11–12. Baudelaire quotes the same passage in his 1861 article "Richard Wagner."

[22] See [Les Frères] Grimm, *Les Veillées allemandes: chroniques, contes, traditions et croyances populaires. Nouvelle traduction* [par Napoléon Theil] *précédée d'une introduction par L'Héritier (de l'Ain)*, vol. 2 (Paris: Huzard, 1838) 367.

experience. In the end, the ideal otherworldliness of Wagner's concert music itself turns out to be a programmatic feature of the music – one that Champfleury thematizes in affective, spatial and geographical terms.

Listening

Wagner: Orchestral Highlights from Operas. The Slovak Philharmonic Orchestra, Michael Halász. Naxos, 1988.

Further Reading

Acquisto, Joseph. *French Symbolist Poetry and the Idea of Music*. Aldershot: Ashgate, 2006.
Baudelaire, Charles. "Richard Wagner and *Tannhäuser* in Paris." *The Painter of Modern Life and Other Essays*. Trans. and ed. Jonathan Mayne. London: Phaidon, 1964. 111–46.
Coleman, Jeremy. *Richard Wagner in Paris: Translation, Identity, Modernity*. Woodbridge: The Boydell Press, 2019.
Deathridge, John. *Wagner Beyond Good and Evil*. Berkeley: University of California Press, 2008.
Dolan, Therese. *Manet, Wagner, and the Musical Culture of Their Time*. Farnham: Ashgate, 2013.
Ellis, Katharine. "Wagnerism and Anti-Wagnerism in the Paris Periodical Press, 1852–1870." *Von Wagner zum Wagnérisme: Musik, Literatur, Kunst, Politik*. Eds Annegret Fauser and Manuela Schwartz. Leipzig: Leipziger Universitätsverlag, 1999. 51–83.
Kieffer, Alexandra. *Debussy's Critics: Sound, Affect, and the Experience of Modernism*. Oxford: Oxford University Press, 2019.
Turbow, Gerald D. "Art and Politics: Wagnerism in France." *Wagnerism in European Culture and Politics*. Eds David C. Large and William Weber, in collaboration with Anne Dzamba Sessa. Ithaca: Cornell University Press, 1984. 134–66.

CHAPTER 10

Locating Elgar: Nationalism, Landscape and Musical Biography

Daniel M. Grimley

Recommended Text

[F.G. Edwards], "Edward Elgar," *The Musical Times and Singing-Class Circular* 41.692 (October 1, 1900): 641–8. Available at *JSTOR*, <https://www.jstor.org/stable/i237436> [Accessed November 1, 2024]. All subsequent references, in parentheses, are to this essay.

Keywords

Colonialism, cultural geography, Edward Elgar, empire, Englishness, landscape, music criticism, nationalism, John Henry Newman, nonfiction, periodicals, poems, reception history, twentieth century

Prelude

Extract 1[1]

[F.G. Edwards], "Edward Elgar," 641.

> In a somer seson · whan soft was the sonne,
> I shope me in shroudes · as I a shepe were,
> In habite as an heremite · vnholy of workes,
> Went wyde in þis world · wondres to here.
> Ac on a May mornynge · on Maluerne hulles
> Me byfel a ferly · of fairy, me-thoute.[2]
>
> Langland's, "*Piers the Plowman.*" ([c.1370], lines 1–6)

---

[1] The essay begins with two short quotations from poems by William Langland and Elizabeth Barrett Browning. The orthography here is exactly as printed in *The Musical Times*.

[2] "In a somer seson": In the summer; "whan soft": when soft; "shope me in shroudes": to don clothes or assume a disguise; "as I a shepe were": as though I were a sheep (or sheep-like in appearance); "In habite as an heremite": in the manner of a hermit (habite: clerical habit or clothing); "vnholy of workes": secular rather than sacred; "wyde in þis world": wide (i.e., travelled) throughout the world; "wondres to here": wonders to hear; "Ac on a May mornynge": ah, on a May morning; "on Maluerne

> While beyond, above them mounted,
>   And above their woods also,
> Malvern hills, for mountains counted
>   Not unduly, loom a-row –
> Keepers of Piers Plowman's visions, through the
>   sunshine and the snow.
>   Elizabeth Barrett Browning. ("The Lost Bower" [1844], IX.41–5)

The Malvern uplands are to be seen, not described. No appreciative mind can fail to be impressed with the bold outline, the imposing abruptness, and the verdant loveliness of these everlasting hills. Nature has left the impress of her smile on this favoured region, and hill and valley combine to produce a landscape of fascinating picturesqueness. It is a steep climb to the hilltop above Malvern Wells, but it more than repays the wayfarer who has eyes to behold and a soul to satisfy. The enjoyment of a quiet stroll along these grassy heights is greatly enhanced by the companionship of one who habitually thinks his thoughts and draws his inspirations from these elevated surroundings. He points out a noble peak once the site of a Roman encampment, and as he tells you that its thereabouts is traditionally associated with Caractacus you instinctively think, "and thereby hangs a tale" – if not a cantata. Not far off is Wind's Point, the charming retreat of Jenny Lind, where the great singer drew her last breath. In descending from the summit, on the Worcestershire side, an exceedingly pleasant detached house is reached. It stands on the steep hillside, and from the little terrace in front of the house the view is as beautiful as its range is extensive. It begins and ends with two cities so long associated with the Three Choirs Festival – Worcester on the left, Gloucester on the right. Between these extremes, through which the Severn flows its tranquil course, lies the vale of Evesham, where Muzio Clementi, "the father of modern piano-forte playing," had his cottage and where he died. The venerable Abbey of Tewkesbury comes within the range of vision, and, on a clear day, even the historic battle-field of Edge Hill, although forty miles distant. Here, in the midst of these delightful Malvern surroundings – how welcome their tranquillity – is located the home of him whom forms the subject of this biographical sketch.

Edward William Elgar was born at Broadheath, four miles from Worcester, June 2, 1857. His patronymic is of Saxon origin, and may be found as Aelfgar, which being interpreted means "fairy spear." He is the eldest son of Mr W.H. Elgar, of Worcester, and of Ann Greening, descended from a fine old yeoman stock of Weston, Herefordshire, and therefore intensely English.

---

hulles": on the Malvern hills; "Me byfel a ferly · of fairy": I experienced a marvel (or wondrous fantasy) created or conjured up by fairies; "me-thoute": I imagined or believed, as though experiencing a vision or dream.

Extract 2

[Edwards], "Edward Elgar," 646.

Personalia

It is now time to refer to the personality of the subject of this biographical sketch, though this is not an easy matter through the medium of cold type. In the first place, Mr Elgar is another instance of success following upon self-help of which so many examples have been furnished in this series of biographical sketches during the last three years. With the exception of those violin lessons from Mr Pollitzer, Mr Elgar is entirely self-taught. He has spared no pains, energy, or trouble in the acquirement of the necessary equipment for his life-work. For instance, in his youthful days he would leave his home at Worcester at six o'clock in the morning, and travel all the way to London, a distance of 250 miles, in order to listen to a Crystal Palace Saturday concert, returning at 10:30 p.m.

Extract 3

[Edwards], "Edward Elgar," 648.

"The Dream of Gerontius"

Before bidding adieu to one of the foremost of British composers of the present day, it is only natural that some information should be sought from him on the subject of his latest work, "The Dream of Gerontius," which is so soon to be produced at the Birmingham Festival. "This is the beginning of it," he says, as he hands us a little copy of Newman's famous poem. "The book was a wedding present to me (in 1889) from the late Father Knight, of Worcester, at whose church I was organist. Before giving it to me he copied into its pages every mark inserted by General Gordon into his (Gordon's) copy, so that I have the advantage of knowing those portions of the poem that had specially attracted the attention of the great hero. It seems absurd to say I have written the work to order for Birmingham. The poem has been soaking in my mind for at least eight years. All that time I have been gradually assimilating the thoughts of the author into my own musical promptings."

It is in this spirit that Edward Elgar conscientiously follows the bent of his genius. A man of high ideals, the possessor of a fine artistic temperament, and an intensely poetical musician, he is known and respected for his kind-heartedness, his modesty, his sincerity, and his steadfastness of purpose. He has already achieved great things in the realm of art and has come into the front rank of English composers.

The Challenge

This chapter focuses on three short extracts from a biographical essay on Edward Elgar (1857–1934), written by the music critic F.G. Edwards and published in *The Musical Times and Singing-Class Circular* in 1900. Elgar is now widely celebrated as one of the most significant figures in English music, but his biography and musical background reveal more complicated issues of social class, religious faith, commercial interest and political affiliation. The challenge lies in understanding how a piece of biographical musical criticism can be understood as a literary text. Edwards's essay is a particularly fascinating case study because of the way it adopts specific literary techniques to create an imaginative framework for contextualizing Elgar and his music. These techniques include the quotation at the head of the essay from two earlier poems, by William Langland (1332–86) and Elizabeth Barrett Browning (1806–61), closely associated with the district (the Malvern Hills in the west of England) where Elgar lived and worked. Edwards's essay further dwells on picturesque notions of landscape and place, the sonorous qualities of the region, constructions of Englishness and national character, and also the complex legacies of empire. These latter issues are referenced through the association between Elgar's latest composition, the oratorio *The Dream of Gerontius* (1900), based on John Henry Newman's poem, and the fate of General Charles George Gordon, who commanded an imperial British force at Khartoum in the Sudan.

Background

The Musical Times and Singing-Class Circular was first printed in London in 1844 and rapidly became one of the most widely circulated music publications of its kind. Edwards's unsigned essay, published as the feature article in the October 1, 1900 issue of the journal, was one of the earliest accounts of Elgar's childhood and musical development, and sought to present the composer as an authentically English figure for a potentially skeptical readership.[3] The article closely followed the breakthrough success in 1899 of Elgar's *Variations on an Original Theme* ("Enigma"), Op. 36, and anticipated the premiere of his ground-breaking setting of Newman's poem at the Birmingham Festival. Edwards's article takes the form of a report following a visit to the composer's residence (a house named Craeg Lea – an anagram of his wife's name, C[aroline] A[lice] Elgar – on the hillside above Great Malvern), and follows a particular pattern of literary allusion, both through direct quotation (the two

---

[3] F.G. Edwards was editor of the journal from 1897 until his death on November 28, 1909. Born in London on October 11, 1853, he studied at the Royal Academy of Music and trained as a church organist. His first article for *The Musical Times*, on Felix Mendelssohn's popular anthem "Hear my prayer" (Psalm LV), was printed in 1891.

epigraphs which precede the main text) and indirect reference (namely, the influence of those two poems upon the specific details of Edwards's argument, and the musical qualities of the poetic texts themselves).

Edwards's introduction pointedly locates Elgar, geographically and aesthetically, within a long-standing sphere of English artistic and literary activity. **Extract 1** provides a framework for mapping Elgar's creative biography with reference to local historical events, institutions and topographic features in the landscape, alongside visionary notions of creative inspiration (Piers Plowman, Gerontius, and the "dream hall" of Barrett Browning's verse). [**Fig. 10.1.**] Edwards's reference to the historical figure of Caractacus, whose last defense against the invading Roman legions was believed to have taken place from the nearby summit of the Herefordshire Beacon, was also a reference to Elgar's recent 1898 cantata on the subject, written for the Leeds Festival with a libretto by a former member of the Indian Civil Service and local Malvern antiquarian, H.A. Acworth. Edwards further underscores Elgar's Englishness with reference to his parents' genealogy: his father's surname is given an Anglo-Saxon (rather than Anglo-Norman) etymology, and his mother is described as coming from "fine old yeoman stock of Weston, Herefordshire, and therefore intensely English."

Edwards's account also stresses Elgar's unprivileged background [**Extract 2**] in a manner that further emphasizes notions of autonomy and self-reliance. Elgar's father owned a music shop in Worcester, and the family therefore belonged to a modest professional trading class. Rather than being presented as a form of social disadvantage, Edwards turns this into a positive asset: Elgar's earliest musical experiences were gained from his involvement in a local "Glee club" (an amateur social music group whose members met informally to perform arrangements of dance tunes, popular songs and favorite movements from symphonies and oratorios) and through his role as organist at St George's Catholic church in Worcester. Elgar was himself a Roman Catholic, at a time when Catholics still experienced discrimination and bias on the grounds of their faith. Edwards presents Elgar's circumstances as a strength, fostering an image of creative fortitude through isolation rather than reliance on continental European professional training, which was the familiar trajectory for many of Elgar's contemporaries. The end of the extract emphasizes lingering tensions of center and periphery, Elgar's occasional journeys to London to attend the Crystal Palace concerts signaling both regional connectivity and the economic and political dominance of the metropolitan capital.

Extract 3 follows a lengthy survey of Elgar's music to date, up to and including the "Enigma" Variations, and concerns work on his Birmingham Festival commission. Elgar's choice of subject was controversial: Newman had been a leading figure in the Oxford movement (which advocated for a more hierarchical form of Anglo-Catholic ritual within the Anglican church) and eventually converted to Roman Catholicism in 1845, founding the Birmingham Oratory –

a Catholic religious community and church – four years later. His powerfully aestheticized poem, *The Dream of Gerontius* (1865), concerns the dying soul's journey toward purgatory and his fleeting encounter with God. Elgar's copy of the poem included transcriptions of General Gordon's annotations on *The Dream of Gerontius*, retrieved after Gordon's death during his unsuccessful evacuation of British-led Egyptian troops from the Siege of Khartoum in 1885.[4] Elgar's reading of Newman's poem through the prism of Gordon's response underlines the entanglement of religious belief, sectarianism, race and British imperial thought. That is, it illustrates how highly essentialized constructions of heroism, territorial conquest, military service and faith could be mediated through a literary text as the basis for musical treatment. Elgar's oratorio eschews overt expressions of militarism (unlike, for instance, *Caractacus*, or his *Pomp and Circumstance March* no. 1 of 1901), and instead focuses on human mortality and divine revelation. Gordon's annotations similarly stressed Newman's preoccupation with intercession ("So pray for me, my friends, who have not strength to pray"), humility ("Be merciful, be gracious; spare him, Lord"), blessed release ("Into thy hands, O Lord"; "I hear no more the busy beat of time, / No, nor my fluttering breath, nor struggling pulse;") and duty ("My work is done, / My task is o'er"). What Elgar appears to have drawn most clearly from Gordon's reading of Newman's poem is an emphasis on the soul's ennoblement through suffering and its relief from worldly care and sorrow.

Case Study

Music, Writing and the Nature of Landscape

A key feature of Edwards's essay is the association between Elgar's music and images of landscape and environment, a trope that has remained highly influential in the composer's reception. Elgar himself frequently invoked such associations in his letters and correspondence, referring for example to his childhood musical inspiration "in the reeds by Severn side," and writing to his publisher in July 1900: "the trees are singing my music – or have I sung

---

[4] Jerrold Northrop Moore, *Edward Elgar: A Creative Life* (Oxford: Oxford University Press, 1984) 119–20. Gordon had given his copy of Newman's poem to a journalist for *The Times* newspaper in London, Frank Power, in Khartoum on February 18, 1884. Power was killed as he returned from the Sudan but had already sent the book to his sister in Dublin, who forwarded it to Newman. Copies of the book with Gordon's annotations were subsequently circulated privately, with recipients including Prime Minister William Gladstone (whose government had posted Gordon to Khartoum), and the volume was reasonably well known by the time Elgar was working on his oratorio. Gordon's original copy, as passed on by Power, is now in the British Library (system no. 013075413).

FIG. 10.1: Henry Guy, "Malvern: View from the Worcestershire Beacon Looking South," color lithograph (c.1880).

theirs?"⁵ Edwards's article draws heavily on literary traditions of nature writing and pictorial forms of representation. Such patterns of association are never neutral or coincidental. Rather, they rely upon a series of assumptions concerning definitions of landscape, literature and music, and the precise quality of their interrelationship. The first assumption is the supposed naturalness of landscape itself: the idea of "nature" as a pure or unsullied medium that invites and benevolently rewards human oversight and habitation. This is the frame for Barrett Browning's "Lost Bower," quoted at the head of Edwards's essay, which situates its female subject within an ecologically rich woodland glade with its green hazels, grazing sheep and apple blossom (IV, VII, II): a site modeled on the poet's own childhood home at Hope End House near Colwall on the Herefordshire side of the Malverns.

The first paragraph of Edwards's account, however, signals the partiality of such an approach: aesthetic contemplation of landscape in fact relies on a highly selective process of scenic prospect, common in nineteenth-century topographic illustrations and panoramas, in which certain details are highlighted at the expense of others. [**Fig. 10.1.**] The opening lines of Edwards's text provide an indicative threshold for this act of survey and representation: the injunction to see rather than merely describe the hills, the "bold outline," and "imposing abruptness" of their appearance, rising suddenly out of the Severn valley on the Worcestershire side of the range, and the "verdant loveliness" of the environment. [**Extract 1.**] These qualities appeal to a particularly privileged observer, the idealized figure of the "wayfarer who has eyes to behold and a soul to satisfy," and who benefits from leisure time that enables the observer to gain the "enjoyment of a quiet stroll along these grassy heights." In other words, Edwards's opening description is a form of elevation or preluding, evoking a heightened state of aesthetic experience, similar to the vision of Piers Plowman and the nature epiphany described by Barrett Browning, that in turn also implies distinctive hierarchies of class and social distinction.

What is absent from his account is any significant trace of modern life: railways, roads, factory buildings, terraced housing or other material signs of urban development. The sites to which the reader's attention is drawn are exclusively ancient and historical: the earthwork encampment on the Herefordshire Beacon, the cathedrals at Worcester and Gloucester, the battlefield at Tewkesbury which was a scene of conflict during the Wars of the Roses in 1471, and a later battlefield (during the English Civil War) at Edgehill on the Warwickshire–Oxfordshire border. Even the paternalistic reference to Muzio

---

⁵ Respectively, letter to Sidney Colvin, December 13, 1921, quoted in *Edward Elgar: Letters of a Lifetime*, ed. Jerrold Northrop Moore (Rickmansworth: Elgar Works, 2012) 403; and letter to August Jaeger dated July 11, 1900, quoted in *Elgar and his Publishers: Letters of a Creative Life*, vol. 1, ed. Jerrold Northrop Moore (Oxford: Clarendon Press, 1987) 212.

Clementi (1752–1832) as the "'father of modern piano-forte playing'" has a quaintly antique flavor for an article published in 1900. Presenting Elgar in such surroundings is a form of naturalization, as well as a civilizing impulse, locating him and his creative work within a highly ideological construction of the English landscape: predominantly rural, scenic, and marked by specific points of historic and topographic significance and their literary instantiations.

Landscape, Class and Privilege

This naturalization points toward a second basic assumption, namely the tension between the idea of landscape as a recreational domain for a privileged upper-middle-class elite (a class to which Elgar's own family did not, economically or professionally, belong), versus the landscape as a creative resource and a space for aesthetic freedom. The town of Malvern, seeking to draw upon the nineteenth-century popularity for spa resorts and health cures, styled itself as a location ideally suited to support the needs of a particular socio-cultural group. Edwards's article hence builds upon a pre-existing body of tourist publications designed to extoll the health-giving virtues and benefits of the location. *The Borough Guide to Malvern*, for example, observes how the town "appeals to three distinct types of humanity – to the invalid, to the holiday-maker, to the resident. [...] Pure air, pure water, and an equitable temperature – these are the three primary things that account for Malvern's healthfulness."[6] Maintaining this level of amenity and provision became a key civic priority. The creation of a local conservation group, the Malvern Hills Preservation Society, in 1876, was followed by the completion in 1884 of the town's Assembly Rooms and Pleasure Gardens, laid out on a site below the abbey church and close to the town's elegant villas and private schools. The Assembly Rooms comprised a purpose-built theater that hosted visiting artists and musicians, including the D'Oyly Carte Opera Company, which catered to the tastes of a community of music-lovers and amateur players who provided a potential source of teaching income for Elgar in the years before his compositional career gained momentum.

The utilitarian conception of the landscape in and around Malvern as a commodious site of consumption for the leisured Victorian middle classes relies also upon a subtly different understanding of the town's significance as a cultural and creative space. The two poetic epigraphs placed at the head of Edwards's essay exemplify this strand of reception. [**Extract 1.**] Langland's poem opens with a feeling of other-worldliness, of the Malvern Hills as the scene of an ecstatic vision and possession by some form of creative spirit: the entrance to a so-called faery-land. Barrett Browning's invocation of Piers Plowman's vision in turn references this same idea of enchantment, the hills' sense

---

[6] E.J. Burrow, *The Borough Pocket Guide to Malvern* (Cheltenham: Burrow, 1905) 24.

of scale and proportion ("for mountains counted / Not unduly") transformed to suggest a cradling frame and also a weight of aesthetic presence ("Keepers of Piers Plowman's visions"). If Langland's *Vision* is essentially allegorical, Barrett Browning's poem is more concerned with remembrance and recollection, and a Miltonic awareness of a landscape lost and imaginatively regained. Elsewhere in her poem, Barrett Browning dwells on both the quietude of the environment – the hills watching "in choral silence" (35) and the "chair of silence very rare and absolute" (130) in which the child-narrator finds herself – and also on the revelation of a magical fairy music ("which was rather felt than heard," 175) that prompts an intimation of the divine ("Mystic Presences of power," 219).[7] The deliberate blurring of temporal boundaries, between waking and forgetfulness, mediates this shift of register from the quotidian reality of the everyday (walking on the hills above Malvern) to a heightened realm of poetic encounter in which local landmarks gain a renewed intensity.

This strategy of intensification is common to other closely contemporary creative responses to the area, for instance in the poetry of John Masefield, A.E. Housman and, later, Ivor Gurney. It is alluded to indirectly in Edwards's highly fanciful etymological derivation of the composer's surname, "Aelfgar" ("fairy spear"), symbolizing an individual who is especially susceptible to vision and enchantment, again referencing both Langland's and Barrett Browning's texts. [Extract 1.] Such images rely in turn on a familiar nineteenth-century construction of the Malvern district as historically contested ground, a borderland or frontier between different worldviews and cultural systems. R.N. Worth's *Tourist's Guide to Worcestershire*, published in 1889, for example, referred not only to the invading Romans, who "either founded or appropriated the city of Worcester as a frontier town, at the time of their defeat of the Silures, who held the Malvern Chain as their great bulwark," once more invoking metaphors of imperial conquest and local resistance, but also claimed that "Keltic [sic] traces are most common near the Malverns, which retained much of a frontier character when the lowlands had long been in Saxon hands."[8] The political status of the hills as a boundary is reinforced by their geological significance, marking a sudden transition between the younger, largely sedimentary rocks of the south-east of England and the harder, older, more crystalline series characteristic of Wales and the north-west. Such differences are accentuated by the weather: the hillier upland areas west of the Severn are more exposed to Atlantic low-pressure systems and the changeable oceanic patterns of the Gulf

---

[7] Elizabeth Barrett Browning, "The Lost Bower," *Poems* (continued), vol. 2 of *The Works of Elizabeth Barrett Browning*, eds Marjorie Stone and Beverly Taylor (London: Pickering & Chatto, 2010) 172, 175–6, 178. The in-text parentheses reference the line numbers in this edition.

[8] Richard Nicholls Worth, *A Tourist's Guide to Worcestershire* (London: Stanford, 1889) 3 and 6.

Stream than the more sheltered country to the east. The simple north–south alignment of the range also provides a particular affective charge: Housman, among others, was moved by the light of the sun setting behind the mountains on the Welsh border to the west, inspiring the wistful evocation of that landscape in the verses of *A Shropshire Lad* (1896). This collection later became the basis for settings by composers such as Arthur Somervell, George Butterworth and Ralph Vaughan Williams, who were especially drawn to the programmatic description of the area in poems such as "On Bredon Hill" and "In Valleys of Springs and Rivers" (which Vaughan Williams titled "Clun") – ballads that gather images of young love, natural beauty and mortality.

The spirit of place that animates Housman's poetry is no less prominent in aspects of Elgar's critical reception. One of the most emotionally charged examples of this association of his work with landscape and nostalgia is an entirely fictional sequence in Ken Russell's biographical documentary *Elgar*, filmed in 1962 for BBC Television's *Monitor* series, which depicts the composer as a young boy riding bareback over the Malvern Hills to the accompaniment of the *Introduction and Allegro* for strings, Op. 47. In strictly historical terms, Russell's choice of score is unjustified: the *Introduction and Allegro* was in fact written in late 1904–early 1905 for the London Symphony Orchestra, after Elgar had left Malvern and was resident in Hereford, and it was initially inspired by a performance of Bach's Brandenburg Concerto no. 3 which Elgar attended at the Lower Rhine Festival in Germany. But the treatment of the so-called "Welsh tune" which constitutes the second subject group in the main part of the work, first heard on the solo viola within the heart of the ensemble and then taken up gradually by the rest of the group, points back toward the idea of landscape. In his program note for the work's premiere on March 8, 1905, Elgar described how the tune was supposedly inspired by the sound of distant singing, overheard "on the cliff, between blue sea and blue sky" during a walking holiday in Cardiganshire on the Welsh coast, and recalled again "far down our valley of the Wye."[9] Elgar suggested that "the work is really a tribute to that sweet borderland where I have made my home," a reading applicable just as much to Malvern as to Herefordshire and the Wye Valley.[10]

Various commentators have focused on the symbolism of that passage and Elgar's meta-textual account of its source. James Hepokoski, for example, has associated the gesture with the tropes of "loss, distance, and yearning" that pervade much of Elgar's music more broadly, translated into an acute awareness of the "loss of the once-whole security of the past, both personal

---

[9] Daniel M. Grimley, "'A sighing with a sigh': The Chamber Music and Works for Strings," *The Cambridge Companion to Elgar*, eds Daniel M. Grimley and Julian Rushton (Cambridge: Cambridge University Press, 2004) 124–5.

[10] Ibid., 125.

and historical."[11] Matthew Riley, meanwhile, describes how, at such points in Elgar's work, "a sense that 'reality' – determined by the conventional frame and form of a movement – gives way, in a sudden moment of transformation, to a magical 'inner' world of pastoral simplicity, childlike innocence, or imaginative vision."[12] Here lies the link between Elgar's work and the enchanted (or figuratively re-sung) vision of the countryside in *Piers Plowman*, through the articulation of such passages that seemingly change both the material body of the listener and their state of mind. As Riley concludes, such "'thresholds' (the word used by the guardian angel in *Gerontius*) – are usually the places where the imitation of natural sounds is heard."[13] It is the point where the landscape seemingly breaks through.

Landscape hence serves as a form of biographical writing: not merely a means of describing the location for the creation of specific works of art but, more deeply, a way of reinscribing and embodying a heightened moment of creative encounter. Landscape thus becomes a shorthand for situating that highly transient, mobile act of embodiment and performance, a process which Edwards's essay attempts to capture in more formalized and conventional terms, just as it frames Langland's and Barrett Browning's work. From a postcolonial perspective, however, it is possible to advance a more troubling reading, namely that it is precisely through the exoticization of particular landscapes and their aesthetic character (whether the Welsh mountains or remoter shores) that a particular form of imperial vision can emerge. According to this imperial gaze, landscape by definition presupposes a seemingly natural order of things, places, peoples, memories and historical events. Its geological layers become a form of political organization and social distinction; it grounds difference. Landscape's full meaning is available only to those fortunate enough to be able to prospect and survey it, preferably from afar, and from a position of privilege that offers them a seemingly sovereign power of dominion and authority: that is, the ability to remember and forget and to record and erase. Elgar's music, from the *Dream of Gerontius* and the *Pomp and Circumstance* marches to the symphonies, *Falstaff* and the Cello Concerto, simultaneously resists and sustains such competing visions, both by invoking images of landscape and also by evading overly deterministic associations with particular times and places. This elusiveness creates a form of subjective dissonance from which his work gains so much of its agency and affect. Contemplating such dissonance is the interpretative consequence of accompanying F.G. Edwards on his literary

---

[11] James Hepokoski, "Gaudery, Romance, and the 'Welsh Tune': *Introduction and Allegro*, op. 47," *Elgar Studies*, eds J.P.E. Harper-Scott and Julian Rushton (Cambridge: Cambridge University Press, 2007) 145.

[12] Matthew Riley, "Rustling Reeds and Lofty Pines: Elgar and the Music of Nature," *19th-Century Music* 26.2 (2002): 177.

[13] Ibid.

excursion as he descends the hill after his visit to the composer, and waits for the train that will carry him back to the offices of *The Musical Times* in London – where he begins to write.

Listening

Edward Elgar. *The Dream of Gerontius*, Op. 38. Janet Baker, John Mitchinson, John Shirley-Quirk. City of Birmingham Symphony Orchestra and Chorus, Simon Rattle. EMI Classics, 2007.

———. *Introduction and Allegro* for strings, Op. 47. Sinfonia of London, John Wilson. Chandos, 2023.

———. *Variations on an Original Theme ("Enigma")*, Op. 36. City of Birmingham Symphony Orchestra, Simon Rattle. EMI Classics, 2007.

———. "Woodland Interlude" from *Caractacus*, Op. 35. London Symphony Orchestra, Richard Hickox. Chandos, 2018.

Further Reading

Adams, Byron. "The Dark Saying of the Enigma: Homoeroticism and the Elgarian Paradox." *Queer Episodes in Music and Modern Identity*. Eds Sophie Fuller and Lloyd Whitesell. Urbana: University of Illinois Press, 2002. 216–44.

———, ed. *Edward Elgar and his World*. Princeton: Princeton University Press, 2007.

Barrett Browning, Elizabeth. "The Lost Bower." *Poems* (continued). Vol. 2 of *The Works of Elizabeth Barrett Browning*. Eds Marjorie Stone and Beverly Taylor. London: Pickering & Chatto, 2010. 167–87.

Crump, Jeremy. "The Identity of English Music: The Reception of Elgar 1898–1935." *Englishness: Politics and Culture 1880–1920*. Eds Robert Colls and Philip Dodd [1986]. 2nd edn. London: Bloomsbury, 2014. 189–216.

Ghuman, Nalini. *Resonances of the Raj: India in the English Musical Imagination, 1897–1947*. Oxford: Oxford University Press, 2014.

Harper-Scott, J.P.E. *Elgar: An Extraordinary Life*. London: Associated Board of the Royal Schools of Music, 2007.

Langland, William. *Piers Plowman*. c.1380. Eds Elizabeth Robertson and Stephen H.A. Shepherd. New York: Norton, 2006.

Matless, David. *Landscape and Englishness*. 2nd edn. London: Reaktion, 2016.

McGuire, Charles E. "Elgar and Acworth's *Caractacus*: The Druids, Race, and the Individual Hero." *Elgar Studies*. Eds J.P.E. Harper-Scott and Julian Rushton. Cambridge: Cambridge University Press, 2007. 50–77.

Moore, Jerrold Northrop. *Edward Elgar: A Creative Life*. Oxford: Oxford University Press, 1984.

Newman, John Henry. "The Dream of Gerontius." *Collected Poems and the Dream of Gerontius*. Sevenoaks: Fisher, 1992.

Riley, Matthew. *Edward Elgar and the Nostalgic Imagination*. Cambridge: Cambridge University Press, 2007.

CHAPTER 11

Musical *Ekphrasis* and Intermedial Form in Walter Pater's "Duke Carl of Rosenmold" (1887)

Elicia Clements

Recommended Text

Walter Pater, "Duke Carl of Rosenmold," ed. Lene Østermark-Johansen, *Collected Works of Walter Pater*, vol. 3 (Oxford: Oxford University Press, 2018) 115–32, and Oxford Scholarly Editions Online. All citations refer to this edition and are given parenthetically in the text. For an open access edition of this story (Boston: Copeland and Day, 1897), see *Internet Archive*, <https://archive.org/details/dukecarlrosenmoooopategoog/page/n11/mode/2up> [Accessed February 25, 2025].

Keywords

Aestheticism, characterization, court cultures, fiction, Germany, intermediality, irony, musical *ekphrasis*, musicality, musicalization, national musics, short story, structural analogy, Victorian Britain

Prelude

Extract 1

Walter Pater, "Duke Carl of Rosenmold," 121–2; original emphasis.

He was thrown the more upon such outward and sensuous products of mind – architecture, pottery, presently on music – because for him, with so large intellectual capacity [*sic*], there was, to speak properly, no literature in his mother-tongue. Books there were, German books, but of a dullness, a distance from the actual interests of the warm, various, coloured life around and within him, to us hardly conceivable. [...]

  In music, it might be thought, Germany had already vindicated its spiritual liberty. One and another of those North-German towns were already aware of the youthful Sebastian Bach. The first notes had been heard of a music not borrowed from France, but flowing, as naturally as springs from their sources, out of the ever-musical soul of Germany itself. And the Duke Carl was a sincere lover of music, himself playing melodiously on the violin to a delighted court. That new Germany of the spirit would be builded, perhaps, to the sound of music. In those other artistic enthusiasms, as the prophet of the French drama or the architectural taste of Lewis [Louis] the Fourteenth, he had contributed himself generously, helping out with his own good-faith the inadequacy of their appeal. Music alone hitherto had really helped *him*, and taken him out of himself. To music, instinctively, more and more he was dedicate; and in his desire to refine and organise the court music, from which, by leave of absence to official performers enjoying their salaries at a distance, many parts had literally fallen away, like the favourite notes of a worn-out spinet, he was ably seconded by a devoted youth, the deputy-organist of the grand-ducal chapel. A member of the Roman Church amid a people chiefly of the Reformed religion, Duke Carl would creep sometimes into the curtained court pew of the Lutheran Church, to which he had presented its massive golden crucifix, to listen to the *chorales*, the execution of which he had managed to time to his liking, relishing, he could hardly explain why, those passages of a pleasantly monotonous and, as it might seem, unending melody – which certainly never came to what could rightly be called an ending here on earth; and having also a sympathy with the cheerful genius of Dr. Martin Luther, with his good tunes, and that ringing laughter which sent dull goblins flitting.

At this time, then, his mind ran eagerly for awhile on the project of some musical and dramatic development of a fancy suggested by that old Latin poem of Conrad Celtes – the hyperborean Apollo, sojourning, in the revolutions of time, in the sluggish north for a season, yet Apollo still, prompting art, music, poetry, and the philosophy which interprets man's life, making a sort of intercalary day amid the natural darkness; not meridian day, of course, but a soft derivative daylight, good enough for us. It would be necessarily a mystic piece, abounding in fine touches, suggestions, innuendoes. His vague proposal was met half-way by the very practical executant power of his friend or servant, the deputy organist, already pondering, with just a satiric flavour (suppressible in actual performance, if the time for that should ever come) a musical work on Duke Carl himself; *Balder, an Interlude*. He was contented to re-cast and enlarge the part of the northern god of light, with a now wholly serious intention. But still, the near, the real and familiar, gave precision to, or actually superseded, the distant and the ideal. The soul of the music was but a transfusion from the fantastic but so interesting creature close at hand. And Carl was certainly true to his proposed part in that he gladdened others by an intellectual radiance which had ceased to mean warmth or animation for himself. For him the light was still to seek in France, in Italy, above all in old Greece, amid the precious things which might yet be lurking there unknown, in art, in poetry, perhaps in very life, till Prince Fortunate should come.

Extract 2

Pater, "Duke Carl of Rosenmold," 123, 124.

It was the desire to test the sincerity of the people about him, and unveil flatterers, which in the first instance suggested a trick he played upon the court, upon all Europe. [...] He determined to assist at his own obsequies. [...]

Surrounded by the whole official world of Rosenmold, arrayed for the occasion in almost forgotten dresses of ceremony as if for a masquerade, the new coffin glided from the fragrant chapel where the *Requiem* was sung, down the broad staircase lined with peach-colour and yellow marble, into the shadows below. Carl himself, disguised as a strolling musician, had followed it across the square through a drenching rain, on which circumstance he overheard the old people congratulate the "blessed" dead within, had listened to a dirge of his own composing brought out on the great organ with much *bravura* by his friend, the new court organist, who was in [on] the secret, and that night turned the key of the garden entrance to the vault, and peeped in upon the sleepy, painted, and bewigged young pages whose duty it would be for a certain number of days to come to watch beside their late master's couch.

The Challenge

Walter Pater (1839–94) is best known for his art criticism. His pivotal work, *The Renaissance: Studies in Art and Poetry* (1873), captured the new conditions of his age by examining the past in relation to the present and proclaiming that "[a]*ll art constantly aspires towards the condition of music.*"[1] Perhaps lesser known is Pater's fictional set of *Imaginary Portraits* (1887), an interdisciplinary fictional genre that he developed. Despite hailing from an earlier time period, the eponymous Duke is remarkably modern in that his appreciation of the arts is paramount, but his penchant for music, indeed his ability to encapsulate the artform in his very personality, is particularly striking. By remaining receptive to moments of musicalization – descriptions of music [*ekphrasis*] and structural analogy – the reader gleans new insights into changing concepts about characterization and the inseparability of subject-matter and form that emerged at the end of the nineteenth century.

Background

Pater's first book was a collection of essays that examined works of art and poetry, explored the significance of the critical act of perception, and reimagined the historical epoch known as the Renaissance in Europe. Pater began the book

---

[1] Walter Pater, *The Renaissance: Studies in Art and Poetry: The 1893 Text*, ed. Donald Hill (Berkeley: University of California Press, 1980) 106; original emphasis.

with late-medieval stories and concluded with a discussion of the eighteenth-century art historian and archaeologist, Johann Joachim Winckelmann. *Studies in the History of the Renaissance* (1873), renamed in the second (1877) and later editions (1888, 1893) *The Renaissance: Studies in Art and Poetry*, contains a controversial Preface and Conclusion;[2] the introductory and concluding material was considered provocative because it espoused aesthetic theories deemed hedonistic and amoral. Nonetheless, Pater's philosophical shift to value the subjective experience of the perceiver and to revel in the flux of impressions and sensation inspired subsequent generations, not only including his younger contemporary Oscar Wilde, but also early twentieth-century modernist writers starting with Joseph Conrad and Henry James and extending to Virginia Woolf, T.S. Eliot and James Joyce.

An outgrowth of Pater's thinking was a new understanding of form as integral to how an artwork, literary or otherwise, makes its meaning. Pater argues in an essay on "The School of Giorgione" from *The Renaissance* that music is an exemplary artform because it seamlessly comingles its subject matter with its form:

> *All art constantly aspires towards the condition of music.* For while in all other kinds of art it is possible to distinguish the matter from the form, [...] it is the constant effort of art to obliterate it. That the mere matter of a poem, for instance, its subject, namely, its given incidents or situation [...] should be nothing without the form, the spirit, of the handling, that this form, this mode of handling, should become an end in itself, should penetrate every part of the matter: this is what all art constantly strives after, and achieves in different degrees.[3]

With music, according to Pater, the distinction between content and form is imperceptible. All other arts strive toward this achievement and manage it to varying levels.

As Lene Østermark-Johansen explains there are substantial connections between the nonfictional writing Pater accomplishes in *The Renaissance* and the generically innovative literary "portraits" he composes between 1878 and 1893. Intermedial links abound. In these short, fictional works, Pater employs the visual art concept of portraiture as well as musicalization to illuminate the vestiges of personality, the perpetual "weaving and unweaving of ourselves"[4] that he also uncovers throughout *The Renaissance*.[5]

"Duke Carl" was first published by itself in *Macmillan's Magazine* in 1887, but subsequently with three other portraits – "A Prince of Court Painters"

---

[2] Because the "Conclusion," especially, was thought to be scandalous, Pater excised it from the second edition, but he returned it, somewhat altered, to the third.
[3] Pater, *The Renaissance*, 106; original emphasis.
[4] Ibid., 188.
[5] See Lene Østermark-Johansen, "Pater and the Painterly: Imaginary Portraits," *English Literature in Transition, 1880–1920* 56.3 (2013): 343–54.

(1885), "Sebastian van Storck" (1886) and "Denys L'Auxerrois" (1886) – in a stand-alone volume, also published by Macmillan, in 1887. Duke Carl is a fictional noble living, according to him, in a culturally provincial duchy in Germany at the beginning of the eighteenth century. The narrative details the Duke's aesthetic predilections and disappointments, his love of and composition of music, his staging of his own death, as well as his travels to France, Greece and throughout his home country – all amidst rising, local political tensions and warfare. Largely through the device of allusion, references to a submerged "plot" about the Duke's love affair with Gretchen the "beggar-maid," a disenfranchised woman from outside his royal standing, bookend the tale. This love story alludes to the sixteenth-century broadside ballad, "The King and the Beggar-maid,"[6] typically employed during the Victorian period as a lesson in class privilege whereby the aristocratic male and the impoverished (or working-class) female live "happily ever after," according to the dictates of courtly romance. Pater's reframing of it, and striking change to its ending, thwarts this popular version: about to elope, the couple ventures outside in the middle of a storm and is crushed to death by a second "storm" – that of an advancing enemy army. Throughout the portrait, character and temperament take precedence over events. Pater questions nineteenth-century ideas about narrative forms, inventing what might constitute a literary portrait and gesturing toward other artforms – painting and music – for guidance.

Case Study

When examining the relationship between literature and music in a text, the first thing to do is establish what type of intermedial connection is being made. The work of Werner Wolf, a theorist of intermedial studies who specializes in musico-literary combination, can be helpful in this regard. His book *The Musicalization of Fiction*, together with intermedial methods outlined by Irina Rajewsky, lay a foundation for the concrete analysis of literature and other artforms.[7] Rajewsky distinguishes three major types of intermediality: medial

---

[6] This ballad was quoted by William Shakespeare several times and in various publications from 1612 and 1765. In the Victorian period, Alfred Tennyson published his poem, "The Beggar Maid" in 1842. Edward Burne-Jones's painting *King Cophetua and the Beggar Maid* was based on Tennyson's poem and first exhibited in 1884. The story is about an African king, Cophetua, and his "love at first sight" infatuation with the "beggar maid," Penelophon, whom he decides to marry despite social barriers; the tale is overladen with stereotypical exoticizations that cut across class, gender and race and is often associated with another re-popularized myth in Victorian culture, the tale of Pygmalion.

[7] See Werner Wolf, *The Musicalization of Fiction: A Study in the Theory and History of Intermediality* (Amsterdam: Rodopi, 1999); Wolf, "Intermediality Revisited: Reflections on Word and Music Relations in the Context of a General Typology

transposition (the transformation of one medium into another, such as film adaptation), media combination (a new medium created from the constellation of two or more medial forms, such as opera), and intermedial reference (gestures toward other artforms from within a single medium, such as *ekphrasis*, the verbal description of a painting).[8] Wolf breaks these larger categories down further to think specifically about the musicalization of fiction. With intermedial reference, one can determine whether or not a text contains overt references (thematization of music within a text), or covert ones (intermedial imitation, whereby the non-dominant medium is imitated in some way, whether on the level of language or structure).

These categories begin to expose the various levels of interaction between two artforms. In the case of Pater's *Imaginary Portraits*, intermedial reference is employed, whereby only one medium is present, that is, literary fiction. But the intermedial references are various, integral to the construction of the imaginary portrait generically and in terms of content, and also integral to at least two different media – both painting and music. The following analysis focuses on the musical connections by exploring the overt thematization of music, chiefly through the mechanism of musical *ekphrasis*, and closes with some connections to the structure of the text to suggest the covert (imitative) links.

A Musical Personality

The more common, utterly apt, reading of the *Imaginary Portraits* is to examine portraiture and the literary/visual art connection. But given Pater's own embedding of music (conceptually) at the heart of *The Renaissance*, examining why, how and to what effect music is enfolded into his fictional imaginary portraits can produce equally thought-provoking analyses. Indeed, music is significant to each "portrait" in the initial volume (and several others written later).[9] Pater seems almost unwilling to write an imaginary portrait without at least some

---

of Intermediality," *Word and Music Studies: Essays in Honor of Steven Paul Scher and on Cultural Identity and the Musical Stage*, eds Suzanne M. Lodato, Suzanne Aspden and Walter Bernhart (Amsterdam: Rodopi, 2002) 13–34; and Irina Rajewsky, "Intermediality, Intertextuality, and Remediation: A Literary Perspective on Intermediality," *History and Theory of the Arts, Literature and Technologies* 6 (2005): 43–64.

[8] Rajewsky, "Intermediality, Intertextuality, and Remediation," 51–2.
[9] "Denys L'Auxerrois" is about a mythological figure set in medieval France. Like Carl, he too is a lover of music, a composer and a musician. Various musical scenes and analogies occur in "A Prince of Court Painters," "Sebastian van Storck" and "The Child in the House" (1878). Apollo figures prominently in "Duke Carl." The protagonist himself is referred to as the "Apollo of Germany!" (123) and the "hyperborean [northern] Apollo" (121, in **Extract 1**). The ancient god and his lyre are alluded to in Pater's "Denys" and "Emerald Uthwart" (1892), and also, of course, in "Apollo of Picardy" (1893).

reference to music, and in "Duke Carl" the echo and specter of Apollo, the Greek god of light and music, loom especially large.

Pater's thematization of music takes various forms. In "Duke Carl," music is described in efficacious terms, as being capable of doing things not typically ascribed to it. Somehow, for example, it aids the protagonist by taking "him out of himself," like a good friend might do. [**Extract 1.**] "Music alone" accomplishes this feat, which is saying something, given that the Duke seems to be plagued by inefficiency and indecisiveness, as the ironically distanced narrator repeatedly discloses. Throughout the imaginary portrait, Duke Carl is also associated with a variety of mythological and historical figures, most of whom have a musical correlation: Balder, the "Nordic counterpart to Apollo";[10] Ludwig II, King of Bavaria, linked with music and, more specifically, the operas of Richard Wagner; as well as the Holy Roman Emperor, Charles V, who, about six months before his actual death, staged his own funeral, complete with shroud and coffin, and then arose from the latter to retire to his apartment, much to the onlookers' shock and dismay.[11] As Mary Tiffany Ferer has documented, it was well known that Charles V was acutely aware of the role that the arts – and music, in particular – could play in the promotion of his leadership.[12] Correspondingly, Duke Carl fakes his own death, and further, writes his own funeral music, in an effort to test the fidelity of his court. This palimpsest of identity is multifarious, creating a flickering sort of perception of the protagonist in which musical associations abound.

Musical *Ekphrasis*

In her study of musical *ekphrasis*, philosopher Lydia Goehr explains that the term can refer to two different types of description or reference.[13] In common usage, *ekphrasis* typically "produces images for the mind's eye by means of words."[14] But Goehr demonstrates that music (sonic references) is part of the history of *ekphrasis* as well. The ancient type, which finds its genesis in the

---

[10] Lene Østermark-Johansen, Explanatory Notes, "Duke Carl," 279.
[11] For more details on these connections see Anna Budziak, "'Duke Carl of Rosenmold': The Self of Romance in its 'Tireless Quest,'" *Text, Body and Indeterminacy: Doppelgänger Selves in Pater and Wilde* (Newcastle: Cambridge Scholars Publishing, 2008) 130–58. See also Maurizio Ascari, "The Mask without the Face: Walter Pater's Imaginary Portraits," *Textus: English Studies in Italy* 12.1 (January 1999): 97–112; and Østermark-Johansen, "Critical Introduction" (1–47) and Explanatory Notes (274–83), from "Duke Carl."
[12] For more on the significance of the arts and music to Charles V's court, see Mary Tiffany Ferer, *Music and Ceremony at the Court of Charles V: The Capilla Flamenca and the Art of Political Promotion* (Woodbridge: The Boydell Press, 2012).
[13] Lydia Goehr, "How to Do More with Words. Two Views of (Musical) Ekphrasis," *British Journal of Aesthetics* 50.4 (October 2010): 389–410.
[14] Ibid., 389.

practices of Ancient Greek rhetoricians, refers to words that describe music. The other type, which Goehr brands modern, enacts the reverse, with music depicting writing (or painting). Pater, who creates verbal impressions of imagined figures from a variety of historical epochs, uses the ancient form of *ekphrasis* (by profession he was a classicist who taught at Oxford). Furthermore, his musical *ekphrasis* is often notional, meaning, as John Hollander has written, referring to purely fictional, or better put, "imaginary," works that do not exist in actuality.[15]

In constant motion throughout the narrative, the Duke "endlessly flits from one narrative to another, and thus fails to acquire any comforting sense of stability in the self,"[16] as Anna Budziak puts it. Correspondingly, the "restless, romantic, eccentric" (115) Duke is described in the portrait in musical terms in reference to the form of the chorale. [**Extract 1.**] Duke Carl regularly attends a Lutheran church – even though he is a "member of the Roman Church" – to hear the chorales being sung by the church choir: "those passages of a pleasantly monotonous and, as it might seem, unending melody – which certainly never came to what could rightly be called an ending here on earth." This musical *ekphrasis* reflects the aimless personality of the protagonist who never settles "here on earth," like the "unending melody" just described.

Moreover, the paragraph starts with an allusion to the "youthful Sebastian Bach," as the savior of German culture (its literature, according to the narrator, is full of dull books); it ends with reference to the chorale compositions of Dr Martin Luther, the formative figure of the Protestant Reformation. Luther advocated for the singing of hymns in German (rather than Latin), integrating music into religious worship on a new and comprehensive scale and signaling the importance of both language and music to social relations. Luther was capable of transcribing folk melodies and harmonizing them himself; he composed over thirty chorales. Like Luther, Pater never underestimates music's capacity to enable meaningful personal and communal experiences, even if he tends to prize the aesthetic over the religious. The Lutheran chorales seem to beckon to the Duke, who "could hardly explain why" he is drawn to listen, surreptitiously, to the "pleasantly monotonous" hymns.

In the next paragraph, notional musical *ekphrasis* is used to link the protagonist with the multidisciplinary artform of opera. Here the duke is inspired by the god Apollo, no less, via the work of Conrad Celtes (1459–1508), a German Renaissance humanist and neo-Platonic poet. In an effort to bring culture to

---

[15] John Hollander, *The Gazer's Spirit: Poems Speaking to Silent Works of Art* (Chicago: University Press of Chicago, 1995). For an excellent discussion of visual notional *ekphrasis* in another of Pater's portraits, "Denys L'Auxerrois," see Kenneth Daly, "Pater's Auxerre Tapestry," *Victorian Aesthetic Conditions: Pater Across the Arts*, eds E. Clements and L. Higgins (Basingstoke: Palgrave Macmillan, 2010) 85–101.

[16] Budziak, "'Duke Carl of Rosenmold,'" 143.

Fig. 11.1: Anon., "Johann Sebastian Bach at the Court of Frederick the Great." Woodcut (c.1892) based on a painting by Hermann Kaulbach.

his court, Duke Carl is eager, albeit only "for awhile," to put on "some musical and dramatic development" based on Celtes's Latin poetry: "It would be necessarily a mystic piece, abounding in fine touches, suggestions, innuendoes." The description not only echoes the Duke's professed values but is also emblematic of his character. He is helped in this musical endeavor by the court deputy organist, "his friend or servant," who was already thinking about composing "a musical work on Duke Carl himself: *Balder, an Interlude*." As the narrator notes, Balder is a Nordic "northern god of light," another allusion to Apollo. These imagined pieces somehow capture the personality of Duke Carl; in fact, "the soul of the music was but a transfusion from the fantastic but so interesting creature close at hand." Yet even this exceptionally solipsistic entertainment is not enough to hold his interest very long, as he dreams still of seeking "the light" in "France, in Italy, above all in old Greece."

The third major instance of musical *ekphrasis* is also notional. Duke Carl, bored again, decides to test his court's loyalty, wondering if those who laud him are sincere in their praise. But Carl is not content simply to watch the ceremony; rather, he is "determined to assist at his own obsequies [or funeral rites]." **[Extract 2.]** Disguised as a "strolling musician," the Duke follows his own procession and overhears a few attendees blessing the dead. He also listens to the "dirge of his own composing" which is "brought out on the great organ with much *bravura*" by his friend, the deputy organist, now court organist, who is in on the trick. Duke Carl is not just a violinist, not just fodder for a musical drama, but also a composer, able to create musically the representation of himself to help, albeit disingenuously, others mourn his loss.

But the portrait does not end where it began, quite, with the ghostly demise of the Duke and his lover trampled under the feet of an invading army. It ends fifty years after Duke Carl's early eighteenth-century death. The narrative concludes with a statement about the Enlightenment and a reference to Johann von Goethe to foretell of the great German tradition in literature that follows the Duke's lifetime. The reader already knows, in contrast, that the German tradition in music is thriving due to Luther and Bach. The allusion to Goethe is another ironic gesture on the part of the narrator who acknowledges his agenda late in the day: that the aspirations of Romantic writers provide the backdrop for "the portrait of Carl" (131). But Carl is a pale version of the "new German citizen and aesthete"[17] embodied by Goethe, the famed poet who ushered in the later eighteenth-century *Sturm und Drang* [Storm and Stress] period and instigated the Romantic epoch in European literature.[18] Yet the narrator's final words suggest there are at least glimpses of the later age in the musical aesthete Duke (perhaps born into the wrong time period): "In that amiable figure [Goethe] I seem to see the fulfilment of the *Resurgam* [I shall rise again] on Carl's empty coffin – the aspiring soul of Carl himself, in freedom and effective, at last" (132).

Conclusion: Structural Analogy and Implications

Quite remarkably, Pater creates a new genre with his imaginary portraits. "Duke Carl" is largely plotless, bound up in perception in terms of character and as process illuminated by the narrator. The text enacts what it speaks about, comingling content and form, as music does so well for Pater. The narrative is seemingly circular in terms of its structure – it looks as though it will end where it began; in musical terms, it will come back to the tonic – the trampling of the Duke and his lover. Yet the final segment on Goethe functions analogously to a coda, suggesting something slightly different. It is an ending that eludes finalization, recalling the "unending melody" of the Lutheran chorale, or even its pleasant monotony. With Pater's imaginary portrait, literary musical *ekphrasis* has become not just a node of intermedial thematization, it has become method, pointing the way for subsequent modernist writers such as Woolf and Joyce to integrate musical forms into their literary experiments.

---

[17] Østermark-Johansen, Explanatory Notes, "Duke Carl," 283.
[18] Gretchen, the Duke's love interest, is also the name of the well-known heroine from Goethe's *Faust*, about whom Franz Schubert composed his *Lied* [German art song] "Gretchen am Spinnrade" ["Gretchen at the Spinning Wheel"] (1814). The narrator also suggests that Gretchen embodies "Die Ruh auf dem Gipfel" ["The rest on the summit"], which recalls one of Goethe's most famous poems, "Wandrers Nachtlied II" ["Wanderer's Night Song"] (1780), also set by Schubert (1823). A notable irony here, however, is that Goethe disapproved of Franz Schubert's settings of his poetry, which, nevertheless, became some of the most well known and representative musical expressions of the Romantic period in music.

Listening

Bach, Johann Sebastian. Chorale. "Ein feste Burg ist unser Gott." SATB. BWV 80, c.1723. *J.S. Bach: Ein Feste Burg Ist Unser Gott*. Chorus Musicus Köln, Das Neue Orchester Spering, Christoph Spering. Deutsche Harmonia Mundi, 2015. Track 1.
Luther, Martin. Chorale. "Ein feste Burg ist unser Gott." SATB. Zahn No. 7377a, 1529. *Reformation 1517–2017*. Choir of Clare College, Cambridge; Graham Ross. Harmonia Mundi, 2017. Track 1.
Schubert, Franz. "Gretchen am Spinnrade." Op. 2, D 118, 1814. *Schubert: Lieder*. Jessye Norman, Phillip Moll. Decca Music Group Ltd, 1985. Track 6.
———. "Wandrers Nachtlied II." Op. 96, D 768, 1822. *Schubert Lieder*. Dietrich Fischer-Dieskau, Gerald Moore. Deutsche Grammophon, 2003. Track 22.

Further Reading

Ascari, Maurizio. "The Mask without the Face: Walter Pater's *Imaginary Portraits*." *Textus* XII (1999): 97–112.
Bucknell, Brad. "Walter Pater: Music and the Aesthetic Resistance to History." *Literary Modernism and Musical Aesthetics: Pater, Pound, Joyce, and Stein*. Cambridge: Cambridge University Press, 2001. 37–50.
Clements, Elicia and Lesley J. Higgins, eds. *Victorian Aesthetic Conditions: Pater Across the Arts*. Basingstoke: Palgrave Macmillan, 2010.
Goehr, Lydia. "'All Art Constantly Aspires to the Condition of Music' – Except the Art of Music: Reviewing the Contest of the Sister Arts." *The Insistence of Art: Aesthetic Philosophy After Early Modernity*. Ed. Paul A. Kottman. New York: Fordham University Press, 2017. 140–69.
Herzog, Patricia. "The Condition to which All Art Aspires: Reflections on Pater on Music." *British Journal of Aesthetics* 36.2 (1996): 122–35.
Higgins, Lesley J. "No Time for Pater: Breaking the Homophobic Silence." *The Modernist Cult of Ugliness: Aesthetic and Gender Politics*. Basingstoke: Palgrave Macmillan, 2002. 79–119.
Leighton, Angela. "Pater's Music." *Journal of Pre-Raphaelite Studies* 14 (2005): 67–79.
Østermark-Johansen, Lene. "Apollo in the North: Transmutations of the Sun God in Walter Pater's *Imaginary Portraits*." *Cahiers victoriens et édouardiens* 80 (2014). <https://doi.org/10.4000/cve.1520> [Accessed November 1, 2024].
Pater, Walter. *Imaginary Portraits*. Ed. Lene Østermark-Johansen. *Collected Works of Walter Pater*. Vol. 3. Gen. eds Lesley J. Higgins and David Latham. Oxford: Oxford University Press, 2018.
———. *The Renaissance: Studies in Art and Poetry: The 1893 Text*. Ed. Donald Hill. Berkeley: University of California Press, 1980.

CHAPTER 12

Women, Music and Tennyson's *The Princess* (1850 edn)

Phyllis Weliver

Recommended Text

Alfred Tennyson, *The Princess: A Medley*, in *Tennyson's Poetry*, ed. Robert W. Hill, 2nd edn (New York: Norton, 1971; 1999) 130–203.

Keywords

Ballad, humor, metaphor, poetic conceit, poetry, recitation, song, Alfred Lord Tennyson, Emily Lady Tennyson, text-setting, Victorian Britain, women's higher education, women in literature

Prelude

Extract 1

Interpolated songs in Alfred Tennyson, *The Princess: A Medley*, 3rd edn (London: Moxon, 1850). Unless noted, subsequent citations refer to this edition and are given in the text.[1]

I ^ II [3rd edn]	I ^ II [anthologized version][2]
As thro' the land at eve we went,	As through the land at eve we went,
And pluck'd the ripen'd ears,	And plucked the ripened ears,
We fell out, my wife and I,	We fell out, my wife and I,
And kiss'd again with tears:	O we fell out I know not why, [added 1851]
And blessings on the falling-out	And kissed again with tears.

---

[1] It is common scholarly practice to label the interpolated songs by two roman numerals and a carrot (^), which indicates where the song fits within the seven parts of *The Princess*. Thus, I ^ II identifies the song that is placed between the first and the second parts. Sometimes, a song is also referred to by its first line, especially when it is printed as an excerpt.

[2] Both the Norton edition (Recommended Text) and Christopher Ricks's edition of the poem give a fourteen-line version of song I ^ II, which offer all of Tennyson's revisions in the third (1850), fourth (1851) and fifth (1853) editions. This layout gives the poem

That all the more endears,	**And blessings on the falling-out**
When we fall out with those we love,	**That all the more endears,**
And kiss again with tears!	**When we fall out with those we love**
For when we came where lies the child	**And kiss again with tears!**[3]
We lost in other years,	For when we came where lies the child
There above the little grave,	We lost in other years,
We kiss'd again with tears.	There above the little grave,
	O there above the little grave, [added 1851]
	We kissed again with tears.

II ^ III
[*Also set by Emily Tennyson; stresses added (bolded)*]
Sweet and **low**, **sweet** and **low**,
    Wind of the **wes**tern **sea**,
Low, **low**, **breathe** and **blow**,
    Wind of the **wes**tern **sea**!
Over the **rolling waters go**,
Come from the **dropping moon**, and **blow**,
    Blow him a**gain** to **me**;
While my **little one**, **while** my **pretty one sleeps**.

Sleep and **rest**, **sleep** and **rest**,
    Father will **come** to thee **soon**;
Rest, **rest**, on **mother's breast**,
    Father will **come** to thee **soon**;
Father will **come** to his **babe** in the **nest**,
Silver sails all **out** of the **west**
    Under the silver **moon**:
Sleep, my **little one**, **sleep**, my **pretty one**, **sleep**.

III ^ IV
  The splendour falls on castle walls
    And snowy summits old in story:
  The long light shakes across the lakes
    And the wild cataract leaps in glory.
Blow, bugle, blow, set the wild echoes flying,
Blow, bugle; answer, echoes, dying, dying, dying.

---

the same number of lines as a sonnet (often a love poem). The 1850 poem was twelve lines; however, the 1851 revision offered ten lines with a stanza break evenly dividing the poem into two parts. The anthologized version reproduced here is from *Tennyson: A Selected Edition*, ed. Christopher Ricks, rev. edn (1969; Harlow, England: Pearson, 2007) 239. Neither it nor the third edition (given in the left column) have stanza breaks.

[3] The bolded lines indicate lines that were omitted in editions from 1851 to 1861. Christopher Ricks, notes, *Tennyson: A Selected Edition*, ed. Ricks, 239. The rest of the lines preserve the indentation of the fourth edition (1851).

O hark, O hear! how thin and clear,
    And thinner, clearer, farther going!
O sweet and far from cliff and scar
    The horns of Elfland faintly blowing!
Blow, let us hear the purple glens replying:
Blow, bugle; answer, echoes, dying, dying, dying.

    O love, they die in yon rich sky,
        They faint on hill or field or river:
    Our echoes roll from soul to soul,
        And grow for ever and for ever.
Blow, bugle, blow, set the wild echoes flying,
And answer, echoes, answer, dying, dying, dying.

IV ∧ V

When all among the thundering drums
    Thy soldier in the battle stands,
Thy face across his fancy comes,
    And gives the battle to his hands:
A moment while the trumpets blow,
    He sees his brood about thy knee—
The next—like fire he meets the foe,
    Strikes him dead for them and thee!
        Tara ta tantara!
	<u>Version set by Emily Tennyson</u>
	    Lady, let the rolling drums
	Beat to battle where thy warrior stands:
	Now thy face across his fancy comes,
	    And gives the battle to his hands.
	
	    Lady, let the trumpets blow,
	Clasp thy little babes about thy knee:
	Now their warrior father meets the foe,
	    And strikes him dead for thine and thee.

V ∧ VI

Home they brought her warrior dead:
    She nor swoon'd, nor utter'd cry:
All her maidens, watching, said,
    "She must weep or she will die."
 	
Then they praised him, soft and low,
    Call'd him worthy to be loved,
Truest friend and noblest foe;
    Yet she neither spoke nor moved.
 	
Stole a maiden from her place,
    Lightly to the warrior stept,
Took the face-cloth from the face;
    Yet she neither moved nor wept.
 	
Rose a nurse of ninety years,
    Set his child upon her knee—
Like summer tempest came her tears—
    "Sweet my child, I live for thee."
	<u>Version set by Emily Tennyson</u>
	Home they brought her warrior dead:
	    They brought him home at even-fall:
	All alone she sits and hears
	    Echoes in his empty hall,
	        Sounding on the morrow.
	
	The Sun peeped in from open field,
	    The boy began to leap and prance,
	    Rode upon his father's lance,
	Beat upon his father's shield—
	    "O hush, my joy, my sorrow."

VI ^ VII
Ask me no more: the moon may draw the sea;
   The cloud may stoop from heaven and take the shape,
   With fold to fold, of mountain or of cape;
But O too fond, when have I answer'd thee?
        Ask me no more.

Ask me no more: what answer should I give?
   I love not hollow cheek or faded eye:
   Yet, O my friend, I will not have thee die!
Ask me no more, lest I should bid thee live;
        Ask me no more.

Ask me no more: thy fate and mine are seal'd:
   I strove against the stream and all in vain:
   Let the great river take me to the main:
No more, dear love, for at a touch I yield;
        Ask me no more.

Extract 2

Tennyson, *The Princess*, iv.18–25, 36–40 (includes first and last stanzas of "Tears, idle tears.")

    Then she "Let some one sing to us: lightlier move
The minutes fledge with music:" and a maid,
Of those beside her, smote her harp, and sang.

    "Tears, idle tears, I know not what they mean,
Tears from the depth of some divine despair
Rise in the heart, and gather to the eyes,
In looking on the happy Autumn-fields,
And thinking of the days that are no more.

    […]

    "Dear as remember'd kisses after death,
And sweet as those by hopeless fancy feign'd
On lips that are for others; deep as love,
Deep as first love, and wild with all regret;
O Death in Life, the days that are no more."

Extract 3

Arthur Sullivan, "I am a Maiden, cold and stately," words W.S. Gilbert, *Princess Ida, Or, Castle Adamant*, vocal score (London: Chappell, 1884) lines 1–9.

HILARION.
I am a maiden, cold and stately,
Heartless I, with a face divine.
What do I want with a heart, innately?
Ev'ry heart I meet is mine!
Ev'ry heart I meet is mine, is mine!

ALL: REFRAIN
Haughty, humble, coy, or free,
Little care I what maid may be.
So that a maid is fair to see,
Ev'ry maid is the maid for me!
[DANCE.]

The Challenge

Alfred Lord Tennyson's long poem, *The Princess: A Medley* (1847, rev. 1848–53) lends itself to multiple approaches to women and word/music relationships: literary analysis, text setting and parodic stage adaptation. Considered one of the most musical poets because of his sonorous language, Tennyson directly addressed the idea of "song" in *The Princess*, and he did so in feminine terms. According to Tennyson, six "songs" by women (poems called songs), intercalated within a verse narrative told collaboratively by seven men about a women's university, make *The Princess* intelligible.[4] Britain's poet laureate thus intended to endow the idea of song with an unusually high exegetical function. However, the six realist songs do not obviously connect to the overarching "mock-heroic gigantesque" (c.11) story about female higher education.[5] The challenges are thus: How can we understand *The Princess*'s argument about equality and education when women are metaphorically called "music" by the male narrators? How do we analyze the intercalated songs themselves? And how do Emily Lady Tennyson's piano/vocal settings of *Princess* songs – collaboratively revised with Alfred Tennyson – relate to her husband's poem?

Background

Tennyson (1809–92) began discussing *The Princess* with his fiancée, Emily Sellwood (1813–96) in 1839 and subsequently revised it more than any of his other long poems.[6] These modifications are normally understood to occur between the first and fifth editions (1847, 1853), with the third edition (1850) being the most heavily revised. "Before the first edition came out," Tennyson explained, "I deliberated with myself whether I should put songs between the separate divisions of the poem; again I thought that the poem would explain itself, but

---

[4] Hallam Lord Tennyson, *Alfred Lord Tennyson: A Memoir by His Son*, 2 vols (London: Macmillan, 1897) 1: 254. Hereafter, *Memoir*.
[5] When referencing *The Princess*, the poem's prologue is typically given line numbers only, the parts are labelled with roman numerals preceding line numbers, and lines in the conclusion begin with a "c."
[6] Edgar Finley Shannon, *Tennyson and the Reviewers* (Cambridge, Massachusetts: Harvard University Press, 1952) 97–140.

the public did not see the drift."⁷ Tennyson therefore relied upon musicality to explain an element that resists narrative paraphrase ("the drift"). An early phonograph recording reveals that he understood poems that he called "songs" as literally musical, for he actually sang parts of "Song of Love and Death" from "Lancelot and Elaine" (unlike his recorded poems without the designation "song" in the title).⁸ But while Tennyson considered the six interwoven songs in *The Princess* to be "the best interpreters of the poem,"⁹ these lyrical utterances seem mostly unrelated in topic or style to the main tale about Princess Ida.

Set in 1840s England, *The Princess* begins with a Prologue. During the summer holiday, the narrator visits Walter, a university friend whose father throws a grand feast for his tenants and the local Mechanics' Institute, covering his park with exhibitions of scientific wonder. This holiday crowd forms a background hum to the spirited chatter of Walter's six undergraduate friends and several female guests. Their banter about college exploits, Walter's female forbear who slaughtered besieging foes, and the idea of a women's college leads to a party-game that Tennyson himself is commonly known to have played at Trinity College, Cambridge. Walter's sister Lilia requests that they play this game as an example of "what kind of tales did men tell men" (177). Each undergraduate will take a turn at telling a story and the ladies will sing "From time to time, some ballad or a song / To give us breathing-space" (217–18). The men thereby begin by underestimating the role of the women's songs, for these ballads and songs are far more than mere "breathing-space."

Framing devices like this Prologue typically provide a realist, contemporary perspective from which to view a more fantastic main story. The title – *The Princess: A Medley* – thus signifies the story-game, but it also implies the blurred topic (Victorian women's education/archaic fairy tale), the method (narrative-poem/sing-song within a frame narrative) and the style (mock-heroic/realist). The "tale from mouth to mouth" (174) then comprises seven parts with six interspersed songs. Set in ancient times like a fairy tale, the plot of the story-game concerns an unnamed prince, betrothed in proxy as a child to Princess Ida. Now adult, Ida has established a women's university and resists the precontract. The prince and his friends (Cyril and Florian) dress in drag, enter the ladies' establishment and are eventually discovered. In the resulting confusion, the prince saves Ida from drowning. The women remain outraged at the deception, battle ensues, the prince is wounded, Ida nurses him back to health, the two discover mutual respect, and the women's university disbands. A Conclusion returns to 1840s England as the feast finishes at dusk and the friends reflect politically on the topic of their tale.

---

⁷ Hallam Tennyson, *Memoir*, 1: 254.
⁸ See Phyllis Weliver, *Mary Gladstone and the Victorian Salon: Music, Literature, Liberalism* (Cambridge: Cambridge University Press, 2017) 227–8.
⁹ Hallam Tennyson, *Memoir*, 1: 254.

Today, Ida's ending can seem troubling because it counters our expectation of women's access to university education and our celebration of pioneering women. In Britain, however, so-called ladies' colleges did not exist until the early 1870s when Girton and Newnham were established at Cambridge. Thus, when poet Elizabeth Barrett Browning heard of Tennyson's project in 1846, she responded: "it is in blank verse & a fairy tale, & called the *University*, the university-members being all females. [...] I dont know what to think – it makes me open my eyes. Now isn't the world too old & fond of steam, for blank verse poems, in ever so many books, to be written on the fairies?"[10] In the industrial ("steam") age, Barrett Browning argues for realism in topic and style; blank verse (unrhymed lines of iambic pentameter) is usually considered closest to English speech rhythms. Still, the narrator's conclusion – "maybe wildest dreams / Are but the needful preludes of the truth" (c.73–4) – is rather close to Barrett Browning's position. The effect of the framing device and mock-heroic fairy tale should certainly be considered in studying this poem (was the sideways approach necessary because the poem was ahead of its time?), along with the added songs and the women's silent influence during the men's story. These last two ultimately dictate an "earnest [...] close" (c.21) to *The Princess*.

Case Study

To understand how *The Princess*'s treatment of women interacts with the overall song structure, let's divide the topic into manageable sections: (1) The poem's representation of women, (2) Musical metaphors, (3) Ballads and songs, and (4) Emily Tennyson's musical arrangements.

These words, part of the prince's final appeal to Ida, reveal the underlying movement of *The Princess*:

> Not like to like, but like in difference.
> Yet in the long years liker must they grow;
> [...]
> Till at the last she set herself to man,
> Like perfect music unto noble words; (vii.251–2, 258–9)

It is relatively easy to paraphrase this passage, but how does the poem communicate beyond plot elements? A distinctive element of this passage is the excessive repetition of the word "like," which draws attention. To grow "liker" suggests both increasing similarity (alikeness) and greater enjoyment (to like). Repetition also reduces the semantic meaning into sound alone; we lose the logical meaning as the words rhyme with themselves (otto rhymes). This sonic

---

[10] Elizabeth Barrett Browning to Robert Browning, January 30, 1846, *The Letters of Robert Browning and Elizabeth Barrett Browning, 1845–1846*, ed. E. Kintner, 2 vols (Cambridge, Massachusetts: Harvard University Press, 1969) 1: 427; original emphasis.

dimension of likeness in the word's meaning and sound – both alike and different – impacts lines vii.258–9 (to which I will return).

The frame narrative begins differently: with shallow flattery. The first compliment paid by an undergraduate man to Lilia – "'Pretty were the sight / [...] / sweet girl-graduates in their golden hair'" (124, 127) – is overlooked. Characters ignore the offensiveness of undergraduate women being measured by their prettiness rather than their intelligence. The *story-game*, however, challenges this sexist ideology by highlighting the insidiousness of "the tinsel clink of compliment" (ii.41) because women are not "pretty babes / To be dandled" (iv.149–50).

The tale seems successful in suggesting change – to a point. By the Conclusion, Walter exclaims of Ida, "I wish she had not yielded!" (c.5), thereby affirming women's rights while ironically revealing patriarchal interpretation because it is *Walter* (a man) who asserts this outcome. To what the prince calls a "two-cell'd heart-beating," Ida at first responds: "A dream / That once was mine!" (vii.278, 279–80). She agrees with the prince's ideal while questioning its realism (seen in the larger context), but her final words in the poem are, "Never, Prince; / You cannot love me" (vii.304–5). Almost twenty-five long-winded lines later, the prince's final appeal concludes the story-game: "Indeed I love thee: come, / Yield thyself up: my hopes and thine are one: / [...] / Lay thy sweet hands in mine and trust to me" (vii.327–8, 330). In the Conclusion, Walter assumes that Ida "yielded" to marriage and this sways the reader's interpretation. Yet what the page actually reveals is Ida's silence.

We must remember that Ida's words (and silences) originate with men's burlesque. Thus, when she finally dubs herself "a Queen of farce!" (vii.217), the pronouncement, hidden behind multiple male voices, is not straightforward. This heterogeneity complicates and confuses the message. Counseling "faith. / This fine old world of ours is but a child / [...] Patience! Give it time" (c.76–8), the narrator ultimately aligns himself with "our wild Princess" and her "wise [...] dream" (c.69).

The Poetic Conceit

The formal construction of *The Princess* (men's blank verse and women's songs) not only names music as women's own expression, but it is also a poetic conceit, or an extended comparison between two unlike things. Heterosexual lovers are "Not like to like, but like in difference"; the inset quotation above compares this relationship to text-setting. This is a poetic conceit, and it also cleverly describes the *process* of a poetic conceit (comparing two unlike things introduces a likeness).

The gender/genre comparison occurred earlier in the poem, too. After being captured, the prince says:

> I cannot cease to follow you, as they say
> The seal does music;
> [...]
>   —yours, yours, not mine—but half
> Without you, with you, whole; and of those halves
> You worthiest; (iv.434–5, 439–41)

This (earlier) passage and the citation from Part VII both compare women with music ("as [...] / music," "Like perfect music"). The passages differ, however, in referring to "music" as first performance and then composition (text-setting). Expressed as causal relations, the woman comes first in the seal/music simile (the seal responds, much as the prince swam to Ida's rescue), while the man/text precedes music in composition. The poem seems to move to the latter (privileging the man) because it comes last.

To comprehend the implications of this poetic conceit for word/music studies, we need to understand how Ida, the narrator, and the prince emphasize the desirability of women's access to higher education, but in Victorian terms. The poem's "diverse" (vii.249) spheres anticipate John Ruskin's famous lecture, "Of Queen's Gardens" (1865): "We are foolish [...] in speaking of the 'superiority' of one sex to the other, as if they could be compared in similar things. Each has what the other has not: [...] the happiness and perfection of both depends on each asking and receiving from the other what the other only can give."[11] Ruskin argues that women and men have separate spheres of influence; educated women make good wives and mothers, which furthers national progress. These concepts, while troubling today, nevertheless advanced women's higher education opportunities at the time.

Antedating Ruskin's lecture, Tennyson's prince emphasizes similar essentialist ideas, but unlike the lecture, the poem expresses this idea melodically. We know that Tennyson word painted when he recited (vocally reproducing the word's meaning, like descending on the word "fall"), and that he enjoyed onomatopoeias (words that recreate their meaning in sound, like "clang").[12] He also chanted lines of poetry in a monotone, making use of extreme changes in pitch (like cadences), dynamics, and pace (*ritardando* and *accelerando*). Knowledge of Tennyson's recitation style can draw attention to certain types of words. Verbs that express altitude, for example, are easily word-painted in rising and falling melodic patterns, as in this passage about the idea, "liker must they grow." To the prince,

---

[11] John Ruskin, *Sesame and Lilies* (1865), ed. Deborah Epstein Nord (New Haven: Yale University Press, 2002) 77.

[12] See Weliver, *Mary Gladstone and the Victorian Salon*, 200–40.

> The woman's cause is man's: they rise or sink
> Together, dwarf'd or godlike, bond or free:
> For she that out of Lethe scales with man
> The shining steps of Nature, shares with man
> His nights, his days, moves with him to one goal, (vii.232–6).

In recitation, Tennyson's pitch likely climbed and fell with the words "rise or sink" and "dwarfed or godlike," and then rose or "scale[d]" with the next line.[13] The lines sonorously communicate the heights to which men and women could ascend (or fall) together. Musical choices (e.g., pitch and rhythm) introduce what *The Princess* terms the female contribution. The goal is masculine (the poet's words), but without the feminine (lyrical), his aspirations would "sink." From a biographical perspective, it is relevant that Tennyson felt considerable anxiety to preserve the sonorous aspects of his poetic meaning.[14]

Of course, music and words are not inherently gendered, just as masculine and feminine nouns in French do not emerge from biology or gender performance. Rather, the music simile relies upon cultural associations. Non-semantic (emotional) meaning is a long-standing, oppressive female stereotype. Here, it potentially undercuts the argument for women's access to higher education (traditionally the purview of reason and logic).

Ballads and Songs

The Princess's interwoven songs are more realistic than the fairy tale story and often more melodic in their sonority than the prince's blank verse. Regular rhyming and metrical schemes in all the songs endow a sonic patterning, augmented in the ballads by their being specific poetic and musical forms. A poem ballad is defined by its alternation of lines of four and three accents, in either an abcb or abab rhyme scheme. Tennyson's ballads align with this older, accentual form of balladry. (Other ballad forms count both a line's syllables and accents.) The ballad meter (the accentual pattern) in three of the interpolated songs makes them sound recognizably "ancient."[15]

These ballads are formally experimental in a way that creates interest to knowledgeable ears, while also specifically fitting *The Princess: A Medley*. The

---

[13] This assertion can be made because there are early sound recordings of Tennyson reciting. Tennyson records, BBC Recorded Programmes Permanent Library, Lib No 18941–45, British Library. As discussed below, Emily Tennyson's text settings are another type of recording since they reveal what she heard in her husband's recitation choices.

[14] See Weliver, *Mary Gladstone and the Victorian Salon*, 200–40.

[15] The ballads are the first, second and fourth interpolated songs in *The Princess*. However, while Emily Tennyson chose the ballad version of IV ∧ V to include in *The Princess*, the alternative text that she set to music is not a ballad. **[Extract 1.]** See the below section on "Setting Songs" for Lady Tennyson's role in choosing and ordering the added 1850 songs.

number of stresses in a ballad (4 + 3) mirrors the seven fairy tale parts, for instance. More broadly, the women's songs are "medleys" (like the subtitle) of literary forms. Today's anthologies often introduce an additional formal blending in the first song by laying out all the textual variants, so that I ^ II appears to combine ballad meter with the fourteen lines of a sonnet (albeit without the sonnet's usual iambic pentameter and break between lines 8 and 9 into two discrete, but related sections). [**Extract 1.**] This unusual formal blending (ballad/sonnet) was introduced after Tennyson's fifth revision to the poem in 1853. More importantly, all versions of this song about two parents and their deceased child sonorously divide into three parts (the 1850 version and the anthologized sonnet have refrains at lines 4, 8, 12, while the 1851 edition introduces a trio of terminal vowel sounds in the rhyme scheme – abccb – as opposed to abcbdb in 1850). Sonically emphasizing the presence of three (the full family) contributes to meaning through what we hear, while other elements align with the survival of two (besides the division of the 4+3 of the ballad into two lines, a stanza break in the 1851 edition visually represents a pair).

The second song, "Sweet and Low," also reveals formal play. [**Extract 1.**] Like other English nursery songs, it is accentually driven,[16] but its stanzas combine the ballad's two quatrains and lengthen the last line to include all seven accents. It seems a variation on a Spenserian stanza (eight iambic pentameter lines followed by an alexandrine [iambic hexameter] and rhyming ababbcbcc, which arose with Edmund Spenser's epic poem, *The Faerie Queen* [1590–5]). Tennyson's rhyme scheme – ababaabb, cdcdccdb – similarly relies upon mixtures of cross rhymes (abab) and rhyming couplets (aa) – and lengthens the last line. Not only are the archaic ballad elements appropriate in the interstices of a fairy tale set long ago, but the long history of the Spenserian stanza also fits.

Tennyson seems especially alive to word-painting in the intercalated songs. The explosive consonants in ballad IV ^ V fit the martial "beat to battle" (line 2), as does "Blow, bugle, blow" in song III ^ IV. [**Extract 1.**] In the latter song, furthermore, "**Blow, bugle; an**swer, **ech**oes, **dy**ing, **dy**ing, **dy**ing" recedes like an echo because the first syllables bear the stress (the line is trochaic; stresses bolded). In stanza 2, the emphatic observations, "O **hark**, O **hear**! how **thin** and **clear**," transform into more echoes in the next line: "And **thin**ner, **clear**er, **far**ther **go**ing!" The multisyllabic words are stressed on the first syllable, which makes the second syllable seem to trail away. The specifically melodic possibility increases with the apostrophes ("O") in stanzas 2 and 3 (see also VI ^ VII in **Extract 1**). Apostrophes – a feeling address – rely upon melodic inflection to communicate meaning, rather than being a word with specified signification.

---

[16] See Bill Gahan, "Ballad Measure in Print," *English Broadside Ballad Archive*, dir. Patricia Fumerton (University of California at Santa Barbara Department of English, 2007) <https://ebba.english.ucsb.edu/page/ballad-measure-in-print> [Accessed October 24, 2024].

More than music as only metaphoric, these lyric aspects blur poetry with highly musical elements.

In their realism, the six interspersed songs from 1850 (assigned to the ladies) [**Extract 1**] differ from the risible songs performed by a man that are contained *within* the fairy tale (which Tennyson included in all editions of the poem). First, the male narrator of Part IV takes the part of a "maid" (iv.19) who responds to Ida's request for music. [**Extract 2.**] S/he renders "'Tears, idle tears,' / [...] / with such passion" that upon its conclusion, "the tear, / She sang of, shook and fell, an erring pearl / Lost in her bosom" (iv.21, 41–3). The sentimental performance, followed by the sudden surprise of a tear falling into cleavage, offers just the sort of sharp contrast that fit mid-nineteenth-century ideas of humor. According to Gerald Massey in the *North British Review* (1860), "The deepest humour and pathos [...] are two sides of the same mental coin."[17] The descent into the ludicrous also underpins the caricature offered by W.S. Gilbert and Arthur Sullivan in their spoof of *The Princess*, "A Respectful Operatic Per-Version of Tennyson's 'Princess,' in Three Acts," more formally titled *Princess Ida; or, Castle Adamant*, which premiered at London's Savoy Theatre on January 5, 1884. In it, the cross-dressed Hilarion (the operetta thus names the prince) exaggerates the sublime, for humorous effect: "I am a maiden, cold and stately, / Heartless I, with a face divine." [**Excerpt 3.**] A seed of truth can be found within the ridiculous, however, for a later musical contribution from the listening ladies in *The Princess* offers a corrective pathos to the bathos of the Part IV male narrator.[18] In the song added between Parts V and VI, a lady responds to her husband's death with the numbness of grief, until her child is placed "upon her knee," at which point "came her tears – / 'Sweet my child, I live for thee.'" [**Extract 1.**] Sung by a woman (not a male impersonator), this song offers a noble example of love and motherhood and, in so doing, seriously accounts for tears of love. Perhaps it also decodes *The Princess* overall, as Tennyson intended. "The child is the link through the parts," explained the poet, "as shown in the Songs (inserted 1850), which are the best interpreters of the poem."[19]

Setting Songs

Another, not unrelated method of approaching the meaning of the (women's) music in *The Princess* is through Emily Tennyson's role in the poem's revision history. Reflecting on his parents, the Tennysons' eldest son Hallam wrote, "With her he always discussed what he was working at; she transcribed his poems: to her and to no one else he referred for a final criticism before

---

[17] Gerald Massey, "American Humour," *North British Review* 63 (November 1860): 472.
[18] Besides "Tears, idle tears," Part IV also includes "O Swallow, Swallow," a courtship song performed in falsetto by the male narrator who impersonates the cross-dressed prince.
[19] Hallam Tennyson, *Memoir*, 1: 254.

publishing."[20] Even before they were married, Emily composed piano/vocal settings of Alfred's poems, eventually producing a total of twenty-four settings between 1832 and his death in 1892, and publishing about half of them.[21] Although we cannot know the full extent of Emily's contribution to *The Princess* specifically, its composition process uncannily echoes the collaboration of men (blank verse) and women (music) in the poem's architecture. Emily chose among variants of the different song lyrics composed by Alfred and wrote the placement of songs into the manuscript for the third edition, composed music for three of the six songs added in 1850, and published these songs with her husband into the 1890s.[22] The revision process thus far exceeded the period between first and fifth editions; it spanned the Tennysons' life together.

In one sense, Emily's songs are a recording. They "give the impression of my Father's reading," as Hallam noted on the fly-leaf of one of Emily's manuscript music books. "My Mother's settings of my Father's Poems were made mostly after she had first heard them read by him."[23] Yet at least once, the "music [was] written before publication of the words," according to a note in Emily Tennyson's hand at the top of the manuscript music.[24] "Sweet and Low" is also notable for setting the same words that appear in the published poem as compared to Emily's two other *Princess* songs, which set alternate texts. [**Extract 1.**] Because the songs do not obviously contribute to the fairy tale plot, the versions are easily exchangeable (like and different). The poem's women, moreover, select their own musical contributions as Emily similarly selects the words to set.

The settings themselves also have fascinating implications for word/music interactions. They seem to focus mostly on the words.[25] As a whole, Emily Tennyson's music is difficult to sing given the vowel settings and how the music

---

[20] Ibid., 1: 331.
[21] See Phyllis Weliver, "Emily Tennyson's Music Manuscript Books" (March 31, 2016), *Sounding Tennyson*, <http://soundingtennyson.org/app.html#/summary/EssayManuscriptBooks> and "Performance and Publication of Emily Tennyson's Music" (March 31, 2016), *Sounding Tennyson*, <http://soundingtennyson.org/app.html#/summary/EssayEmilysMusic> [Accessed November 1, 2024].
[22] Ewan Jones and Phyllis Weliver, "*The Princess* and the Tennysons' Performance of Childhood," *The Edinburgh Companion to Literature and Music*, ed. Delia da Sousa Correa (Edinburgh: Edinburgh University Press, 2020) 462–75. Emily Tennyson's manuscript music album suggests the date "September 30 1880[?]" as when fifteen songs were sent to Natalie Janotha to arrange, but 1890 is likelier. See Natalie Janotha to Hallam Tennyson, January 23 and September 8, 1890, TRC/Letters/3815–6, Lincolnshire County Council.
[23] Unknown hand despite Hallam's "signature," in Emily Tennyson, manuscript music album, TRC/Music/5321, Lincolnshire County Council, f 1.
[24] Emily Tennyson's hand, note on Emily Tennyson, "Sweet and Low," in ibid., f 149v.
[25] See Emily Tennyson's settings on the *Sounding Tennyson* website. Sung by Phyllis Weliver and accompanied by Francesco Izzo on Prince Albert's piano, <http://soundingtennyson.org/app.html#/music> [Accessed October 24, 2024].

FIG. 12.1: Albumen print of Alfred Lord Tennyson and Emily Lady Tennyson with their sons at Farringford, by Oscar Gustav Rejlander, c.1862.

lies in the voice. Victorian composer Charles Villiers Stanford addressed Lady Tennyson's choices of keys when he transcribed her version of "Hands all Round" for baritone Charles Santley in 1882: "The lie of the notes is [...] too low [...] that is if you wish the same voice to sing the high notes as well. [...] the song won't be so effective when sung as it looks upon paper or sounds on the piano."[26] Was Emily simply a better pianist than singer, or did the aim to

---

[26] Charles Villiers Stanford to Emily Tennyson, February 20, 1882, TRC/Letters/7394, Lincolnshire County Council. Reproduced by permission of Lincolnshire

duplicate Alfred's recitation choices trump basic musical considerations? Certainly, when seven of Emily's songs (arranged by a Clara Schumann student, Natalie Janotha) were performed at St James's Hall in London, the press noted "the irregular rhythms" of the melodies, "apparently being the result of an attempt to fit the words."[27] Two of these pieces were from *The Princess* ("Home they brought him" and "Lady let the rolling drums").[28] Similarly, the under-composed piano parts suggest that the scored notes may have functioned as reminders to the player, who filled them out in performance.[29] Regardless, the page and performance rely upon each other to make a whole, as *The Princess* similarly conceives of heterosexual marriage.

This gap between words and music stirred the imagination of nineteenth-century authors and composers. So, too, was the space between women's and men's roles examined and addressed in Victorian Britain. It is only to be expected that the two invite comparison in creative practice and product, as the Tennysons exemplify.

Scored Music

Sullivan, Arthur and W.S. Gilbert. *Princess Ida, Or, Castle Adamant*. Vocal score. London: Chappell, 1884. *International Music Score Library Project* [*IMSLP*], <https://imslp.org/wiki/Princess_Ida_(Sullivan%2C_Arthur)> [Accessed October 24, 2024].

Listening

Sullivan, Arthur. *Princess Ida*. Jeffrey Skitch, John Reed, Kenneth Sandford, Philip Potter, Donald Adams, Elizabeth Harwood, D'Oyly Carte Opera Company, Royal Philharmonic Orchestra, Malcolm Sargent. Decca, 2003.

County Council in Weliver, "Performance and Publication of Emily Tennyson's Music," *Sounding Tennyson*, <http://soundingtennyson.org/app.html#/summary/EssayEmilysMusic> [Accessed November 1, 2024].

[27] Press clipping from *Truth* regarding the March 13, 1891 concert at St James's Hall, London, TRC/Catalogue/6877, Lincolnshire County Council.

[28] Emily Tennyson, arr. Natalie Janotha, words Alfred Tennyson, *Songs by Lord Tennyson* (London: Chappell [1892]). See Weliver, "Emily Tennyson's Music Manuscript Books," *Sounding Tennyson* <http://soundingtennyson.org/app.html#/summary/EssayManuscriptBooks> [Accessed November 1, 2024]. For the publication history of "Sweet and Low," see Jones and Weliver, "*The Princess* and the Tennysons' Performance of Childhood," 467–72.

[29] My thanks to musicologist and professional pianist Francesco Izzo for this observation, which he made while we were recording the music for the *Sounding Tennyson* project (December 8, 2015).

Tennyson, Emily. "Break, Break, Break." *Sounding Tennyson*. Phyllis Weliver. <http://soundingtennyson.org/app.html#/music> [Accessed October 24, 2024].

Further Reading

Clapp-Itnyre, Alisa. "Marginalized Musical Interludes: Tennyson's Critique of Conventionality in *The Princess*." *Victorian Poetry* 38 (2000): 227–48.

Fiss, Laura Kasson. "'This Particularly Rapid, Unintelligible Patter': Patter Songs and the Word-Music Relationship." *The Cambridge Companion to Gilbert and Sullivan*. Eds David Eden and Meinhard Saremba. Cambridge: Cambridge University Press, 2009. 98–108.

Gahan, Bill. "Ballad Measure in Print." *English Broadside Ballad Archive*. Dir. Patricia Fumerton. University of California at Santa Barbara Department of English. 2007. <https://ebba.english.ucsb.edu/page/ballad-measure-in-print> [Accessed November 1, 2024].

Griffiths, Eric. *The Printed Voice of Victorian Poetry*. Oxford: Oxford University Press, 1989.

Helsinger, Elizabeth K. *Poetry and the Thought of Song in Nineteenth-Century Britain*. Charlottesville: University of Virginia Press, 2015.

Jones, Ewan and Phyllis Weliver. "*The Princess* and the Tennysons' Performance of Childhood." *The Edinburgh Companion to Literature and Music*. Ed. Delia da Sousa Correa. Edinburgh: Edinburgh University Press, 2020. 462–75.

Prins, Yopie. "'Break, Break, Break' into Song." *Meter Matters: Verse Cultures of the Long Nineteenth Century*. Ed. Jason Hall. Athens, Ohio: Ohio University Press, 2011. 105–34.

Ricks, Christopher. *Tennyson*. (1972). 2nd edn. Berkeley: University of California Press, 1989.

Santonja, Blanca. "Musical Lights: Illuminating the Shadows in Tennyson's *The Princess*." *Victorian Poetry* 62.3 (2024), forthcoming.

Tennyson, Alfred. *Tennysons Archive: Digitising the Work of the Tennysons, Plural*. PIs Ewan Jones and Phyllis Weliver. <https://www.english.cam.ac.uk/research/tennyson/2017/02/20/tennysons-archive/> [Accessed October 24, 2024].

Weliver, Phyllis. *Mary Gladstone and the Victorian Salon: Music, Literature, Liberalism*. Cambridge: Cambridge University Press, 2017.

CHAPTER 13

Reading Whitman, Hearing Vaughan Williams: Sexuality, National Politics and the Role of the Artist in Society

SARAH COLLINS

Recommended Texts

Walt Whitman, *Leaves of Grass* (Boston: Osgood, 1881–2). Further citations are given parenthetically in the text. A transcription of the 1881–2 edition, as well as images of scanned pages from this edition, are available to view at *The Walt Whitman Archive*, <https://whitmanarchive.org/item/ppp.01663> [Accessed October 24, 2024].[1]

Ralph Vaughan Williams, *A Sea Symphony* [Symphony No. 1] (London: Stainer & Bell, n.d. [1918]). Score available in Canada and the USA for free download through *International Music Score Library Project* [IMSLP], <https://imslp.org/wiki/A_Sea_Symphony_(Symphony_No.1)_(Vaughan_Williams,_Ralph)> [Accessed October 24, 2024].

Keywords

Democracy, difference, empire, masculinity, modernism, nationalism, nineteenth-century America, poetry, politics, queerness, symphony, text-setting, transatlantic, twentieth-century Britain, Ralph Vaughan Williams, Victorian Britain, Walt Whitman

---

[1] A useful note on the context for this edition can be found in Dennis K. Renner, "*Leaves of Grass*, 1881–82 edition," *Walt Whitman: An Encyclopedia*, eds R. LeMaster and Donald D. Kummings (New York: Garland, 1998), available at *The Walt Whitman Archive*, <https://whitmanarchive.org/criticism/current/encyclopedia/entry_26.html> [Accessed October 24, 2024].

Prelude

Extract 1

Walt Whitman, "As I Ebb'd with the Ocean of Life," *Leaves of Grass*, 202 (sec. 2, lines 4–7); 203 (sec. 4, lines 1–4).

> As the ocean so mysterious rolls toward me closer and closer,
> I too but signify at the utmost a little wash'd-up drift,
> A few sands and dead leaves to gather,
> Gather, and merge myself as part of the sands and drift.
>
> […]
>
> Ebb, ocean of life, (the flow will return),
> Cease not your moaning you fierce old mother,
> Endlessly cry for your castaways, but fear not, deny not me,
> Rustle not up so hoarse and angry against my feet as I touch you
>   or gather from you.

Extract 2

Whitman, "Songs for All Seas, All Ships," *Leaves of Grass*, 208 (sec. 2, lines 1–11).

> Flaunt out O sea your separate flags of nations!
> Flaunt out visible as ever the various ship-signals!
> But do you reserve especially for yourself and for the soul of man one flag above all the rest,
> A spiritual woven signal for all nations, emblem of man elate above death,
> Token of all brave captains and all intrepid sailors and mates,
> And all that went down doing their duty,
> Reminiscent of them, twined from all intrepid captains young or old,
> A pennant universal, subtly waving all time, o'er all brave sailors,
> All seas, all ships.

Extract 3

Whitman, "On the Beach at Night Alone," *Leaves of Grass*, 207, full poem.

> On the beach at night alone,
> As the old mother sways her to and fro singing her husky song,
> As I watch the bright stars shining, I think a thought of the clef
>   of the universes and of the future.
> A vast similitude interlocks all,
> All spheres, grown, ungrown, small, large, suns, moons, planets,
> All distances of place however wide,
> All distances of time, all inanimate forms,
> All souls, all living bodies though they be ever so different, or in
>   different worlds,
> All gaseous, watery, vegetable, mineral processes, the fishes, the brutes,

All nations, colors, barbarisms, civilizations, languages,
All identities that have existed or may exist on this globe, or any globe,
All lives and deaths, all of the past, present, future,
This vast similitude spans them, and always has spann'd,
And shall forever span them and compactly hold and enclose them.

The Challenge

For British writers working during the final decades of the nineteenth century, the American poet Walt Whitman (1819–92) became an emblem of male–male friendship and desire. Yet British composers – who began to create musical settings of Whitman's verse some years later – largely eschewed the sexual implications of his thought, preferring its politically democratic and egalitarian associations. It may be tempting to read the turn from the "sexual" or homoerotic Whitman to the "democratic" Whitman as part of a broader narrative in British music history about the reaction against *fin-de-siècle* Aestheticism, with a corollary shift in the popular conception of the artist – from an apolitical, cosmopolitan, metropolitan, dandy figure in the late-Victorian period, toward a patriotic, rough-cut, "voice of the people" figure in the years prior to World War I. Yet looking more closely at Ralph Vaughan Williams's *A Sea Symphony* for orchestra and chorus (which includes text excerpts from Whitman's *Leaves of Grass*) can reveal continuities between ideas about sexuality and national culture that belie this stark shift. This case study asks: In what way does the musical treatment of a poetic text reveal surprising intersections and continuities across areas of public discourse that are often considered to be separate?

Background

At the time of Walt Whitman's death in 1892, the poet was more widely celebrated in Britain than in his own country, with his poetry being lauded by the likes of Algernon Charles Swinburne, Alfred Tennyson, William Michael Rossetti, John Addington Symonds and Edward Carpenter. Although Whitman's work was considered by many on both sides of the Atlantic to be overly "coarse" and "sensual," the cultural value placed on these characteristics differed, and within British literary circles an appreciation for Whitman became a marker of forward-thinking, as well as of homosocial friendship. The noted scholar of queer theory Eve Sedgwick has described Whitman as an "English (far more than as an American) prophet of sexual politics for the nineteenth century."[2] She highlights, for example, how "*Leaves of Grass* operated most characteristically as a conduit from one man to another of feelings that had, in many

---

[2] Eve Kosofsky Sedgwick, *Between Men: English Literature and Male Homosocial Desire* (New York: Columbia University Press, 1985) 204.

FIG. 13.1: Walt Whitman by Samuel Hollyer. Engraving of a daguerreotype by Gabriel Harrison (original lost), 1854, printed as the frontispiece for the 1855 self-published edition of *Leaves of Grass*.

cases, been private or inchoate," and even how "photographs of Whitman, gifts of Whitman's books, specimens of his handwriting, news of Whitman, [and] admiring references to 'Whitman' [...] seem[ed] to have functioned as badges of homosexual recognition."[3]

Whitman's deliberate projection of a rough-hewn self-image attracted particular class associations that shaped his British reception as a "prophet of

[3] Ibid., 205–6.

sexual politics," leaving room for multiple versions of male–male relations in British literary culture between the 1860s and 1880s. On the one hand, there was an aristocratic, feminized, cosmopolitan, apolitical model that drew inspiration from "Catholic Europe."[4] And on the other, male bonds among the "educated middle classes" eschewed associations with femininity, casting the absence of women as a virilizing force, and one that promoted manly brotherhood as an exemplar of democratic egalitarianism, drawing inspiration from classical Sparta and Athens.[5] It is important to note, for the purposes of this chapter, that this second version of manly bonds was explicitly about political participation, in contrast to the apolitical, feminized model. In Sedgwick's account, the development of the second, middle-class model, was substantially facilitated by the reception of Whitman by British writers such as John Addington Symonds and Edward Carpenter. Through these writers, this model of interaction was extended well beyond homosexual relations towards the broader concepts of egalitarianism, democracy and human brotherhood that underpinned Whitman's eroticized political philosophy. Carpenter wrote for example, "Eros is the great leveler [that] unites in the closest affection the most estranged ranks of society,"[6] reflecting the indivisibility of the political and sexual ideologies at play here.

This middle-class conception of male bonds – expressed through masculine virility, strong political agency and democratic ideals – was ultimately subverted by the moral panic surrounding the trials of Oscar Wilde in 1895.[7] At this critical moment, the many nuanced renderings of a Whitman-inspired male comradeship forged in the service of democracy were flattened out into the more singular, apolitical, aristocratic model for which Wilde became an icon, and which has become the enduring male homosexual stereotype.

Although British writers had been reading Whitman since at least 1856 (only one year after the publication of the first edition of *Leaves of Grass* in North

---

[4] Ibid., 207.
[5] Ibid., 206–7.
[6] Edward Carpenter, *The Intermediate Sex* (London: Sonnenschein, 1909) 114, quoted in Richard Cavell and Peter Dickinson, "Bucke, Whitman, and the Cross-Border Homosocial," *American Review of Canadian Studies* 26.3 (1996): 426–7.
[7] The first trial was brought by Wilde himself, a claim of libel against the Marquess of Queensberry, who had accused Wilde of engaging in homosexual practices. Homosexual acts between men were criminalized by the Criminal Law Amendment Act 1885, and this remained the law in the UK until 1967. As part of Queensberry's defense against Wilde's libel case in 1895, he marshaled evidence of Wilde's homosexual associations, which were persuasive enough to acquit Queensberry of libel, while at the same time opening the way for a criminal prosecution of Wilde for "gross indecency" under this Act (s11). The result of this second trial was a hung jury, resulting in a further criminal trial which ultimately saw Wilde prosecuted and imprisoned. The three trials have become a flashpoint in the history of public discourse about male homosexuality.

America), the concentration of settings of Whitman's poetry by British composers did not occur until the turn of the century.[8] During this time, Whitman's verse was set by composers such as Vaughan Williams, Gustav Holst, Frederick Delius, Cyril Scott, Percy Grainger, Rutland Boughton, Frank Bridge, Samuel Coleridge-Taylor, Ivor Gurney, Charles Villiers Stanford, Charles Wood, Arthur Bliss, Hamilton Harty and W.H. Bell, among others. By the time these musical settings began to appear, not only had the political and sexual landscape shifted dramatically within a burgeoning modernism, but new editions of Whitman's verse were already evincing a degree of editorial sanitization, driven by the author himself and his British devotees such as William Michael Rossetti.

The impact of these sanitizing efforts is reflected in the shifting critical response. In the 1870s, for example, music critics were calling Whitman the "wild word-monger of the West, who [...] preaches the supremacy of carnality: the flesh he deifies above the spirit, the life above him who lives it."[9] Yet by the turn of the century, the associations were quite different. The critical response to Vaughan Williams's *A Sea Symphony*, in which he set fragments of Whitman's poetry, gives an indication of the extent of this change, one critic noting, "When we think of music in association with Walt Whitman we imagine something of the sustained spirituality, of the fleshless grandeur, of Palestrina – an exaltation of senses pouring out in music of a grand, yet simple, continuity. Whitman is the purest spirit among poets."[10] It seems almost unfathomable that after acting as such a powerful symbol of homosocial relations in the Victorian literary sphere, and being thereby implicated in the moral controversies of the 1890s, Whitman's poetry could come out of the other side of the Wilde trials somehow purified for British composers, so that they were able to simply ignore this key feature of Whitman's politics. That Whitman could go from being described as the "supremacy of carnality" to being considered the apotheosis of "fleshless grandeur" in the musical sphere speaks to an astounding shift.

In addition to changing attitudes toward homosexuality and political participation, another factor shaping the reception of Whitman was the position of British culture with respect to the geopolitical changes that were occurring during this period. Britain's imperialist endeavors were not only the result of economic and political motivations, but were also predicated on a universalist view of humanity and a paternalistic vision of culture as a civilizing force. By

---

[8] According to Byron Adams, this highpoint dated from 1884–1936. Byron Adams, "'No Armpits, Please, We're British': Whitman and English Music, 1884–1936," *Walt Whitman and Modern Music*, ed. Lawrence Kramer (New York: Garland, 2000) 25.

[9] Anonymous, "The Advent of the Uncouth," *The Orchestra* 18 (1872): 378. The musical impact of Whitman's "decadence," according to this critic, was manifest in opera composition as the rejection of melody and the democratic pre-eminence of chorus singers above soloists, both of which s/he equated with Wagner.

[10] "Dr R. Vaughan Williams," *The Musical Herald* 781 (1913): 99.

contrast, many European nations experienced an intensified sense of nationalism during the nineteenth century, and they cultivated national forms of cultural expression with more urgency than in Britain. The years before World War I were therefore a time of cultural recuperation for many British artists, a putative "turn inward." Yet the clash between the national and "universal" was not as pronounced as it was elsewhere. The work of both Vaughan Williams and Whitman became very much a part of an equipoise that elsewhere presented starker binaries.

Case Study

Ralph Vaughan Williams (1872–1958) once described Whitman as being "too fond of the smell of his own armpits."[11] The comment – if indeed it was reported accurately – refers to the fecundity of Whitman's poetic imagery, which often plays upon bodily metaphors. Despite this apparently dismissive sentiment, the composer became enthralled with Whitman after being handed a copy of *Leaves of Grass* at Cambridge in 1892 by philosopher and mathematician Bertrand Russell, who was at the time experiencing his own sexual awakening via Whitman's text.[12] Vaughan Williams went on to acquire *Leaves of Grass* in several editions and a range of sizes and formats, and it was described as "his constant companion."[13] He even took a pocket-sized version with him during his military service in World War I, jotting down reminders in the book jacket relating to his work running the ammunitions wagon.[14] Forty years (and twenty Whitman settings) later, in the last month of his life, when his biographer

---

[11] Oliver Neighbour, "The Place of the Eighth among Vaughan Williams's Symphonies," *Vaughan Williams Studies*, ed. Alain Frogley (Cambridge: Cambridge University Press, 1996) 216, n.10.

[12] Indeed, Ray Monk has commented that "the effect of lines [from Whitman's *Leaves of Grass*] upon Russell – who previously had nearly swooned when his teacher used the word 'breast' – was electrifying, and served to confirm him in his view of America as 'a land of promise for lovers of freedom.' Whitman – or 'Walt,' as Russell always called him, conferring upon him the intimacy of a close friend – became one of his idols. The first place he visited when he went to America three years later was the house in which Whitman had lived. It was a gesture of respect and gratitude for Whitman's having brought out into the open, and declared healthy and normal, desires that, by the spring of 1893, had become so strong in Russell that he considered them a threat to his sanity." Ray Monk, *Bertrand Russell: The Spirit of Solitude, 1872–1921*, vol. 1 (New York: The Free Press, 1996) 53.

[13] Ursula Vaughan Williams, *R.V.W.: A Biography of Ralph Vaughan Williams* (London: Oxford University Press, 1964) 65.

[14] This list of reminders included: "1.) six gun teams / 800 rounds of amm. / Officers kit, wagon / Water cart to be up here at 6pm; 2.) Lewis guns with am." Quoted in Ursula Vaughan Williams, *R.V.W.*, 128.

and friend Michael Kennedy asked him about Whitman, Vaughan Williams apparently answered, "I've never got over him, I'm glad to say."[15]

That Vaughan Williams's clear devotion to Whitman might have been tempered in some way by an underlying unease with the poet's corporeal associations may signal his awareness of the shifting anxieties about homosexuality at the time. Yet it also points toward the composer's sense of positioning in relation to certain cultural and political shifts during the decades around the turn of the twentieth century. Vaughan Williams spoke and wrote passionately about his concern for the role of Britain in international politics, and while he supported the idea of a federated Europe, he was committed to fostering a strong national culture for Britain.

With this collection of ideas in mind, we can begin to discern why in the Victorian literary context Whitman generated an alternative model of male-male bonds, while in the early twentieth-century British musical context his work generated an alternative model of national affiliation. This model was essentially a form of rooted cosmopolitanism – an ethic that was associated with strong political commitment, and which attracted masculine connotations. Both models developed from Whitman's essential reimagining of the relationship between self and other, or between sameness and difference, and from Vaughan Williams's musical sensitivity to this theme in Whitman's work, as we shall see.

The Sea as an Emblem of Sameness and Difference

In an autobiographical reminiscence, "Specimen Days," Whitman wrote of the seashore, variously as both a border – namely, a "dividing line, contact, junction"; a point of reconciliation – a "blending" or "marrying"; a point of transformation – from "objective form" to "subjective spirit"; and a point of mutual interpenetration – "each made portion of the other."[16] It is in the last sense that the seashore functions in Whitman's poetry as a point where the apparent unity of the whole is shown to be underpinned by multiplicity.

This function of the seashore in Whitman's poetry is especially clear in the first two poems of the eleven-poem *Sea-Drift* cluster, prepared for the 1881 edition of *Leaves of Grass*, parts of which were set to music by both Delius (*Sea Drift*, 1903–4) and Vaughan Williams (*A Sea Symphony*, 1903–9). Here, the sea embodies a sense of pre-subject union from which individual subjectivities emerge, and back into which they eventually recede with the ebb and flow of the tide. Issuing from the "fierce old mother" of the sea, Whitman imagines the individual as "chaff, straw, splinters of wood, weeds, and the sea-gluten / Scum,

---

[15] Michael Kennedy, *The Works of Ralph Vaughan Williams* (Oxford: Oxford University Press, 1964; new edn 1980) 100.
[16] Walt Whitman, "Sea-Shore Fancies," *Prose Works 1892, Vol. 1 Specimen Days*, ed. Floyd Stovall (New York: New York University Press, 1963) 138–9, lines 1–5.

scales from shining rocks, leaves of salt-lettuce, left by the Tide" ("As I Ebb'd with the Ocean of Life," sec. 1, lines 13–14), whose separateness or distance is strikingly precarious.

Likewise, in **Extract 1**, the sea here signifies death, but also the eternal recurrence of life, or the immortality of the soul ("and merge myself as part of the sands and drift"). The sea embodies wholeness in contrast to the "wash'd-up drift" of humanity, yet its function involves both synthesis (namely in subsuming the individual upon death) and atomization (by being the organ of birth or individuation). In this sense, the unit is always already present in the whole, and should logically undermine its unity. For Whitman though, it is only through this realization that the speaker is able to become truly himself, truly individual, indeed truly human ("Now in a moment I know what I am for, I awake").[17] Significantly, it is the seashore – "The rim, the sediment that stands for all the water and all the land of the globe"[18] – that provides the site for and instigator of this revelatory incongruity.

Quite apart from Whitman the man, this conception of the point between land and ocean – the seashore – as a point of "blending" rather than a border, might also offer an understanding of the ideological function that his poetry came to play in various national contexts. We can see this in the literal sea-crossing of Whitman's poems – namely, his transatlantic reception within a British nation geographically bounded by the sea, and with a powerful tradition of seafaring and colonization. The relationship between the putative "center" and "peripheries" of the British Empire, and its implications for constructions of Otherness and difference, was an active political concern at the turn of the twentieth century.[19] This concern becomes important when we consider that Whitman's poetic evocation of the concept of retaining diversity within unity, evoked both explicitly and metaphorically in the imagery of the sea and seashore, underpins the text chosen by Vaughan Williams for *A Sea Symphony*.

This concern is most aptly demonstrated in the relationship between the first and second movements of the Symphony. The portions of text that Vaughan Williams chose to highlight in the first movement, titled "Song for all Seas, all Ships" [**Extract 2**], seem to forward an all-encompassing humanism, with the most direct reference to the unifying impulse of commemoration being introduced by the first appearance of the solo soprano voice: "Flaunt out O sea your separate flags of nations!" This rallying cry is immediately echoed by the chorus, with an extraordinary *a cappella* choral unison on the phrase "separate flags of nations!" The setting of this choral unison to a phrase that directly

---

[17] Walt Whitman, "Out of the Cradle Endlessly Rocking," from "Sea-Drift" in *Leaves of Grass* (Boston: Osgood, 1881–2) 200, line 148.
[18] Whitman, "As I Ebb'd," 202 (sec. 1, line 9).
[19] For the musical implications, see Eric Saylor and Christopher M. Scheer, eds, *The Sea in the British Musical Imagination* (Woodbridge: The Boydell Press, 2015).

refers to separateness is noteworthy, given that Vaughan Williams's intention here was clearly to convey the sense of unity that underpins the text as a whole. Also, there are a range of explicit references to unity in the text that might seem more obviously to warrant such special treatment – such as "one flag above all the rest" (which upon its first appearance receives a particularly ambivalent harmonic treatment); "signal for all nations" (given a contrapuntal setting); and "a pennant universal" (first exclaimed by solo baritone). This choice to preserve unison choral treatment for textual references to diversity is again exemplified a short while later at "various flags and ship-signals."

The musical high point of this movement occurs at the setting of the words "one flag," though even here the sense of grandeur quickly disintegrates into the uncertain singularity of the solo soprano, who descends quietly into her lower register at "above all the rest." She then gives a still and solemn repetition of the very line of text that received such a cataclysmic setting at the opening of the movement: "behold the sea itself, and on its limitless, heaving breast the ships." The fragile fading *pianissimo* D major chord with which the movement ends seems again, in such contrast to the heroic opening, to undermine the notion that Vaughan Williams intended his setting of Whitman here to be an unbridled exaltation of "oceanic unity" and brotherhood.

The juxtaposition provided by the second movement, "On the Beach at Night, Alone" [**Extract 3**], only deepens the sense of stillness and solitude left by the first movement, though again it is not a simple divisibility with which Vaughan Williams seems concerned. Rather, the solitude of the second movement is a solitude of revelation in the idea of the indivisibility of time and space, with the solo baritone line maintaining an awe-struck monotone, with only narrow deviations.

Gradually, the celestial voices of the soft chorus join the solo quester, as if echoing from a great distance.[20] Again in monotone, though becoming more insistent: "all nations, all identities"; leading to "All lives and deaths, all of the past, present, future"; finally being reinforced by the unified *a cappella* chorus, beginning in monotone: "This vast similitude spans them, and always has spanned, / And shall forever span them and compactly hold and enclose them." The heroic brass fanfare that follows is violently cut off, as the movement recedes back into the solitariness of the opening solo monotone "on the beach at night alone."

Political Participation and the Function of the Artist

By examining the relationship between music and text in *A Sea Symphony*, we have seen how Vaughan Williams's musical setting of Whitman's verse draws out the theme of multiplicity within unity. The process has also shown us that

---

[20] The quotations that follow reference Vaughan Williams's orthography. He also excerpts Whitman's text at this point.

what appears to be a stark shift in reception of Whitman's verse from the sexual to the political belies the interconnection of these spheres of discourse at the turn of the twentieth century. Whitman's eroticized political philosophy, and Vaughan Williams's musical setting of Whitman's verse, offer insight into these interconnections.

One further piece of evidence in this case study can be gathered from Vaughan Williams's own essay writing. This additional set of sources suggests a deep integration of Whitman's aesthetic and political concerns within Vaughan Williams's own thinking about the role of the artist in society, and the national character of the English composer in particular. Drawing from Whitman's "Song of the Exposition" (1876), in which the poet tells us to stop wandering among the classics, and instead "know a better, fresher, busier sphere, a wide, untried domain."[21] Vaughan Williams argued in his article "Who Wants the English Composer?" (1912) that the composer should act as a voice of the people. Yet he also emphasized what he termed "personal individualism," which he saw as a constituent part of communal participation, rather than its opposition.[22] His understanding of the function of music in society and the responsibilities of the composer incorporated an aspect of contemplative isolation prior to community expression. After all, the composer's role was not merely to voice the will of the people, but also to activate the latent aspirations of the *polis* – to be "their own voice speaking through his art those things which they can only dimly grope for."[23] In this way, the realm of private experimentation was seen as enhancing rather than subverting the broader democratic system, in the same way that a strong national identity made one a more effective citizen of the world – thereby maintaining difference within sameness, and fending off the threat of "emasculated standardization" of the type he attributed to cultural internationalism.[24] Rather than being considered solely as a "code-word for illicit desire" in the Victorian literary sphere, and as an emblem of national or cosmic union in the musical sphere, then, Whitman should be considered in both instances as an advocate of the interdependence of difference and sameness – difference being associated with withdrawal and independence, and sameness indicating participation and communal identification.[25] By listening to Vaughan Williams while reading Whitman, and in the

---

[21] Whitman, "Song of the Exposition," *Leaves of Grass*, 158 (sec. 2, lines 6–7).
[22] Vaughan Williams, "Nationalism and Internationalism" (1942), included in his *National Music and Other Essays* (London: Oxford University Press) 154.
[23] Vaughan Williams, "Who Wants the English Composer," *Royal College of Music Magazine* 9.1 (1912): 12.
[24] Vaughan Williams, "Nationalism and Internationalism," 154.
[25] Richard Dallamora notes how Victorian aesthetes were accused of using Whitman in this coded manner. See Richard Dellamora, *Masculine Desire: The Sexual Politics of Victorian Aestheticism* (Chapel Hill: University of North Carolina Press, 1990) 87.

music-text relationships exhibited within *A Sea Symphony*, we can discern the interrelationship between these spheres of thought and practice.

Further Reading

Adams, Byron and Daniel M. Grimley, eds. *Vaughan Williams and his World*. Chicago: University of Chicago Press, 2023.

Collins, Sarah. "Nationalisms, Modernisms and Masculinities: Strategies of Displacement in Vaughan Williams's Reading of Walt Whitman." *Nineteenth Century Music Review* 14.1 (2017): 65–91.

Dellamora, Richard. *Masculine Desire: The Sexual Politics of Victorian Aestheticism*. Chapel Hill: University of North Carolina Press, 1990.

Esty, Jed. *A Shrinking Island: Modernism and National Culture in England*. Princeton: Princeton University Press, 2004.

Kramer, Lawrence. *Walt Whitman and Modern Music: War, Desire, and the Trials of Nationhood*. London: Routledge, 2018.

Prettejohn, Elizabeth. "From Aestheticism to Modernism, and Back Again." *Interdisciplinary Studies in the Long Nineteenth Century* 19.2 (2006). <https://19.bbk.ac.uk/article/id/1723/> [Accessed October 24, 2024].

Riley, Matthew, ed. *British Music and Modernism, 1895–1960*. Farnham: Ashgate, 2010.

Saylor, Eric and Christopher M. Scheer, eds. *The Sea in the British Musical Imagination*. Woodbridge: The Boydell Press, 2015.

Sedgwick, Eve Kosofsky. *Between Men: English Literature and Male Homosocial Desire*. New York: Columbia University Press, 1985.

Coda

Shafquat Towheed

Walter Pater (1839–94) famously claimed in *The Studies in the History of the Renaissance* (1873) that "[a]ll art constantly aspires towards the condition of music," noting its unity of matter and form.[1] While many critics have seconded Pater's elevation of music as first among equals, fewer have commented on the extent to which he also stressed the mutual interrelationship between the arts and their ability to inspire each other: "the arts are able, not indeed to supply the place of each other, but reciprocally to lend each other new forces."[2] Pater's emphasis on the mutually enriching relationship between the arts, not least between literature and music, is the approach taken throughout *Reading Texts in Music and Literature of the Long Nineteenth Century*. Within the volume, Elicia Clements in Chapter 11 provides an exemplary analysis of this interdependency in relation to Pater and *ekphrasis*, using Pater's "Duke Carl of Rosenmold" (1887) as the core text. As the editors note in their introduction, human responses to music and literature are "sometimes so closely linked that [...] they are impossible to separate" (1).

My own background as a historian of reading practices with a literary training puts me firmly on the textual rather than the musical side of things, but the fact is that the history of reading cannot be separated from the history of listening, and that words and notes have been in coexistence since the invention of writing (and music, of course, preceded words). All reading carries with it the cadence and rhythm of speech, and even silent reading is voiced in the imagination. Just as there can be no text without speech (whether implicit or explicit), there can be no literary work that does not have a relationship to music, whether through literary allusion, the representation of music (instrumental and vocal) in the work, or the more subtle implications of the soundscapes within the text. Beyond the text itself is the aural environment and the implications of reading a text in relation to the act of listening, whether passive or active. While directing the pioneering *UK Reading Experience Database*,

---

[1] Walter Pater, *The Renaissance: Studies in Art and Poetry: The 1893 Text*, ed. Donald Hill (Berkeley: University of California Press, 1980) 106; original emphasis.
[2] Ibid., 105.

1450–1945 at The Open University, one of the things that struck me immediately was the extent to which the responses of readers and listeners drew upon each other, that the coextensive nature of silent and voiced reading experiences meant that the same person could be both a reader and a listener in their engagement with a written text.[3] It also became evident to me that readable texts existed in a voiced and musical world, a soundscape both natural and manmade, and those reactions to reading literary works so often mirrored reactions to listening to music. While UK-RED could not include responses to listening to music in its 34,000 or so records, it soon led colleagues to develop a sister project at the same university and housed in the same school, the *Listening Experience Database*, which has since collected and curated over 12,000 records of listeners' responses to music.[4] This research synergy led to changes in pedagogy: both databases were embedded in curriculum, and colleagues at The Open University worked together to produce a third level interdisciplinary module, *Words and Music* (2008), with its own dedicated teaching texts. Similar initiatives in other universities also developed innovative curricula and put new pedagogical methods into practice, much of it increasingly making use of online digital platforms. This is the substrate which has nourished this particular volume.

Building upon their own prior work on interdisciplinary research projects and their considerable collective teaching expertise, contributors to *Reading Texts in Music and Literature of the Long Nineteenth Century* draw upon the rich synergy between these two arts, by normalizing "the study of music as a literary topic of the nineteenth century" (1) while also facilitating the interrogation of literature by music students. The editors of this volume have been innovative and thoughtful in their careful organization of material throughout. The editors modestly claim that *Reading Texts in Music and Literature of the Long Nineteenth Century* is a "cross between a reader, a workbook and a DIY manual for students and instructors" (1), but in fact, this book does all these things and much more, by offering an excellent model of pedagogical practice. The logically structured progression of material takes reader-learners from close reading of extracts of nineteenth-century primary-source material to independent research, via carefully constructed case studies and a wealth of contextual and background material. Eschewing the penchant for specialist technical terms that has plagued some interdisciplinary work on music and literature, this volume provides clear guidance to students and instructors at all levels, without making assumptions about prior knowledge.

---

[3] *UK Reading Experience Database, 1450–1945* (UK-RED), <https://www.open.ac.uk/Arts/reading/UK/> [Accessed October 24, 2024].

[4] *Listening Experience Database* (LED), <led.kmi.open.ac.uk/> [Accessed October 24, 2024].

Reading Texts in Music and Literature of the Long Nineteenth Century promises to open up new vistas for interdisciplinary teaching and research. This inclusive, generous and highly facilitating book brings together the best aspects of teaching and research in interdisciplinary nineteenth-century literature and music studies.

Index

acousmatic, 26, 34–5, 38
activism, Chapters 3, 4, 5 (*passim*)
aestheticism, 139, 188–90, 196 n.25, Chapter 11 (*passim*)
America, 4–13, Chapters 3, 4, 8, 13 (*passim*)
   Black America, 64 n.7, 88 n.9, 95, Chapter 8 (*passim*)
   Louisiana, Chapter 8 (*passim*) *see also* Creole
   Native America, 6–13, 64 n.7, 127–8
animal-welfare movement, Chapter 3 (*passim*)
anthropology, Chapter 7 (*passim*)
Auber, Daniel-Esprit, 129–31
auto/biography, 50, 66, 67, 98, 114, 141, 143, Chapters 2, 8, 10 (*passim*)

Bach, Johann Sebastian, 24, 114, 156, 166–8
ballad, 52, 109, 156, Chapters 5, 12 (*passim*)
   ballad meter, 52, 179–80
   broadside ballad, 84–5, 163
Bildungsroman, 33, 37
body, Chapter 1 (*passim*)
   political body, Chapters 3, 4, 5 (*passim*)
Bonnin, Gertrude Simmons, *see* Zitkála-Šá
Browning, Elizabeth Barrett, 176, Chapter 10 (*passim*)

cantata, 6–9, 150
castrati, Chapter 1 (*passim*)
Celtes, Conrad, 169–70
Champfleury, Jules (*pseud.*), Chapter 9 (*passim*)
Coleridge-Taylor, Samuel, 6–9, 191
Collins, Wilkie, 3–6

Courbet, Gustave, 138–9, 142
Creole, Chapter 8 (*passim*)

Decadence, 138–9, 191, Chapter 1 (*passim*)
democracy, Chapter 13 (*passim*)
digital humanities, 69–70, 73 n.24, Chapter 3 (*passim*), Coda
drag, 175, 181
Dupin de Francueil, Amantine Lucile Aurore, *see* Sand, George

education, 10, 115 n.17, 199
   children's, 112, Chapter 3 (*passim*)
   women's, Chapter 12 (*passim*)
Edwards, F.G., Chapter 10 (*passim*)
ekphrasis (musical), Chapter 11 (*passim*)
Elgar, Edward, Chapter 10 (*passim*)
empire, Chapters 0, 6, 7, 8, 10 (*passim*)
empowerment, Chapters 3, 4, 5 (*passim*)
ethnomusicology, Chapter 7 (*passim*)
exile, 135, 143

fairy tale, 144, Chapter 12 (*passim*)
feminist criticism, Chapters 4, 12 (*passim*)
Fétis, François-Joseph, 137–40
fiction, Chapters 0, 1, 2, 8, 11 (*passim*)
   prose romance, Chapter 5 (*passim*)
   short story, Chapters 1, 8, 11 (*passim*)
Fleury-Husson, Jules François Felix, *see* Champfleury, Jules
folk music, 9, 67–8, 109, 127, 138, 140, 166, Chapter 2, (*passim*)

gender, Chapters 1, 4, 13 (*passim*)
   gendered language, Chapter 12 (*passim*)

Goethe, Johann von, 168

Hoffmann, E.T.A., 36, 38, 138
humor, Chapter 12 (*passim*)
hybridity, Chapter 6 (*passim*)
hymns/chorales, 10, 54, 68–9, 109, 110, 112, 166, Chapter 6 (*passim*)

improvisation, 126–7
Indigenous music, Chapter 7 (*passim*)
interart/intermediality, 6, 9, Chapters 11, Coda (*passim*)
irony, 26, 48 n.9, 71, 85, 127, 177, Chapter 11 (*passim*)
isiXhosa, Chapter 6 (*passim*)

Jobey, Charles, Chapter 8 (*passim*)

Kiribati, Chapter 7 (*passim*)

landscape, Chapter 10 (*passim*)
Lee, Vernon (*pseud.*), Chapter 1 (*passim*)
listening, 52, 71, 166, 167, 181, 196, Chapters 0, 1, 2, 5, 7, 8, 9, 10, Coda (*passim*)
Liszt, Franz, 33, 136, 142
Longfellow, Henry Wadsworth, 6–9

masculinity, Chapter 13 (*passim*)
metaphor, 22, 37, 51, 81, 99–100, 101, 115, 143, 155, Chapters 12, 13 (*passim*)
missionaries, 109, 110, Chapter 6 (*passim*)
modernism, 162, 168, Chapter 13 (*passim*)
Morris, William, 63, Chapter 5 (*passim*)
musicalization, Chapter 11 (*passim*)
music criticism, 25, Chapters 9, 10 (*passim*)
musical structure 19, 181–4, Chapters 3, 4 (*passim*)
narrators/narrative voice, 3–4, 111–12, 155, Chapters 1, 2, 5, 8, 11, 12 (*passim*)
nationalism, 1, Chapters 10, 13 (*passim*)
national musics, 64, 67, 69, Chapters 0, 11 (*passim*)

Newman, John Henry, 149, 150–1
noise, 38–9, 113
non-fiction, *see* prose, non-fictional
non-Western music, 96, Chapter 7 (*passim*) *see also* Indigenous music
Ntsiko, Jonas, Chapter 6 (*passim*)

Oceania, Chapter 7 (*passim*)
opera, 6, 9, 10, 65, 66, 81 n.2, 114–15, 116, 164, 165, 166, 181, 191 n.9, Chapters 1, 8, 9 (*passim*)
Otherness, 2, 9, 34, 194, Chapters 2, 7, 8 (*passim*)

Paget, Violet, *see* Lee, Vernon
Pater, Walter, 198, Chapter 11 (*passim*)
poetry, 1, 6–13, 66, 84 n.7, 89, 108, 109, 110, 122, 128, 161–2, 163 n.6, 166–7, 168, Chapters 3, 10, 12, 13 (*passim*)
    see also prose poem, *see also* rhyme, *see also* rhythm
    and metrical hymn categorisation for music, Chapter 6 (*passim*)
    and performance, 182, Chapter 7 (*passim*)
    poetic conceit, 177–9
    poetic meter, 7, Chapters 3, 6, 12 (*passim*)
    as sonorous, 141, Chapter 12 (*passim*)
power, 6, 95, 97, 107, 157, 194, Chapters 2, 8 (*passim*)
program music, 24–5
prose, nonfictional, 161–2, Chapters 7, 9, 10 (*passim*) *see also* travel writing
prose poem, Chapter 9 (*passim*)

queerness, Chapters 1, 13 (*passim*)

race, 3–13, 64 n.7, 68, 151, 163 n.6, Chapters 7, 8 (*passim*)
reading, history of, Coda (*passim*)
recitation, 46 n.2, 47, 84, 109, 143, Chapter 12 (*passim*)
rhyme, 6, 50, 66, 67, 81–4, 85, 89, 125, 176–7, 179–80
rhythm, 6–8, 67, 81, 83, 85, 88–9, 100, 114, 176, 179, 198
Romanticism, 168, Chapters 1, 2, 9 (*passim*)

and illness, Chapter 1, 2 (*passim*)
Romantic virtuoso, Chapter 2 (*passim*)

Sand, George (*pseud.*), Chapter 2 (*passim*)
and Frédéric Chopin, 33, 39
Scotland, Chapter 7 (*passim*)
sexuality, Chapters 1, 13 (*passim*)
simile, 37, 111, 140, 178, 179
Smyth, Ethel, 27, Chapter 4 (*passim*)
Socialism, Chapter 5 (*passim*)
song, 2–3, 10–13, 23, 36, 125–8, 138 n.5, 168 n.18, 194, 196, Chapters 3, 4, 5, 7, 12 (*passim*)
spiritual, African American, 9, 52, 95
soundscape, 34, 38, 129–31, 155, 198
South Africa, Chapter 6 (*passim*)
Stevenson, Robert Louis, Chapter 7 (*passim*)
Sublime, the, 129, 131, 181
symbolism, 35, 37, 72–3, 98–9, 101, 156, 191
Symbolism, 139, 141

Tennyson, Alfred Lord, 163 n.6, 188, Chapter 12 (*passim*)

Tennyson, Emily Lady, Chapter 12 (*passim*)
text-setting, 6–13, Chapters 3, 4, 5, 12 (*passim*)
torture, 37–8
travel writing, Chapters 7, 8 (*passim*)

Vaughan Williams, Ralph, Chapter 13 (*passim*)
visual, 128–9, Chapters 7 (*passim*)
visual art, 138–9, 142, 164, *see also* interart/intermediality
voice, Chapter 1 (*passim*)

Wagner, Richard, 18, 19, 24–6, 68, 114, 165, Chapter 9 (*passim*)
Whitman, Walt, Chapter 13 (*passim*)
Wilde, Oscar, 162, 190, 191
women, Chapters 4, 12 (*passim*)
and equality, 33
women's fashion, 48, 49, 53
women's suffrage, Chapter 4 (*passim*)

Zitkála-Šá (*pseud.*), 10–13